Down-to-Earth Spirituality

Encountering
God in
the Ordinary,
Boring Stuff
of Life

R. PAUL STEVENS

InterVarsity Press
Downers Grove, Illinois

InterVarsity Press
P.O. Box 1400, Downers Grove, IL 60515-1426
World Wide Web: www.ivpress.com
E-mail: mail@ivpress.com

InterVarsity Press® is the book-publishing division of InterVarsity Christian Fellowship/USA®, a student movement active on campus at hundreds of universities, colleges and schools of nursing in the United States of America, and a member movement of the International Fellowship of Evangelical Students. For information about local and regional activities, write Public Relations Dept., InterVarsity Christian Fellowship/USA, 6400 Schroeder Rd., P.O. Box 7895, Madison, WI 53707-7895, or visit the IVCF website at <www.ivcf.org>.

All Scripture quotations, unless otherwise indicated, are taken from the Holy Bible, New International Version®. NIV®. Copyright ©1973, 1978, 1984 by International Bible Society. Used by permission of Zondervan Publishing House. All rights reserved.

Cover design: Kathleen Lay Burrows

Cover image: © Sonja Paravano/Photonica

ISBN 0-8308-2383-2

Printed in the United States of America ∞

Library of Congress Cataloging-in-Publication Data

Stevens, R. Paul, 1937-
  Down-to-earth spirituality: encountering God in the ordinary, boring
stuff of life / R. Paul Stevens.
     p. cm.
Includes bibliographical references (p.   ).
   ISBN 0-8308-2383-2
   1. Spirituality. 2. Spirituality—Biblical teaching. 3. Jacob
(Biblical patriarch)—Family. 4. Bible. O.T. Genesis XXV-L—Biography.
I. Title.
   BV4501.3 .S75 2003
248—dc21

2002014450

P 17 16 15 14 13 12 11 10 9 8 7 6 5 4 3 2 1

Y 15 14 13 12 11 10 09 08 07 06 05 04 03

Contents

Foreword

What follows is the story of Jacob, told in a way that will take you by surprise.

It is no mere sermon, even though the author has drawn many significant implications for present-day Christian living. Nor is it a scholarly commentary that fills the mind with historical information with fine literary style, even though the gentle touches of the scholarly brush are everywhere evident. It is a profound reflection on the fascinating biblical story of Jacob, with its drama and intrigue, its grace and folly.

For decades, Paul Stevens has been captivated by the story of this father of the faith of Israel. And besides a careful scholarly reading, he has brought to bear on this biblical story many of his diverse experiences: as urban missionary, staff worker with university students, pastor, husband and father, carpenter, marriage counselor, crosscultural educator, and professor of marketplace theology at Regent College.

As a result, the person of Jacob does not remain frozen in an ancient religious world. Rather, his story gains a pristine relevance for contemporary Christian spirituality. Jacob's story, in some sense, becomes our story.

Two powerful themes play themselves out in this retelling of the Jacob tale. The first is theological. The other is ethical and practical.

While there is much that is exemplary about the hoary figure of Jacob, there is equally much that is shabby about this schemer and deceiver. The deeper texture of this story is not so much about the example of Jacob as it is about the God of covenant faithfulness who shows his mercy and grace to a deeply flawed man. God, with the firmness of love, transforms Jacob into a person of faith and humility. Thus, theologically this story celebrates God's mysterious hand in the biography, setting and movement of one of Israel's patriarchs.

The second significant theme revolves around human and social embeddedness and embodiment. The Jacob tale is told at the fulcrum of life — eating, sleeping, dreaming, working, courting, marrying, reproducing, raising a family, dying. Played out in this complex and dramatic biblical story we see the tapestry of life with all its human ingenuity, prowess and weakness, and the surprising participation of the God who journeys with us.

This book will surprise you. In its passionate telling and its often lyrical language lie the contours of the story of life which we are all called to live: a story that sees all human activity as sacred, all of life as a symphony to God's glory, all of life as prayer and sacrament, and all of life as purposeful in shaping the human community and as blessing to family, friends, neighbors and strangers.

This book is written not simply to inform. It is written to incite us to take life in full stride.

Charles Ringma
Regent College

Introduction

The Earthy
Spirituality of Jacob

*I once read a Hasidic story about a teacher who
was said to have lived an unusually abundant life.
After his death one of his pupils was asked,
"What was most important to your teacher?" The pupil replied,
"Whatever he happened to be doing at the moment."*

— SUE MONK KIDD

Just to be is blessing. Just to live is holy.

— ABRAHAM JOSHUA HESCHEL

Some years ago I read a fascinating book on the passages of a person's life. I felt that the book was reading me. Each stage of my life was cataloged and targeted with psychological precision, like a heat-seeking missile — the twenties when I married, the thirties when I established myself in a career, and so on, with all the sensitive transition points (around thirty, forty and fifty) characterized by major changes, deep questions and attempts to reformulate my life. I was following the pattern, conforming to the norm. Then I suddenly thought, *This does not explain my life at all.*

What makes sense of my journey — the everyday experiences as well as the passages — is God. The *providence* of God means that God oversees me and my life is not a bundle of accidents. The *purpose* of God means that God engages me for a compelling, world-transforming mission. And the *welcome* of God means that I know continuously and deeply that God accepts me, approves of me and — most amazing of all — finds pleasure in me.

All this I have known since eighteen years of age, when I was first touched by the love of Christ. But these revelations have come, by and large, through more than forty years of brooding on one portion of Scripture—the story of Jacob. There I have discovered a down-to-earth faith wrung from an Old Testament character that helps me live in the center of everyday things, rather than at the circumference in retreats and religious activities.

Normally, however, we would not look to Jacob as a model of the holy life. He is not a porcelain saint to be displayed on a shelf of spiritual heroes.

Jacob's name can mean "cheat," and he lives up to his name. He is manipulative, deceptive and aggressive—not someone who could qualify as a well-scrubbed member of First Church. Jacob is a seriously flawed person growing up in a dysfunctional family. He seems to be always getting into trouble or just getting out of it or about to make some more trouble.[1] We wouldn't let him teach a course on prayer or become our spiritual director in order to get our life centered on God. But he has one redeeming quality that dominates the whole story—he wants God. He has a passion to be blessed by God. He wants his life to be saturated with blessing. And who wouldn't?

Jacob has a "prodigal" passion because, as the word implies, Jacob's heart toward God is extravagant, exuberant and even wasteful. He will lie and cheat to get the blessing if that is the only way. Jacob is anything but apathetic.

But so is God. God is always after Jacob, seeking and finding him, continuously apprehending him, repeatedly calling his telephone number, always showing up in the most unlikely places, especially when things get dangerous. And so we can only say (reverently) that God's love is prodigal too—wonderfully extravagant.

The Necessary, the Menial and the Mundane

All this happens in very ordinary circumstances, the necessary, the menial and the mundane: eating, sleeping, traveling, experiencing sexual appetite, finding a life companion, raising children and going about our daily work. We see God illuminating all the passages of a person's life—birth, youth, emerging adulthood, leaving home, establishing a career, getting married, becoming a parent, returning to one's roots, becoming a grandparent and finally saying goodbye to this world. The story of Jacob takes us from the womb to the tomb or, more accurately, from conception to resurrection. It reveals an earthy spirituality such as that demonstrated in the life of Jesus, who was the most human person who ever walked across the stage of history. Jesus was Jerusalem's favorite dinner guest; he rubbed shoulders with tax collectors, was touched by prostitutes, went fishing and worked in a carpenter's shop. True spirituality does not make us angels but fully human—like Jesus.

God is with Jacob not only in the special epiphanies of the ladder to heaven and the all-night wrestling match with the angel of the Lord but in all the everydayness of his life. We do not see Jacob "going to church," though he does erect altars and worship memorials. Mostly we discover that God is with Jacob in the home, traveling on the dusty roads that lead to Haran, working on his father-in-law's ranch, engaging his neighbors and being reconciled with his brother. Looking through the lens of Jacob's life, we see how temptation and spiritual victory, how spiritual darkness and God-revealing revelation, happen in all our waking and sleeping hours in the home, office, factory, church, school and streets.

For Jacob, these soul-nourishing events are located (as we will be exploring chapter by chapter) in the womb (Rebekah), at the dinner table (with Esau), in the home (with Isaac), out in the field (the angels of God), by a well (Rachel), in a tent (Leah), by the farm feeding trough (Laban), beside a brook (the angel of the Lord), in a pagan city (Dinah), in a foreign palace (Joseph), through a bad friendship (Judah) and on a deathbed (Ephraim). Jacob, and we the readers, meet God at home and abroad, at work and play, in company and in solitude. We are found by God in naming a new baby, eating a meal, relating to family, working hard, falling in love, getting married (and finding we married the "wrong one"), having children and facing the ultimate unmentionable topic: our own death. With Jacob we look not merely *at* life but *into* it. Thus everyday life is re-enchanted, and we are given a spirituality for the road rather than the sanctuary.

The Bible is not an instruction manual that contains principles of spirituality—how to get right with God and yourself, how to make your daily work into a holy ministry. It is not a self-help guide for the perplexed and the spiritually hungry. It is a story—a story about God in search of humankind and a story about God's progressive establishment of his kingdom on earth. And this over-arching Story is told through stories (like the one we are about to explore). The Bible tells us about God and faith by saying, "Once upon a time . . ." Narrative is the dominant form of the Bible.[2] Henry R. Luce, founder of *Time* magazine, quipped, "*Time* didn't start this emphasis on stories about people; the Bible did."[3] And these stories engage us not simply because they were "once upon a time" but because they address us in our own real time. They have a primary meaning related directly to the characters involved, their struggles and joys, and a secondary meaning that has a universal value and feeling that engages us.

The inspired narrator tells it like it is with searing honesty and with consid-erable artistry. He lets us draw our own conclusions, inviting us to exercise dis-cernment. Thus, rarely do we find a moralistic comment such as "Jacob did wrong in trying to get his brother's blessing by deceit." Instead we are exposed to the boomerang effect whereby Jacob the beguiler becomes deceived.[4] So the indirect method of the inspired author turns out to be the most direct. Faith, hope and love get wrung out of us serendipitously. We are found by God right where we are, especially in our relationships. We will explore this story through each of the persons surrounding Jacob—his mother (Rebekah), brother (Esau), father (Isaac), wives (Rachel and Leah), father-in-law (Laban), children (Dinah, Joseph and Judah), grandchildren (Tamar, Ephraim and Manasseh), strangers he meets along the way (Shechem) and even angels.

THE UNIVERSAL STORY

In the book of Genesis we learn more about Jacob than about Abraham and Isaac (his grandfather and father) put together. Jacob is the first lover in the Bible, that is, the first to show us what it is like to be in love as an all-consuming passion. He is also the first worker in the Bible—not just one whose work is mandated (as in the case of Adam and Eve) but one whose daily expenditure of energy is actually described in its toilsome agony and breathtaking creativity. He is the first entrepreneur, the first to show us what it is like to exercise faith in the workplace, to envision, invent and implement. Jacob is the first dreamer whose nocturnal visions are explicitly described. He is the first to give us the intimate details of the deathbed experience, the first to reveal his last will and testament. But there are other reasons why this story engages us personally.

Jacob is one of the most compelling characters in the Bible because he is so psychologically present to us.[5] He is one of us. He has the same weaknesses, longings, yearnings, ambiguities and neediness. As it turns out, his vulnerability is his opening to God. As German philosopher Adolf Alexander Schroeders put it, enigmatically, in a way that Jacob could affirm, "My burden carries me."[6]

Jacob's story is so universal because it is so personal. He grows up with an emotionally distant father and bonds deeply with his mother. The family is fragmented and messy. While his parents' marriage began in love, his mother and father grew emotionally distant from each other, and each parent sought intimacy and solace in a favorite child. A distant father, an overbearing mother, an overpowering brother, wives he cannot please, a manipulative father-in-law, children alienated from each other—this is the stuff not only of Jacob's story but all too often of our own. It is in this messy complexity of family life that Jacob's own identity, his vocation and his spirituality are forged and hammered. We are privy to every detail, from whispers in the honeymoon tent to panic prayers on the eve of a fateful rendezvous. But most important, we get inside Jacob himself to discover what makes him tick.

THE BLESSING

What drives Jacob is the desire to know the blessing of God.[7] Blessing is not simply well-wishing or speaking well of another but the actual transmission of a positive and spiritual good. Admittedly his motives are mixed—just as ours are—but he wants blessing with all his heart. Some of the characters seem determined to divert this blessing. And it is only by scheming, or better still, by shrewd initiative that God's will is done. Rebekah makes sure the younger son actually gets it. Jacob schemes to provide for his family as a tangible aspect of the blessing. The sons of Jacob rescue their sister by deceit when she is kidnapped and raped. One thinks of the words of Jesus, expressed in the parable of the servant who made friends for himself with his master's money before he was fired, that he was commended for his *shrewdness*. Jesus lamented that the people of this world are "more shrewd in dealing with their own kind than are the people of the light" (Lk 16:8). Jacob is a shrewd believer.

The pursuit of blessing is the engine of faith in the story. Jacob wants his father's blessing. Esau, his brother, wants it too. In fact, Esau wants *both* his parents' blessing, and he tries to get it by marrying women he thinks will be progressively more acceptable to his mother and father (they are not!). Leah wants Jacob's blessing. Jacob wants Esau's blessing, but he had cheated Esau and run away from him. The sons of Leah (the less loved wife) want their father's blessing. They are driven to desperate ploys to try to make things right in this imbalanced family, including retaliating against the rape of Dinah and having Reuben sleep with Leah's maid (who was also Jacob's concubine) to obtain rights and blessing in the family. But ultimately it is the desire for the blessing of God that is the primary motivating power.

To get this blessing, Jacob takes God on rather than passively waiting. Jacob's name means "grabber" or "he who grabs by the heel" and arises from his birth circumstances (he came out after his twin brother, grabbing his brother's heel).[8] But the intensity with which Jacob seeks the blessing of God makes him truly a God-wrestler. He hounds God, even hustles God.[9] The epicenter of Jacob's passion for God is found in the poignant and pivotal scene by the Jabbok Brook, where Jacob wrestles with God. He says to God, "I will not let you go until you bless me."

THE STORY WITHIN THE STORY

For those unfamiliar with Genesis 25—35, I have provided a family tree and brief summary in appendixes A and B. Jacob is, of course, a patriarch. And the story is put in the Pentateuch (the first five books of the Bible) precisely to tell us about the unfolding of the promise of God. That promise has three parts: to make us fruitful, to give us an earthly vocation in the land (in the world) and to bless all the nations. God intends that we should have a life saturated with blessing.

Genesis reveals God's irrevocable covenant with the patriarchs to make them a nation that would be a light and blessing to the earth and to all nations. The three parts of the promise—the people, the land and the blessing of the world—get passed on from Abraham, to Isaac, to Jacob and ultimately to Jacob's sons, including his half-Egyptian grandsons, Ephraim and Manasseh. This is the driving force of the narrative. It begins with (surprisingly) "This is the account of Abraham's son, Isaac" (Jacob's father, Gen 25:19), but it was the custom in this form of literature to tell the story of the heads of the family through their children.[10] The story is not primarily a psychological study or even a spiritual biography (though, interestingly, Genesis 25—50 does these things). As we live our way into the text, I will sometimes suggest contemporary explanations that were probably not in the author's mind but that are illuminating to our everyday spirituality.[11] The heart of the story—which I endeavor to keep always in the center—is God's utter determination to bless the human race. God does this by concentrating on a family that would embody that blessing so that through them the whole human race up to our own generation would be blessed.

That God wants to bless in spite of unworthiness, and place in the family constellation is one of the great themes of the book. God's passion is prodigal, totally wasteful. Indeed the apostle Paul (in the New Testament) affirms that Jacob, and not Esau, was blessed "in order that God's purpose in election might stand: not by works but by him who calls" (Rom 9:11-12). To say, as is repeated over and again in the Bible, "the God of Abraham, Isaac and Jacob," while knowing the characters involved, is to say that God associates with very imperfect people. In other words, we are in good news territory. All this happens not by being exposed to propositions about God but by being included in a story that has a beginning, a plot line and an ending.

AN ORAL MASTERPIECE

This is a work of oral art constructed beautifully around a cycle that starts and ends but has internal symmetries. In the endnotes I have suggested in more detail just how the author has done this and other scholarly matters. An example of the pattern is how Genesis 25:19-34 starts with the seeking of an oracle from God (Rebekah going to a prophet or the family altar to find out what God would be saying about the struggle in her womb); it ends with another oracle, this time fulfilled, and Rachel struggling in childbirth (35:1-22).[12] As Jacob leaves the land, he encounters angels on a ladder between heaven and earth; as he returns to the land, he meets two companies of angels and calls the place Mahanaim—"Two Camps." The author(s) (whether Moses alone or Moses along with his disciples)[13] has masterfully interwoven themes to form a seamless fabric—deceit, barrenness, struggle, stolen blessing, wrestling and reconciliations.

It is a masterpiece of storytelling that invites us to embrace the God-soaked worldview of the narrator. And in the process we become more human, more whole. As Bruce Waltke suggests, "Because personhood emerges as life unfolds, the possibility of grasping personal identity arises by seeing another's life whole and clear."[14]

Jacob is known "whole and clear." Through all the vicissitudes, schemings, manipulations, shrewdness and entrepreneurial activity, it appears that human beings are getting their own way. Indeed this God-wrestling seems to be something quite central to the human quest for God. God does not want compliant servants but sons and daughters who are passionate about him. There is a mystery in this—a passionate God who looks for people with passion.

In reality, however, it is God who has the last word. Michael Fishbane summarizes this brilliantly:

> Accordingly, no unpromised fire is stolen from heaven. To the contrary—those whom God has chosen succeed. But in the thickness of historical time, and because of limited divine interventions, realization of the divine promises appears

to rest with human action. Just this narrative perspective—the ambilateral givenness and hiddenness of divine grace—give to the Jacob Cycle its most fulsome power.[15]

Faith is a gracious conspiracy between God and the seeking person, a hounding on both sides and a symphony of wills. We are involved. The kingdom of God, as both Jacob and we know all too well, is not for the mildly interested but for the desperate. Jesus said as much: "Forceful men lay hold of it" (Mt 11:12). While Jacob's method is not always right, in the depths of his heart Jacob wants the blessing of God—and wants that blessing not in a superspiritual way but in the realities of everyday life: the menial, the necessary and the mundane.

Along the way I acknowledge my indebtedness to many who have helped me (many authors are quoted in the endnotes) and to my students at Regent College who have heard this story as part of my "Everyday Life" course. I especially appreciate the help rendered on the Hebrew text by my colleague, David Clemens, and my pastor-friend Brian Morgan. I am still discovering its depths. My experience over the years of reading, pondering it and teaching it is well described by a Jewish author, Isaac Bashevis Singer. "Whenever I take the Bible down from my bookcase and I begin to read it," Singer said, "I cannot put it down. I always find new aspects, new facts, new tensions, and new information in it. I sometimes imagine that, while I sleep or walk, some hidden scribe invades my house and puts new passages, new names, new events into this wonderful book."[16]

Jacob is the Old Testament prodigal who, like the one described by Jesus in the New Testament (Lk 15:11-32), got his inheritance in advance, went to a far country where he suffered, came to himself and came home. He finds himself and the Father at the same time. This wonderfully evocative story invites us to a double homecoming that is parallel to the double homecoming Jacob experiences: home to God and home to ourselves. We cannot have one without the other.

Birth — the Story of Rebekah
Genesis 25:19-28

> *The point of marriage and family is to make us realistic.*
>
> — MICHAEL NOVAK

Jacob's story, like ours, begins in a double womb: a mother's womb and the womb of a loving Creator God. As Eve said long before, "With the help of the LORD I have brought forth a man" (Gen 4:1). But Adam was involved too. Virgin births are rare. Conception usually takes place through the loving embrace of a man and woman who contribute as subcreators in a divine-human conspiracy.

Two sperms penetrated two ova to form Jacob and Esau. They were far from being identical twins. They were not only genetically but also spiritually distinct. The great mystery of the story is why the more attractive Esau should in the end never wrestle with angels or hear God speak, and why the bad boy, Jacob, should wrestle with angels, see visions in the night, inherit the land and experience the promise and the blessing of God. Was it nature or nurture? Or both? Or something more?

WHERE DO WE COME FROM?

Conception — the beginning of it all — is a truly awesome thing. It should lead us to cry, "God!" DNA has the unique ability to replicate itself, preserving as it divides a blueprint from one cell to another. During replication, the DNA spiral staircase cleaves equally, like a zipper parting, and forms (as the ancient book of Job metaphorically suggests) a firm embryonic body from milky semen, just as milk curdles into cheese.[1] The DNA is a self-propagating molecule of life, determining hair color, personality, shape and size, predispositions to disease and even addictions. And once the ovum is penetrated by the sperm, a miraculous change occurs in the outer coating of the ovum to prevent another sperm from entering even before the two nuclei have fused, which is a paradigm of betrothal and monogamy. The dividing and differentiating cells are embedded in a fleshy fertile soil, taking root in the womb like a seed.[2]

Roots and wings are the two gifts parents can give to a child, and without the roots there will be no wings—no cleaving, no leaving. But the addictive bonding of Jacob to his mother and she to him (today we would call it "enmeshment"), and the attachment of Esau to his father, is another great mystery of this dysfunctional family, which is nevertheless a grace-saturated God story. Sometimes enmeshment and addiction emerge where there has been insufficient bonding: no roots means no wings. But there is more than genetic determination in this story. There is a special act of God.

That conception should happen to anyone is a miracle—a miracle somewhat clouded today by modern technology. The original sin in the Garden of Eden reveals our desire to be "as gods" and is perhaps being repeated in this age of the new reproductive technology and the mapping of the human genome. That this should happen to the infertile and aging Isaac and Rebekah was a miracle of miracles. Isaac himself was a "son of laughter" (for that is what his name means),[3] a joke or, perhaps better put, "worshipful hilarity" that delights in the fact that God is God and we are not. His mother had cracked up laughing when the angel visitor told this old lady that she would carry a child.[4] So it is hardly surprising that Isaac would pray when his loving embrace with Rebekah time and again was fruitless. He prayed for twenty years—no small testimony to his persistence. But prayer does not stop with a successful pregnancy. The whole process of child rearing that follows is fraught with hope and danger. It was so with me.

When I was twelve, my father took my brother and me aside to explain "the family story." I had always wondered why my father coddled my mother—"walked on eggshells," as we would say, not to offend, provoke or disturb her. "When your brother John was born, Mom went into a deep depression." She was kept alive by verses from the Bible she memorized as a young girl in the Salvation Army corps in her fishing outpost in Newfoundland, then a British colony. The doctor said, "No more children; it is too risky." "But then," Dad said, "there was another child—a girl—who was born dead." And mother slipped once again into the depths. "No more children." "But then," Dad said, looking at me with a twinkle in his eye, "you came along."

He could have said I was a mistake, that I was unplanned (a phrase that captures the arrogant and idolatrous tendency in the human heart ever since the Garden). Or he might have said I was a frightening possibility—which I was. But he said, "You were a love baby." So I was. So are all of us, created not only in our mother's womb but also in the loving heart of God, the love community of Father, Son and Spirit. God made the world in love and fashions human beings in love.

So conceiving a child is a work of God that should evoke worship in our hearts. It is a ministry—parents giving life to a child "with the help of the Lord." But the gift goes two ways. Children are a gift to parents. They are the means of helping parents mature. God gives children to parents to help them grow up. As Michael Novak has so wisely observed, many people today refrain from having children because they know intuitively that they will, when they become parents, have to cease being children themselves.[5] We are not told what effect having these twins had on the personal maturity of Isaac and Rebekah except that in the sad declension of their lives it appears they found solace and spiritual center in one of the children instead of the living God. They fused themselves addictively and idolatrously each to a favorite child. And it all started with naming.

What Is in a Name?

Children do not come from the womb with name tags. They are nameless, like animals. And the first gift of parents to children as they begin to human-ize them is a name. As a permanent gift, it lasts for a lifetime. Indeed, even after the person has died, it is often carved in a tombstone and evokes mem-ory layered on memory. Isaac and Rebekah must have looked on the wrin-kled little faces of these two boys and, as is customary in ancient societies and older cultures today, named them by their appearance and the circum-stances of their birth.

The first boy came out red and covered with hair as though he were wearing an animal skin. So they named him Esau, which may mean "hairy." And afterward "Hairy" was called Edom, which means "red." "Hairy" implies an animal nature, and "Edom-Red" suggests earthiness or passion.[6]

Jacob, the second to come out of the womb, emerged (as it appeared to the midwife) grasping the heel of his brother, the first born, with his extend-ed hand. So they named the smooth one "he who grabs the heel"—Jacob—with the possible figurative meaning of "deceiver" and "crooked cheat," though the name may also mean "God Protects" or "God Is Your Rear Guard (at your heel)."[7]

Our dear friends in Kenya, where we have spent parts of ten years, named their first son Budget. When I asked Mololo why he and Mama Kalundi chose this name, he said, "Because he was born on the day that the government brought down the budget."

Another time we were driving along a dusty country road and encoun-tered a *matatu*—a private bus normally burdened with colorful people going to market. But the bus was drawn up by the side of the road with all the men standing outside, the women inside. I asked the men, "What's happening?"

"A baby is being born on the bus."

"What will the baby be named?"

"Born Along the Way" (in the tribal language).

Names not only describe but also prescribe. They have life-shaping power. A name can point to a destiny, as it did for Martin Luther King Jr., who was a pivotal figure like his namesake. Christian parents sometimes

name their children prophetically, anticipating that their children will embody "Faith," "Hope" or "Joy." Sadly, some thoughtless parents name their
children after a soft drink ("Pepsi") or a celebrity—a burden to bear.

True to his name, Esau grew up trying to conquer nature, in the fields,
gaining skills in hunting—an animal. True to his name, Jacob would grow
up trying to conquer people—a manipulator. Jacob would spend his life
grasping after his brother's heel to get the advantage, to be first rather than
second, to get his own way. But names also reveal the parents.

Naming the Parents

Names often express the humility or pride, the hopes and fears of the parents. They can reveal their will to bless. A name gives both identity and in-
dividuality within the family. As Amy and Leon Kass insightfully suggest,
"Naming a child thus anticipates exactly the central difficulty of child-rear-
ing altogether: how to communicate unconditional love for the child-just-
as-he-now-is, at the same time as one is doing all in one's power to encourage and to help him become better."[8]

Rebekah clearly intended to shape Jacob by his name. For when she was
carrying the twins and found them smashing each other in the womb,[9]
deeply distressed as to what this conflict should mean, she consulted the
Lord—probably through a prophet at the family altar. She was told that
there were two nations in her womb, that the two nations would be separated (a darkly prophetic anticipation of a wider conflict) and that one people coming from one of the twins would be stronger. The battle that began
in the womb would escalate. Then—most surprising of all—she was told
that the younger, the second, would be the leader, making the first serve the
second. Did this mean the older would serve, or that the older would be
made to serve, the younger? And so Jacob was given the name "Second, but
determined to overcome."

In naming, Rebekah wanted to make the prophecy come true, to make
God's blessing happen, to grab what could only be given—something Jacob
would emulate for twenty or more years in adulthood. Clearly, of Jacob's

two parents, Rebekah is presented by the narrator as "a continuous whirl of purposeful activity," while Isaac is presented as the "most passive of the patriarchs."[10] (We will get to know him better in a later chapter.) Prior to the birth of Jacob and Esau, Isaac is described as waiting in Canaan for a surrogate (Abraham's servant) to find him a wife back in Haran. This is symptomatic of his entire career. As a boy, he was a bound victim lying compliantly on the altar. As a young man, he was waiting for someone to provide a bride for him. As a father, he prefers the son who will go to the field and bring back food. And his one extended scene as an old man pictures him lying in bed "weak and blind, while others act on him."[11] So in the various genealogies *(toledoth)* there is no extended account of Isaac under the heading of "This is the story of Abraham's family."[12]

Rebekah was not much better, though she had (as did Isaac) many commendable features. She was raised in a godly family that had emigrated from Ur in response to the word of God. Her marriage to Isaac was arranged by a godly servant who saw in her qualities of hospitality, courtesy, graciousness, beauty, quiet self-possession and unimpeachable virginity (Gen 24:14, 20-21). The narrator deliberately pictured her as a whirl of activity, energetic and entrepreneurial. She goes down to the well, draws water, pours it and gives drink to Abraham's servant (here to find a bride for Isaac).[13] These same qualities will come up shortly when there is a rapid chain of events surrounding the blessing by Isaac—cooking, dressing Jacob and orchestrating the ruse, so much so that Robert Alter says that she is "the shrewdest and most potent of the patriarchs."[14] When she was courted by Abraham's servant, Rebekah agreed on short notice to take the long journey to Canaan with this stranger in obedience to what must have seemed a divine calling (vv. 57-58).

Each of the wives of the patriarchs had the equivalent of a call to "leave all and follow." With Sarah it was the call to emigrate from the security of Haran to a campsite in Canaan and to trust God for the fulfillment of his promise to bless her with a child though she was barren. Rebekah, her daughter-in-law, had been sent off from Haran with a ceremonial flourish:

Our sister, may you increase
　　to thousands upon thousands;
may your offspring possess
　　the gates of their enemies. (Gen 24:60)

But she was infertile. Rachel, in the next generation, also had to trust God
for children because she, too, was barren. Eventually she and Leah also had
to leave the security of Haran to make a pilgrimage to Canaan, not knowing
what would await them there. For Rebekah, it was the call to marry a man
she had never met and to live in a distant country she had never visited—all
this on the strength of a stranger's word with the breath of God in it!

Rebekah was a remarkable woman. Her marriage started in faith, hope
and love (Gen 24:67). But like her husband, Rebekah diminished as the
years went by and became in the end a jealous wife plotting with her darling son to get around the old man by a clever ruse so that the leadership of
the family and the inheritance attendant on it could pass to Jacob rather
than Esau. Chapter 27 speaks volumes about the quality of their marriage.
Far from being mutually submissive, she appears to have controlled her
husband, who in turn appears to have complied rather than submitting in
loving freedom. Politics rather than grace ruled the home, and Rebekah determined to be, as the Bedouin say today, "powerful in the tent." One woman, on hearing that the husband is the head of the family, said, "I am the
neck and I can turn the head any way I like." Rebekah could have said it.

Rebekah, powerful in the tent, keeps her darling son close to her, as he is
a "quiet man, staying among the tents" (Gen 25:27). Jacob is stuck between
a strong-willed mother and a distant father. He must either defy his mother
or deceive his father. Under his mother's control, he chooses the latter.

Rebekah paid dearly for this. She lost her favorite son, who had to run
for his life, again through the clever strategy of persuading her compliant
husband that Jacob needed a wife from the old homeland rather than from
the surrounding pagan Canaanites (Gen 27:46—28:5). Her shrewdness
saved her from seeing her son murdered. She did not see Jacob for at least
twenty years and never informed him that his brother's fury had subsided

(27:44), for perhaps it never had. Indeed she might have died during the interim, as we do not hear of her again. The boys are finally reconciled at their father's funeral (35:29). Rebekah's nurse, Deborah, is mentioned in the narrative (v. 8), but not Rebekah.

The Jewish psychiatrist Naomi Rosenblatt reflects, "The womb where Jacob and Esau contest for supremacy becomes a symbol of the constricting confines of any sibling relationship. Anyone who's ever seen a sonogram of prenatal twins can appreciate just how physically Jacob and Esau competed for nurture in their mother's womb. There never seems to be enough space, enough food, enough attention." She argues that the truth of rival siblings, which Esau and Jacob demonstrate, is that they do not "so much compete so much *with* each other as *for* their parent's attention."[5]

"Second and not satisfied with being second" was Jacob's name—"Determined to overcome my brother and get the blessing that comes to the head of the family," "Grabbing at advantage and making the good purpose of God happen." But behind it was the desire for his father's blessing and presence—things that Esau enviably had in abundance. Jacob would live out his name until, much later, bruised by God and hurt by himself, he would find rest in simply being a child of God. God wanted to bless Jacob, but he could not do it until Jacob was prepared to be real, and that desperate discipline in reality therapy would take the patriarch through two marriages, thirteen children and three different countries. God wanted to *give* Jacob what Jacob, the grabber, wanted to *get* by his own manipulative, controlling schemes. The next scene shows us just how desperately Jacob wanted the blessing, and the action all happens in the grand ordinariness of life.

Eating—the Story of Esau
Genesis 25:27-35; 27:1-40

*In humanized eating we can nourish
our souls even while we feed our bodies.*

—LEON KASS

*A meal is still a rite—the last "natural sacrament"
of family and friendship, of life that is more than
"eating" and "drinking." To eat is still something more
than to maintain bodily functions. People may
not understand what that "something more" is,
but they nevertheless desire to celebrate it.
They are still hungry and thirsty for sacramental life.*

—ALEXANDER SCHMEMANN

God's first gift to humankind in the book of Genesis is food![1] No wonder it is a delight to eat. But it is also dangerous. Ask Esau, Jacob's brother.

As with animals, human beings must eat to live. Leon Kass reflects on our basic physicality:

> The bodies of higher animals are, in fact, highly complex variations of a sim-
> ple plan: a thick-walled solid cylinder built around a hollow tube that runs
> through its center. In schematic cross-section, the organism is like a dough-
> nut, nourished from its hole, here and there armed with appendages that
> work either to keep that hole filled or to keep the doughnut from filling some
> other doughnut's hole.[2]

WHATEVER HAPPENED TO THE FAMILY MEAL?

Unlike animals, God-imaging creatures discover almost by accident that eating is not mere feeding. In today's fast-food society—where food is calculated to take an average of fifty seconds to "get" and a few minutes to consume—eating is often reduced to in-flight refueling. In the United States the majority of all meals (52 percent) are now purchased in a restaurant and eaten either there or in the car. The most rapid growth in supermarket sales is in take-out food.[3] Many have given up having meals and "graze" through the day on snacks. Yet all of us started eating as the experience of the intimate communion of mother and child at the breast or bottle, getting strength (for that is the real meaning of "comfort") from the relationship and not merely the milk.[4] It is a relational and spiritual sacrament.

We progress to assisted feeding, to self-feeding, to full meals and finally, in many cases, to emergency feeding through intravenous tubes. Some end their lives, as my father did, being sustained by a gastric tube inserted in his stomach through which essential nutrients were put in his body without the joy of eating—no taste, no odor, no company. The meal trays in his hospital (where he spent most of the last two years of his life) would pass by his room.

Eating was meant for communion, for multilevel fellowship, and in its deepest meaning, it is a sacrament of the presence of God. Old Testament saints "saw God, and they ate and drank" (Ex 24:11)[5]—an evocative anticipation of the experience of Christians of covenant renewal in the presence of the Lord as they eat bread and drink wine in Communion. But Old Testament saints also "sat down to eat and drink and got up to indulge in revelry," that is, idolatry and sexual immorality (32:6)—the very thing Esau and Jacob did. So it is not so much that "you are *what* you eat" as it is that "you are *how* you eat." The emphasis today is on what eating does to the body, either giving it dangerous fats or making the body too fat. But we will need to consider what food does to the soul.

Because of this inundation of life with grace and God-presence, eating is fraught with spiritual consequences. It is a particularly direct way to the soul. It is sometimes said by women that the way to a man's heart is through his stomach. Teasingly I say I was won to my wife, Gail, by her mother's bar-becued chicken and homemade French fries. My mother-in-law enticed a poor, hungry student into her home for Sunday dinners and made it possi-ble for him to meet her two lovely and available daughters (it was not unlike the home of Laban to which Jacob came, homeless, penniless and hungry, and was introduced to two eligible women). But there is more at stake than mere romance.

It is significant that Esau lost his place in the family (the birthright) and the actual transmission of the promise of God's blessing at the supper table. Hebrews 12:16-17 says, "See that no one is sexually immoral, or is godless like Esau, who for a single meal sold his inheritance rights as the oldest son. Afterward, as you know, when he wanted to inherit this blessing, he was re-jected. He could bring about no change of mind, though he sought the blessing with tears." Actually, in Esau's case there were two meals that re-vealed (as Heb 12:16 says) his godlessness. The first was a stew and the sec-ond a steak.

A Most Revealing Stew

The stew prepared by Jacob was tailor-made for "Red," his brother. Esau came in from the hunt, a man of the open field. Today he might be presi-dent of a hunters' club or a mountain ranger. Like his father, Isaac, Esau loved the open country. And like his father, Esau lived to eat rather than ate to live. It was said of Isaac, literally in the original Hebrew, "Venison was in his mouth" (Gen 27:4); this means he really liked it, lived for it![6] Like father, like favorite son. Esau's palate controlled his soul. His god was his stomach, his senses and his physical appetites—as people today live for golf, sex, gourmet meals, physical beauty or speed—whatever gives an adrenaline rush, whatever satisfies the demon in your jeans.

The stew did not cause Esau's sensuality; it revealed it. So the famous Bible biographer Alexander Whyte notes:

No man sells his birthright on the spot. He who sells his birthright, sells it many times in his heart before he takes it openly as that to the market. He belittles it, and despises it, and cheapens it, at any rate to himself, long before he sells it so cheaply to another. . . . Everybody knew that Esau's birthright was for sale, if anybody cared to bid for it. Isaac knew, Rebekah knew, and Jacob knew; and Jacob had for long been eyeing his brother for a fit opportunity.[7]

Never, warns Whyte, "sell to man or woman or devil your divine birthright. Your birthright of truth, honesty, and especially of chastity." But if you have, "Who is a God like unto Thee, that pardoneth iniquity, and passeth by the transgression of the remnant of His heritage?"[8]

Not surprisingly, Esau has been held as a symbol through Christian history of a "believer" (in name) who is nevertheless given over to sensuality and is weak in hunger for God.[9] Esau was godless. It is not that he had never heard of God or seen evidence of God's eternal power and deity. Like the kind of godlessness we see day by day along the street where we live, Esau's godlessness was a practical atheism—living as though God does not exist, living for sensual satisfaction, living for instant gratification, living without ultimate accountability to God, driven by lust rather than love.[10]

When Esau spots the pot of red stew, he says to Jacob (who has his gourmet cook's hat on, candles on the table and a place set for his brother), "Quick, let me have some of that red stew! I'm famished!" (Gen 25:30).[11] Literally, "Red" says, "Give me some of that red stuff." (That is why, once again, Esau was called Edom, or Red—the name given to the people east of the Jordan, where Esau eventually settled.)

Jacob, a heel grabber, sees his opportunity to take advantage of his brother's hunger and tries to buy (through an exchange) what should have been given (by God). What he wants is good; the way he goes about getting it is not good. "First sell me your birthright," he says to his brother (Gen 25:31). The birthright was the right of the first-born to give leadership to the clan, a position of honor and responsibility.[12]

Esau can't think beyond his next meal, as some cannot think beyond their next sexual encounter, so he says, "Look, I am about to die. . . . What good is the birthright to me?" (Gen 25:32). It is the characteristic of an addiction that one becomes totally preoccupied with the next fix, whether alcohol, drugs, sex or work. But the real meaning of addiction is that it is an alternative god—people are using a substance or an experience to fill the God-shaped vacuum of the soul. Gerald May deals with this perceptively:

> For me, the energy of our basic desire for God is the human spirit, planted within us and nourished endlessly by the Holy Spirit of God. In this light, the spiritual significance of addiction is not just that we lose freedom through attachment to things, nor even that things so easily become our ultimate concerns. Of much more importance is that we try to *fulfill our longing for God* through objects of attachment. . . . From a psychoanalytic perspective, one could say we *displace* our longing for God upon other things; we cathect them instead of God. . . . Thus the more we become accustomed to seeking spiritual satisfaction through things other than God, the more abnormal and stressful it becomes to look for God directly.[13]

Essentially, addictive behavior is a failure in imagination, being unable to envision what it will be like after the fix has worn off, just as the adulterer cannot (or rather does not) imagine the sober reflection after the sexual encounter—and the remorse when one considers the implications of what one has done. But as I have said, it is also a failure in faith.

Esau spurns his birthright, effectively canceling himself out of future leadership of the clan by his commitment to instant gratification. As Bruce Waltke notes, "At the heart of Jacob and Esau's differences are clashing worldviews: deferred prosperity versus immediate satisfaction."[14] In contrast, Jacob is one who thinks about and plans for the future. Physically weaker, Jacob relies on his cunning. The real reason for his competition with Esau is Jacob's desire for his father's blessing and the promise that goes with it. Not able to get this directly, and having a physically stronger brother, Jacob must resort to subterfuge.

So Jacob, knowing his brother's Achilles' heel, says, "Swear to me first" (Gen 25:33). Jacob will not wait to negotiate a deal after the meal but needs assurance in advance. He cannot trust that God will give in God's own time the blessing that he promised even before Jacob was born. Jacob is leaving nothing to chance and nothing to God's providence. He must be in control. So Esau swears an oath to him, selling his birthright to Jacob. Esau's thoughtless haste is noted by a string of short verbs: "ate," "drank," "got up" and "left" (v. 34).

That was the stew. But there was another fateful meal.

A STEAK DINNER

The steak dinner takes place many years later when father Isaac is getting old, his eyes being dim. Though he will not die for decades, he is already anticipating his own parting. Isaac is determined to bless his favorite son, Esau. His palate controls his life. What is there left for him in the restricted life of old age other than the enjoyment of a good meal? So Isaac instructs Esau to hunt some wild game and prepare a meal so he can give Esau his blessing before he dies.

Rebekah, for her part, may have more than crass favoritism in her heart as she schemes to get the blessing for Jacob. As Walter Brueggemann writes, "The two parents who prayed so passionately for a son have now chosen sides."[5] She may have been haunted by the prophecy revealed to her by God during her painful pregnancy—"the older will serve the younger." Rosenblatt suggests, "For two decades Rebekah had carried this secret inside her heart, watching and waiting for this promise from God to be fulfilled. Now Isaac lay dying. . . . If God had elected Jacob to lead, who was Isaac to deny her younger son what God had promised?"[6]

So Rebekah endeavors to get the blessing for her favorite, Jacob, roasting a goat, preparing it just the way Isaac liked, dressing up Jacob with skins to simulate Esau's hairy skin, and clothing Jacob in Esau's fire-smoked smelly clothes. Dressed in a charade, Jacob brings the dish to his father. His father confronts him with his own identity—the issue that cracks open his spiritual search—by asking, "Who is it?" (Gen 27:18). Jacob cannot say his own name, is not yet content to be himself, does not know who he is, is evading confrontation with himself. So he answers elusively, "I am Esau your first-

born" (v. 19). Jacob is now asking for the love and blessing from his father
that he has always craved. Jacob is a classic study of a man who grew up in
a home with an absent or emotionally distant father and who strives in all
of his achievements to win a father's blessing. In Jacob's case he tries to *be*
his brother.[7]

He even takes on the name of the Lord to explain why he got back from
the hunt so quickly, lying through his teeth as he attributes his success to
God (Gen 27:20). As Jacob gets nearer to his father, Isaac gets confused: the
voice is the voice of Jacob, but the hands (now covered with animal skins)
are hairy to the touch. Jewish expositors have always seen that Isaac does not
trust words, or let words come into his heart, especially the word of God,
but goes with his tactile senses—touch and smell.[18] Smell breaks the tie between touch and hearing. It is a tense moment. "Are you really my son
Esau?"[19] is asked twice (vv. 21, 24). Would Jacob be found out? Martin
Luther said that at this point in the drama he, if he had been Jacob, would
have dropped the dish!

Apparently convinced, and having consumed the meal, Isaac asks Jacob (as Esau) to "come . . . and kiss me" (Gen 27:26). Does Jacob dare
risk detection? Imagining the confusion in Jacob's mind, Rosenblatt describes what may have been going on: "Jacob buried his head in his father's neck and kissed him, searching his mind in vain for memories of
this fatherly embrace."[20]

Isaac goes ahead with the blessing—an act that he could not recall, as
he had given himself through his words. Esau comes in shortly after with
the game and prepares the steak for his father. When Isaac realizes he has
blessed the "wrong" son, whom he knows intuitively is the "right" son (because of the prophetic word given to his wife before the twins were born,
though we are not sure she ever revealed this), he "tremble[s] violently"
(Gen 27:33). He knows that through the ruse, through even his own determination to choose one whom God has not chosen, God has the last word:
"I have made him lord over you" (Gen 27:34). And "Esau wept aloud" (v.
38),[21] knowing in his heart that the deal he had made with Jacob over the

stew was now fulfilled over the steak. The steak dinner was the logical outcome of his godlessness. With deep insight the author of Hebrews links the
two acts, the two tables and the two deceptions as one seamless and godless
act: "Afterward, as you know, when he wanted to inherit *this* blessing, he
was rejected" (Heb 12:17).[22]

So Esau allowed hunger and sensuality to become his center and therefore his idol. Idolatry is simply making something one's ultimate concern
other than the One who is ultimate. The other, Jacob, used the hunger of
another for his own selfish ambition, as is the case in the consumer culture
of the Western world.

This would not be the last time that a meal would become a fellowship
in deception. Over the wedding supper, Laban would slip his older daughter, Leah, into Jacob's marriage tent. Later, when Jacob is fleeing Laban
with his two wives and twelve children, he would sit down to a reconciliation meal with Laban. Why are meals so important, so dangerous and so
fraught with spiritual consequences?

THE FIRST AND THE LAST MEAL

The first gift to Adam and Eve, the first command and the first blessing of
God, is to eat. "I give you every seed-bearing plant . . . for food" (Gen 1:29).
But the first sin also took place in the context of eating. Adam and Eve were
placed in a sanctuary garden to enjoy communion with God, to build community and to be cocreators with God—all in the presence of God. But as
the serpent pointed out, the tree of knowledge represented the temptation
to be independent of God—"godless" like Esau, to quote Hebrews again.
The first couple could dine with the devil and break fellowship with God,
which is exactly what happened. When they saw it was "good for food" (a
matter of provision), "a delight to the eyes" (aesthetically beautiful) and
"desirable for gaining wisdom" (giving power), they ate. Why did sin enter
the human family through a common meal? Is it because there is no such
thing as a *common* meal?

Speaking to this with great depth, Leon Kass says:

Though the tree of knowledge of good and bad is only metaphorically a tree—knowledge does not grow on trees—the image suggests an explicit connection between human autonomy and human omnivorousness, by representing the limit on the former in the form of a limit on the latter. . . . God sought to protect man from the expansion of his desires beyond the naturally necessary, or from the replacement of desire given by nature with desires given by his own mind and imagination. These tempting but dangerous prospects—of autonomy, choice, independence, and the aspiration to full self-command, and of emancipated and open-ended desire—lay always at the center of human life. . . . When the voice of reason awoke, and simple obedience was questioned (and hence no longer possible), the desires of the man began to grow. Though he did not know what he meant exactly, he imagined that his eyes would be opened and he would be as a god—that is, self-sufficing, autonomous, independent, knowing, perhaps immortal, and free at last. Such did the serpent promise—the smooth voice that asked the world's first question and so disturbed its peace forever.[23]

Jesus was similarly tempted in the context of eating. Having fasted for forty days in the wilderness, he was hungry, and Satan invited him to use his Sonly power to turn stones into bread. Jesus' answer is profound: "It is written: 'Man does not live on bread alone, but on every word that comes from the mouth of God' " (Mt 4:4). In fact, Jesus was quoting from Deuteronomy 8, where the issue is not living on Scripture but depending on God's self-giving (which is the real meaning of God's speech). "He humbled you, causing you to hunger and then feeding you with manna . . . to teach you that [humankind] does not live on bread alone but on every word that comes from the mouth of the LORD" (Deut 8:3). So the table is a test: can we trust God for provision and live in constant thanksgiving to God?[24]

Because Jesus was and is God, indeed God's self-giving (the Word), he defines himself and his mission by using eating imagery: "I am the bread of life." He invites us to eat him up. Significantly, when Jesus wants to leave a memorial of himself, he does not leave a book but a meal.[25] It, too, was a place of temptation for Judas, to accept that Jesus would bring in the kingdom through suffering weakness on the cross rather than through military insurrection. It is a test of James and John, who wanted to use the table for personal advantage the way Jacob did. But like the Old Testament covenant renewal, it is seeing God and eating and drinking once again—a sacrament.

The famous Russian iconographer Andrew Rublev captures the essence of the communal meal in his rendering of Genesis 18, where Abraham and Sarah entertain three strangers and discover, eventually, that they are angels—messengers bringing the presence of God. Rublev shows three angels, representing Father, Son and Holy Spirit, at a table of invitation with a chalice in the middle, thereby showing the double hospitality that takes place in table fellowship—our welcoming God into our hearts and God welcoming us into his house of love. The three appear to be enjoying each other's company, and they visually form an oval of communion with one another. But their bodies are turned toward the viewer as a gesture of invitation. We are wanted at the table of God, and the member sitting closest has his hand in the bowl, as God mixes his hand in the world. And it all happens in the context of eating.

Jesus pictures the final end of the salvation story as a party. This is suggested over and again by his parables—from the welcome-home party of the prodigal son to the wedding supper to which he had invited all the ragtags of the world. And even his own work style is soiled in the minds of the religious because he ate with tax collectors and sinners and appeared to be, in comparison to the ascetic John the Baptist, "a glutton and a drunkard" (Mt 11:19), like the profligate son in Deuteronomy 21:20.

And the Bible ends with a double vision of eating—our final destination. There will be a wedding and a wake. Revelation 19 tells us that the saints will enjoy "the wedding supper of the Lamb" (v. 9), and for the permanently godless (like Esau), there will be a wake after the judgment (vv. 11-21). The way we eat tells it all. It certainly did for Esau and Jacob. Each was covetous of what the other had. Esau coveted Jacob's food; Jacob coveted Esau's position in the family. Each person's heart was revealed in eating. We are vulnerable at the table.

SOULFUL EATING

Parents know that discipline prohibits digestion. The dinner table, if one bothers to have one, is the worst place to discipline children. Friends know that one cannot sit down and eat together if there is estrangement, unforgiven sin. It becomes the table of manipulation and deception. Food is not only for nutrition but also for fellowship, and not only fellowship between people but also fellowship with God. In most cultures of the world a business deal is sealed over a meal. It is where lovers discover companionship (*com-* means "shared" and *-panion* comes from the word that means "bread"). When we want someone's company, we share bread. And when we want God's company, we come to table. Indeed the purpose of the Eucharist in church is to empower us to live eucharistically in the whole of life. Thus we discover God in work, family and neighboring and at a common kitchen table (feeding on God and food at the same time). Robert Capon advises that we should eat "festally, first of all, for life without occasions is not worth living. But ferially, too, for life is much more than occasions, and its grand ordinariness must never go unsavored."[26]

So why eat? We eat for *satisfaction*. We also meet for *ministry*. Hospitality at the table is one of the primary ways we show the love of God. Reuven Kimelman, a professor of Talmud and Midrash, explores the impact of the Exile on every member or "lay" ministry within Israel. They were separated from the temple and its formal liturgy but not separated from God-in-life. So they multiplied blessings — blessings for eating and blessings for making love, as many as one hundred for each day like the hundred sockets required to hold the tabernacle together. In this way the rabbis attempted not to make the Jewish community into a democracy but to raise all the people to become priests together.

Mealtimes were especially viewed as occasions for the ordinary to be inundated with heaven. According to the Talmud, "As long as the Temple stood, the altar atoned for Israel, but now a man's table atones for him."[27] Part of that atonement was receiving strangers and the poor at one's table — a principle that led to the practice in medieval Spain of burying the benevolent rich in coffins prepared from their table. Tables thus become rabbinic altars. "When two sit together and the words between them are of Torah, the divine presence is in their midst" (Avot 3:3).[28] So we eat for *mission,* extending God's kingdom of love and transformation into the world.

We also eat as a *sacrament,* meeting with God. Each meal is a remembrance of God's creational provision (so we pray "Give us this day our daily bread"). But it is also a confession of worship (so we pray, "Hallowed be thy name"). Each meal is a rumor of the incarnation, that God enfleshes himself, that God comes in the ordinary. Each meal is a hint of redemption as we welcome one another around the table, showing the hospitality of God and, amazingly, experiencing that welcome as we give it—getting what we give.

And finally we eat as a *prophecy.* Each meal drives our stake into the future, anticipating the final end to which the whole travail of human history yearns, the second coming of Christ and the full consummation of the kingdom of God, the new heaven and the new earth, and—guess what?—a wonderful meal.

So eating is a window on eternity and a way to God.[29] Leon Kass comments perceptively:

> The hungry soul seeks satisfaction in activities animated also by wonder, ambition, affection, curiosity, and awe. We human beings delight in beauty and order, art and action, sociability and friendship, insight and understanding, song and worship. . . . All these appetites of the hungry soul can in fact be partially satisfied at the table, provided that we approach it in the proper spirit. The meal taken at table is the cultural form that enables us to respond simultaneously to all the dominant features of our world: inner need, natural plenitude, freedom and reason, human community, and the mysterious source of it all. In humanized eating, we can nourish our souls even while we feed our bodies.[30]

3

Family—the Story of Isaac
Genesis 26—27

> *Nothing can replace a parent's loving attention,*
> *and no child can get too much of it.*
>
> — NAOMI ROSENBLATT

> *I feel myself so much a part of you all that I know we live*
> *and bear everything in common, acting and thinking*
> *for one another even when we are separated. . . . Although I am*
> *utterly convinced that nothing can break the bonds between us,*
> *I seem to need some outward token or sign to reassure me.*
> *In this way material things become vehicles of spiritual realities.*
>
> — DIETRICH BONHOEFFER
> (A LETTER TO HIS PARENTS WHILE IN PRISON)

Most families are messy. But God is at work in them, even the most dysfunctional ones like Jacob's. Family life itself is a spiritual discipline (not simply the locale for devotions and family religious practices); it is a furnace of transformation. In Jacob's case it was his relationships with his parents, with his brother, Esau, and with his wives and children that served as the hammer and heat of spiritual formation.

A THREATENED CALLING

Parenting is a threatened calling. It is threatened both from within and from without. On the inside is the erosion of confidence that ordinary people can actually nurture children into maturity and enable them to leave home and form another family. On the outside is the professionalization of parenting with expertise and technology so that daycare centers, schools and trained counselors are expected to do the job that once was undertaken in the home. People unwisely look forward with dread to children's coming teen years. Not able to give "quantity time" to their children, many parents claim to give "quality time," though the possibility of planning quality time is a myth. *Kairos* (the Greek word for opportune time—in contrast with *chronos*, or clock time, which is manageable) is given, not organized. Particularly tragic is the situation that occurs when a parent, like Eli in the Old Testament (1 Sam 2:12-36), is a religious leader who sees his or her calling to be outside the home and regards family life as an auxiliary activity, if not a distraction, to really important work.

Great cultural shifts taking place in the world are powerfully affecting the parenting experience. In most societies children have always been prized. In the developing world, to have as many children as possible has been a way to increase wealth and gain help for working on the farm. But even in the Third World, having more children (ironically) now leads to less wealth and more expenses (for example, in school fees). And the children are the losers in all this. Most tragically, in countries ravaged by AIDS, many children, orphaned at an early age, are literally bringing up themselves. Meanwhile, in the so-called developed world, parenting is considered by many to be an unfortunate diversion from the real business of life, which is to actualize oneself and one's potential. Many couples are electing not to have children at all.

With all the pressures of the surrounding narcissistic culture, parenting is, according to some psychiatrists, reduced effectively to the first two years of a child's life. Whereas the family used to be an economic, social, spiritual and relational unit, family life is now effectively reduced to meeting primary physical and emotional needs. People go outside the home (or bring it in through the media) for almost everything else. We are in desperate need of recovering a spirituality of parenting.

SIX DIMENSIONS OF PARENTING

Looking at parenting biblically, we find there are six dimensions.[1]

First, parenting is *vocational*. It is a calling of God, a holy vocation that involves us in serving God's purposes and building the human race. It is equal, and in most cases is joined to, callings like being a businessperson, a doctor, a pastor or an artist.

Second, parenting is a matter of *stewardship*. Parents are trusted with children from God. They are stewards. As Eve said, "With the help of the LORD I have brought forth a man" (Gen 4:1). Parents do not "own" their children. They are charged to create a welcoming space for children where they can be free to be themselves. As Stanley Hauerwas suggests, in a sense a child is always adopted, since the child belongs to the parents in a provisional and limited way.[2]

Third, parenting is a *ministry*. It is a way of serving God and God's purposes in the context of everyday life. It touches people for God and touches God on behalf of people, in this case those who are nearest and dearest. The parable of the two prodigals (Lk 15:11-32) shows us that the gospel is pleaded in the context of family life. The younger son finds unexpected grace as his father welcomes him home. The older son, embittered and feeling cheated, does not know the father's heart or the father's welcome until he welcomes his good-for-nothing but homebound brother, even though the father goes outside the party to plead with him to come in. Family life is shot through with intimations of God and God's grace. In the same way Paul's instructions to parents and children (Eph 6:1-4) suggest that not only are children to be brought up in the nurture and admonition of the Lord but even so are the parents. They, too, need to know the Lord's unconditional love, the Lord's correction and the Lord's affirmation.

In this way, fourth, parenting is also a *priestly function*. It is priestly not only because the child's view of God is being shaped by his or her experience of Father and Mother at home but also because, as priests, parents represent God and God's purposes to children, and bring children to God in intercession. In reality parents enjoy a mutual priesthood with their children. Children "priest" their parents as well as the other way around, creating a "priesthood of all believers" at home.

Fifth, parenting is *discipling*. It is essentially an imitation process. We see this powerfully at work in the family of Abraham, Isaac and Jacob. Even Jesus said, regarding the process of forming people in relationships, that the "student is not above his teacher, but everyone who is fully trained will be *like* his teacher" (Lk 6:40).[3] The same imitation process as takes place between Jesus and the disciple occurs in the home. Parents and children are learning continuously through life-on-life relationships and mostly in unscheduled situations.

Sixth, parenting is a form of *community building*. Healthy families are covenant communities that belong together not on the basis of stipulated agreements and contracts but "for better and for worse." Day in and day out, parents are teaching, often without realizing it, what it means to belong. And even a dysfunctional family (like Jacob's), if properly processed, can be an asset for life and for establishing a new covenant community through marriage.

CHILDREN HELP PARENTS GROW UP

One of the questions we need to ask at the end of it all is "How did the parents turn out?" In Isaac's case we must conclude, "Not too well." Did he resist the learning and growth that God had in mind for him in the thick and thin, the tears and pleasure of family? And if so, why? And why, in the four generations of the family of promise that are described in Genesis 25—50, does Joseph become the one who is most healthy and most health-giving to the family of Jacob?

The pregnant phrase in the book of Genesis—"Isaac, who had a taste for wild game, loved Esau, but Rebekah loved Jacob" (Gen 25:28)—was not merely a statement of the differing genetic makeup of the boys. This cryptic phrase expresses a humanly perpetuated fault line in the family of promise that runs generation after generation, carrying its seeds of favoritism and envy from mother and father to children, until much later there is reconciliation in the family of Jacob's son Joseph.

Isaac was a sensuous, self-indulgent man of whom it could truly be said that the way to his heart was through his stomach. The only place where the word *love* appears in his vocabulary is not between father and son or between husband and wife but rather between father and food. The high point of his life appears to have been in his childhood, when he voluntarily submitted to his father's extraordinary obedience in offering him on the mountain (Gen 22:1-18), though Isaac was the only observable means of fulfilling the promise given to Abraham. As Waltke notes, "A son who was strong enough to carry on his back a load of wood sufficient for a sacrifice was certainly able to resist an aged father had he been so minded."[4]

THE DOWNHILL RUN

It is downhill from that point on.[5] When a famine comes, Isaac goes to the land of the Philistines to get food. God speaks to him directly, confirming that God will be with Isaac and will bless him (Gen 26:3) and that the promise of Abraham was passed on to him. God tells him not to go to Egypt. But then, like his father in a foreign palace, he fears for his life because of his beautiful wife. So he persuades her to claim she is his sister rather than his wife. This ruse almost leads Isaac into a marital and social disaster. But fortunately Abimelech, the Philistine king, happens to see him fondling his wife and concludes that this is not Isaac's sister.[6] As with the parallel story in the case of Abraham and Sarah (have they learned from one generation to another?), Abimelech fears God (20:9, 11), understands the solidarity of the group and wants to do the right thing—a matter that signals that God is at work in the so-called secular marketplace. Often those outside the family of promise have a higher moral standard than those inside.

Then Isaac digs some wells. There is more conflict with the local people, until Isaac comes to Beersheba. Once again God speaks to him and blesses him—a blessing that includes protection (Gen 26:9, 11, 31), enjoyment of his wife (vv. 8, 11), yield of a hundredfold (vv. 12-13), herds and servants (v. 14), water supply (vv. 17-22, 32), space (v. 22) and triumph over his enemies (vv. 25-31).[7] And just as his father had done, Isaac builds an altar and responds with worship.

Then Isaac makes a pact with Abimelech in a way that makes this account a parallel with the story of Dinah in a foreign palace in Genesis 34. For all of his complicated deceptions, Isaac proves his faith by staying in the land during a famine rather than going to Egypt for a bellyful. As Waltke notes, "Isaac manifests his faith by his willingness to accept 'stones' (i.e. famine) in God's will rather than search for bread outside of God's will. His greater son manifests his faith in both ways (see Mt. 4:3-4)."[8] God rewards that faith by speaking an unconditional commitment to bless him.

How different is the action of Esau! This son of Isaac, without any spiritual sensitivity, marries two women who are from a nation (the Hittite nation) that God had condemned for their wickedness and who would undoubtedly lead Esau astray from the holy purpose of the family of Abraham. Thus Esau's two wives are a source of grief for Isaac and Rebekah (Gen 26:35).[9] This should be a signal to Isaac that Esau is spiritually unsuitable to bear the birthright and the blessing.

As an old man, dimly aware that long ago God had chosen his younger son, Isaac goes ahead in secret with his plan to bless his favorite, Esau, whose wild game he loves. In this he rejects God's word (Gen 25:23). It is a challenging example for those facing old age and retirement.[10] Alexander Whyte comments: "When I read Isaac's whole history over again, with my eye upon the object, it becomes as clear as a sunbeam to me that what envy was to Cain, and what wine was to Noah, and what lewdness was to Ham, and what wealth was to Lot, and what pride and impatience were to Sarah—all that, venison and savoury meat were to Isaac."[11]

Truly remarkable, however, is what the author of the letter to the Hebrews selects as Isaac's superlative act of faith (Heb 11:20)—the fateful blessing of Genesis 27, clouded as it is with wilful disobedience, sensuality and secretiveness.[12] How can this be?

Isaac believes he is mediating God's irrevocable blessing and that he speaks (what he thought was to Esau but actually was to Jacob) in the power of God and for God's purposes. When he discovers the ruse, "he trembl[es] violently" (Gen 27:33), undoubtedly realizing that God is in this in spite of his own devious plan. His dream of a peaceful closure to his life with his favorite son to take his place is shattered forever.[13] The blessing cannot be undone, and he has "made [Jacob] lord over" Esau, sustaining Jacob with grain and wine (v. 37). There is irony in this.[14] As Waltke says, "Isaac and his vice are treated as a joke, but God and virtue have the last laugh."[15]

THE SINS OF THE FATHERS TO THE THIRD GENERATION

The text contains some psychological notes that should send up red flags. For one, Genesis 24:67 says that Isaac "brought [Rebekah] into the tent of his mother Sarah . . . and Isaac was comforted after his mother's death." Did they ever bond as husband and wife? Was Isaac himself a "mommy's boy"?

Going beyond the isolated clues in the text and offering illuminating insights from psychology,[16] Naomi Rosenblatt suggests, "There is a natural temptation to use our relationship with a favourite child to compensate for emotional disappointments in our marriage. The story of Jacob and Esau is a strong warning to us of the danger to children when parents draw them into the shifting power balance of their marriage. Children need to grow and develop without feeling responsible for the emotional well-being of the adults in their lives." She continues, "This new surrogate 'marriage' between parent and child is fundamentally unequal and frustrating for the child, who needs the balance of both male and female role models."[17]

I have seen this dynamic at work in African homes, where mothers, lacking intimacy with their husbands, bond with their oldest male child. When that child marries, he brings his bride into his mother's home. His mother teaches the young bride how to cook and care for him. But husband and wife do not bond, and thus the surrogate "marriages" get passed on generation to generation. One cannot "cleave" with a man who has not "left father and mother" (Gen 2:24).

Whatever the cause, it is clear that both Isaac and Rebekah found alternative companions in a favorite son rather than each other—Isaac with Esau, Rebekah with Jacob (Gen 25:28). As with most family sins, this one was passed down generation to generation (Ex 20:5): Jacob had a favorite wife, Rachel, and son, Joseph. In each case envy and jealousy ripped the family apart and led to family secrets, devious practices and, once, attempted murder.

Rosenblatt comments, "In the few moments he spends in his father's tent, Jacob tastes the sweet love from his father that Esau has enjoyed for years. . . . Jacob's tragedy is that by glimpsing the wonderful father-love he never received, he feels more deprived than ever. The guilt of deceiving his father and brother will haunt him for the next twenty years." Rosenblatt's extrapolation on this is that "we all need to feel loved by our parents [and] that by externalizing the blessing of our parents' love we acquire self-esteem and self-confidence." She further notes, "Judaism acknowledges the importance of ritualizing this implicit parent-child bond by instructing parents to bless their children every Friday night at the beginning of the Sabbath."[18]

What went wrong, and what can we learn from it? What went right, and what can we gain from this family?

FAMILY INHERITANCE

Every person comes into life with baggage from his or her family, some good and some bad. Jacob had a rich store. He inherited a family covenant, a godly heritage in the family of promise, born into a family where God is God and the parents are not. He was given a personal promise at birth that the elder would serve the younger and that the weak would be strong. He had a domestic and pleasing personality.[19] Jacob was the kind of person it is hard to dislike. The flip side of his pleasant personality, though, was his ambition, his determination to make things happen. These are all rich gifts of nature and nurture. And we do well to add up the good baggage from our own past. In practice we tend to amplify the negatives, such as our parents' divorce or being sexually molested. We tend to ignore the prayers before we were born, or even, in my own case, the fact that night after night my parents would kneel beside their bed praying for me and my brother, John.

The family inheritance of Abraham-Sarah and Isaac-Rebekah was certainly a mixed bag. James R. Koch has done a masterful study of the family of promise, showing how seeds of fear, distrust and low self-esteem gave rise to deception, exploitation, marital discord, manipulation, triangulation, power alliances and family secrets. Koch finds coherence between the relational "hints" in Genesis and insights gained from family systems theory now widely used by therapists in helping families gain health. In the family of promise the strains of relational illness were passed on and added to, until by the third and fourth generations they had mushroomed into a series of full-blown atrocities that few family lineages would ever want to claim. Koch maintains that the course and eventual cure of their family pathology provide an ancient but valid link between modern psychology and Christian theology.[20] The passing on of this pathology from generation to generation is a phenomenon now well explained by family systems theory.[21]

One example of multigenerational sin in the story of Jacob is deception, especially family secrets. The story is riddled with it. Abraham and Sarah deceived Pharaoh and other kings while in Egypt, pretending Sarah was his sister (this would have required the whole tribal group to keep the family secret). Isaac and Rebekah did the same thing. Isaac and Esau set up a secret session for the blessing. Secretly, Rebekah and Jacob planned their own deception of Isaac. Laban deceived Jacob on the wedding night. Simeon and Levi deceived Shechem and Hamor with a covenant they never intended to keep (but would disable the Shechemites and make them vulnerable, Gen 34). Joseph's brothers deceived Jacob about their brother's "death." Tamar deceived Judah, pretending to be a prostitute (Gen 38). Even Joseph ended up deceiving his brothers for a while about his real identity.

In the same way, sexual abuse, work addictions, family secrets and the addict-enabler syndrome get passed on intergenerationally unless there is an end to the denial. To move out of dysfunctionality into health, there must be insight, support and persistent determination. In all families there is a process rather than a case of instantaneous flight into health. But it never happens unless there is recognition and repentance. In the case of Jacob's family, this was a long time coming.

DECEPTION, TRIANGLES, FAMILY SECRETS
AND SIBLING RIVALRY

Koch notes that there was an escalation of deception in the covenant family. While Abraham and Sarah began with a half-truth in telling a foreign leader that Sarah was Abraham's sister (for Sarah actually *was* Abraham's sister, in addition to being his wife), Isaac and Rebekah were guilty of a full lie when they claimed a brother-sister relationship under similar circumstances (they weren't siblings at all). Then Jacob lied five times to his own father, in the blessing scene, and even introduced blasphemy by indicating that it was the Lord who had granted him success in hunting the game and getting it to his plate so quickly.[22]

Analyzing the grand deception of Isaac by Rebekah and Jacob, Koch notes that instead of the traditional interpretation that there were two villains (Rebekah and Jacob), there were in fact three (including Isaac), with all becoming both victims and villains. When Isaac feared that he might die without seeing his favorite son blessed (he could not trust God to do this for his son as Abraham had for him), he planned a secret session. Had he simply blessed him on the spot, he could have pulled off the whole thing undiscovered. But his desire to be spoiled, to have his savory food, meant the passage of time, which gave Rebekah and Jacob the opportunity to cook up their own plan. In the end Isaac did not see Esau blessed and had to live another twenty-five years with that disappointment; Jacob ran for his life; Esau kept trying to win his parents' blessing and esteem; Rebekah never saw her son again—four victims in all.[23]

Family triangles abounded. A triangle is a power alliance in which two members "gang up" on a third. The classic biblical example is Martha trying to "triangle" Jesus into an alliance against Mary, and Jesus' refusal to be so drawn in (Lk 10:38-42). Rebekah and Jacob aligned themselves against Isaac. When Jacob later married both Rachel and Leah, Leah triangled each of her three sons (Reuben, Simeon and Levi) to gain, if she could, her husband's affection. Koch notes, "Leah's triangulation of them set them up for rejection, which later manifested itself in gross action of displaced anger

([Gen] 34:25-31, 35:22). Leah finally gave up the dream of winning Jacob's love, and turned her focus ever so temporarily on God with the birth of her fourth son."[24] The name of Leah's fourth son, Judah, means "This time I will praise the Lord."

Devaluation and exploitation of persons was passed on for four generations. Abraham devalued and exploited Sarah to protect his own life when they lived in Egypt (Gen 12:10-20). Sarah exploited Hagar to have a son through a "baby machine." Isaac exploited Rebekah in the same way as his father had exploited Sarah while in a foreign court (chap. 26). Laban exploited Leah, putting her in the marriage tent to get more years of work out of Jacob (29:27). Rachel exploited Bilhah to have children, as Leah did with Zilpah (30:3, 9). Rachel exploited Jacob to get Reuben's mandrakes (30:15). Judah exploited Tamar to gratify his sexual desires (chap. 38). Arguably, Joseph exploited the people of Egypt by enslaving them all to Pharaoh during the famine (47:13-26).[25]

In each generation there was marital disillusionment that arguably contributed to triangulation. Abraham and Sarah had no children; thus Abraham was caught between Sarah and the maidservant Hagar (the latter giving him a child). But Hagar "triangulated" Ishmael to increase her status, while Sarah did the same thing with Isaac. Isaac appears to have expected Rebekah to take over his mother's role (Gen 24:67); Rebekah resisted Isaac's expectations and found solace in her favorite son, Jacob. Meanwhile Isaac triangulated Esau to meet needs that should have been met within his marriage. Jacob loved Rachel and wanted only her as his wife. But Jacob hated Leah because she reminded him of being tricked on the marriage night.[26] Rachel turned against Jacob because of her barrenness and even traded Jacob's lovemaking for mandrakes. (It seems Rachel did not love Jacob with the same adoration he gave her.) Jacob was caught between his two wives, who were bitter rivals. When Rachel finally did give birth, she even triangulated Joseph to increase her status (giving him the name that means the "gateway" to more children, thus giving her competitive advantage over Leah).[27]

The obvious result of all of this was sibling rivalry, escalating as it did to the point where Esau intended to kill Jacob (as soon as his father would be off the scene), and the brothers of Joseph tried to eliminate this younger brother with his dreams of greatness. Koch concludes:

> With an atmosphere of competition, division, and alliances all around them, the children learned to pour their energies into the sibling rivalries. This vicious sequence evolved into a vicious generational cycle when the children became parents and continued to perpetuate the identical atmosphere with their children. Of all the strains of family pathology, this cycle was the subtlest, the most enduring, and the most undermining of the "covenant family's" relational health.[28]

This continued tragically until there was a breakthrough in the fourth generation when Joseph was whisked away to Egypt. There, in the cooking pot of a pagan country, isolated from his family, Joseph discovered God in a new way, and through a process of recognition, repentance and restoration, he was not only reunited with his brothers when they came to Egypt for food but also brought unity and health once again to the family.[29]

GOD AT WORK IN THE HOME

At the heart of the family pathology is a refusal to trust God. When the family members have their esteem or possessions threatened, they do not trust God to protect them. Consequently they scheme and manipulate, even using those closest to them in the family to promote their own ambitions. Isaac cannot trust God to bless the right son after he dies, as his father Abraham had (Gen 25:11). Rebekah cannot trust that God will fulfill the prophecy his own way and in his own time. And on it goes.

Our families could be merely a vicious circle, an unending cycle of sin passed down generation to generation. But with God, our family life is a gracious circle, a furnace of transformation. Where was God in this family? Where was God not present? God was there in family life, as he is in ours, infusing, saturating our family life with reality and a gospel-seasoned hope.

First, God had given a promise to this family, a promise that would not be revoked (Gen 17:4-8). God was faithful to the promise, protecting them from imminent danger (as in the case of Abraham and Sarah in Egypt), steering them toward the Promised Land and providing for them in the coming famine through sending Joseph down to Egypt. In Christ all the promises of God find their "yes" in him (2 Cor 1:20).

Second, God was with them even when they did not know it. Three times Jacob heard God say, "I am with you" (as Jesus similarly promises in Mt 28:20). At least once Jacob reflected that God had been with him even when he was unaware: "If the God of my father, the God of Abraham and the Fear of Isaac, had not been with me, you [Laban] would surely have sent me away empty-handed" (Gen 31:42).

Third, God took them through a desperate discipline to bring them to real faith and maturity. God allowed them to experience the consequences of their own actions. Michael Novak says, "The point of marriage and family is to make us realistic."[30] Sensuous Isaac lived to see his hunter son choose pagan wives that made his life bitter (Gen 26:34-35). Manipulative Rebekah lost her favorite son. Esau despised his birthright and lost it, though he later sought it with tears (Heb 12:17). Jacob schemed to get the blessing but had to run for his life, was outwitted by Laban and was given the less lovely daughter on the marriage night. Jacob was chased by his father-in-law. His only daughter, Dinah, was raped, and his beloved Rachel died in childbirth. His favorite son, Joseph, was kidnapped and sold into slavery. James Koch remarks that God's " 'covenant family' was given the choice at all times to either honor God and each other or to destroy, exploit, manipulate, or reject each other. But beyond the element of choice, God was allowing His 'covenant family' to learn the lessons that could be learned and appreciated from the school of natural, long-term consequences."[31] Eventually, God intervened to bring health through Joseph.

Fourth, God graciously saved them. This is the divine surprise. Rachel the childless miraculously bore Joseph and later Benjamin. Leah the unloved wife was the one responsible for building up the family of promise.

She, and not Rachel, was buried beside Jacob. Jacob was graciously brought to himself, like the prodigal son coming home from the far country, though limping. He was reconciled to his brother (and so saw the face of God) and was reconciled with himself (and so got a new name). When he finally blessed his grandchildren, he could say, "I know" (Gen 48:19). God redeemed the broken life of Jacob and poured grace into his woundedness.

Finally, God was bringing each of them to the point of knowing that their needs could not be met ultimately by anyone but God himself, for whom they were created. If we live for our children, we will be bitterly disappointed. Each parent looked to a child and was left bitter or empty. Jacob married for the wrong reasons, but it did not solve his problems; he was still Jacob, the heel grabber. But he had, in the end, the pearl of great price—faith in the living God. Walter Brueggemann sums up the matter:

> There are no natural guarantees for the future and no way to secure the inheritance of the family. It must trust only to the power of God. . . . Promise requires an end to grasping and certitude and an embrace of precariousness. It is only God who gives life. Any pretense that the future is secured by rights or claims of the family is a deception.[32]

4

Sleep—the Story of the Angels
Genesis 28:10-22

> *Now I lay me down to sleep,*
> *I pray thee Lord my soul to keep;*
> *If I should die before I wake,*
> *I pray thee Lord my soul to take.*

— TWELFTH-CENTURY *ENCHIRIDION LEONIS*

We spend about one-third of our lives sleeping, yet few of us have inquired about a theology and spirituality of sleep—what it means, how it relates to our life in God, what it does for us, why we should sleep and, most important, how to sleep, especially when we are stressed, as Jacob was.

Strange and wonderful things happen when we sleep. Dreams are only one of them. There is the mysterious ministry of sleep that accomplishes the renewal not only of the body but also of the soul, a renewal some people seem determined to shortchange.

THE PROBLEM OF A GOOD NIGHT'S SLEEP

In the high-pressure Western world and the newly industrialized world, people forgo sleep to squeeze a few extra hours in the day for work. Many people are quite simply tired all the time, not just during the early parenting years when infants may wake us two or three times a night, but continuously. So people keep themselves going with the help of caffeine. It is well known to marriage counselors that one of the greatest problems couples encounter in having a healthy sexual relationship is quite simply that they are too tired. Stress also plays its part as people go to bed only to writhe and turn on the mattress, worrying about their bills, their children, their unfinished tasks and the future. Not surprisingly, insomnia is one of the most common medical problems in the industrialized world and the emerging information society.

But the problem is not restricted to the Western world. In war-torn countries and among the very poor and homeless, sleep is fitful, often punctuated with noise and interruptions.

Yet sleep is important—important enough for us to spend a third of our life doing it, important enough to realize why it is such a valuable service to ourselves. As Thomas McAlpine notes, "People who do not get enough sleep . . . have less psychological stamina, make poorer decisions and find it difficult to concentrate and think effectively. They also lose out on the equilibrium and, at times, insight that comes from regular dreaming."[1]

In Korea one of the most severe problems of pastors is fatigue. They are up almost every morning leading prayer meetings at 5:00 or 6:00 a.m. and proceed through the day with meetings and pastoral care. So when I was addressing a large group of pastors on Monday morning in Seoul, many in the auditorium were falling asleep (always an embarrassing thing in a public place). I tried everything I could to keep them awake. But then I decided to teach on the ministry of sleep and told them to enjoy that ministry right then and to bless themselves. They did. A fruitful ministry!

Sleeping is not only a ministry; it is also an expression of faith. Psalm 127 notes:

> In vain you rise early
>   and stay up late,
> toiling for food to eat—
>   for [God] grants sleep to those he loves. (v. 2)

But verse 2 is explained by verse 1:

> Unless the LORD builds the house,
>   its builders labor in vain.

Unless the LORD watches over the city,
the watchmen stand guard in vain.

We cannot afford to sleep if we are running the world, if we are taking ourselves too seriously! But if we trust God, we can afford to pass into uncon-
sciousness. Psalm 3:5-6 says:

I lie down and sleep;
I wake again, for the LORD sustains me.
I am not afraid of ten thousands of people
who have set themselves against me round about. (RSV)

Of course, sleep will sometimes be lost in order to pray, as witnessed in
the Psalm 63:6. As with Paul, we may lose sleep because of our anxiety over
the church (2 Cor 6:5). But essentially, sleep is a God-given ministry we give
to ourselves. Thus refreshed, we work and care for others the next day. Personally, I need eight hours of sleep each night and find that if I deny myself
this for more than one or two nights, I have little emotional and physical
energy to invest in the coming day.

But sleep is not only a matter of personal nurture but also a matter of justice, to see that others can sleep too. As McAlpine proposes, "Following the
lead of the biblical witnesses [such as Psalm 44:23-24], we should . . . cry out
to God until we can all sleep securely."[2]

THE SLEEPING PILGRIM

In Genesis 28 Jacob leaves home, plagued by guilt, fearful of his brother's
rage (planning to kill him when their father died) and propelled by yearnings to hunt for a wife. Jacob is actually a runaway, though one having his
mother and father's "permission" artfully contrived by Rebekah, who, to
save her darling's skin, manipulated Isaac into sending Jacob to the old
homeland to find a wife from the right family. In one sense, after traveling
two or three days from Beersheba, Jacob's lying down in the field with a
warm stone as a pillow was simply yielding to fatigue. But there is more to
this than merely a tired traveler taking rest. Jacob must "go" from his home

in order to find himself and God, just as his grandfather Abraham had to "leave" Haran and "go" to Canaan to rise to power and influence and to fulfill God's purpose.

The pattern of relinquishment ("leave your country, your people and your father's household") and movement ("go to the land I show you"—Gen 12:1) is woven into God's mission call not only to Abraham but to all who follow him in faith. Even God "leaves" and "goes." The Son of God relinquished heaven and moved to earth to become the suffering servant for us all (Phil 2:6-8). So Jacob is becoming an adult, becoming mature by taking this journey, just as much later his son Joseph will "leave" and "go" to Egypt, where he will "find himself" away from his kith and kin.

One of the metaphors for the spiritual life is a journey. But there is more to meeting God than simply traveling from one place to another; that is tourism. Essentially, Jacob is a pilgrim. Years later he speaks to Pharaoh about "the years of my pilgrimage"—implying wanderings with temporary shelters (Gen 47:9). Were it merely a journey, he could have stayed at Beersheba or even Egypt. Pilgrimage is more. Pilgrimage means there is a destiny, a homeland and an inheritance in view—though Jacob, like his forefathers, was obliged to live his life as a stranger on earth, a resident alien. Above all, pilgrimage means living so that one looks "forward to the city with foundations, whose architect and builder is God" (Heb 11:10).

So the pilgrim Jacob leaves with just a staff in hand and a few provisions. Alexander Whyte imagines the staff had been given to him by the hunter Esau at one of their shared birthdays, E and J carved into a true lover's knot under the handle. And he both cherished and used that staff for over twenty years, "though it sometimes burned his hand to a red-hot cinder" until Jacob, while praying to God and wrestling with God on the eve of his meeting Esau, reflected, "I had only my staff when I crossed this Jordan" (Gen 32:10).[3] It is possible this is the same staff that Jacob leaned on in the final deathbed blessing scene pictured by Hebrews 11:21: by faith, Jacob, "when he was dying, blessed each of Joseph's sons, and worshiped as he leaned on the top of his staff."

Staff in hand, leaving home, Jacob has nothing. It is possible he spent the first night in a herdsman's hut and the second with a hospitable stranger, because he would need three days to make it to Luz, later called Bethel, about sixty miles from home. But now Jacob is in the open country, sleeping out, with only a flat stone for a pillow, lonely, in a strange land, with a contract on his life, a man with overweening ambition but no one around with whom he can compete—except God. Much later he would be again "left alone" (Gen 32:24)—one of the prerequisites for seeing the world and life itself transparently. Jacob needs to be geographically separated from his passive father, his manipulative mother and his competitive brother in order to connect with God.

Brian Morgan offers, "Now that Jacob is off stage and his only friends are the demon of fear pursuing him, and the weight of unresolved guilt pressing in upon him, his soul becomes very sensitive to the voice of God. I have found the same principle at work in my own life. My richest experiences of heaven occurred when I was 'exiled' in some unknown place."[4] Pilgrimage transforms loneliness into solitude. It also allows us to see the invisible, to find God in ordinary, run-of-the-mill places.

Leaving home is stressful—as every first-year college student knows, as brides leaving the family home to make a new home experience and as people going off to war or to work in a faraway place realize. But to leave home under a cloud of fear and guilt, despised by one's brother, shamed before one's dying father, is to be especially vulnerable to loneliness. As Rosenblatt suggests, "The stolen blessing and birthright hung on him like a millstone."[5] So as Jacob escapes into sleep, it is not surprising that his dreams should be revelatory. Brueggemann notes, "The gospel moves to Jacob in a time when his guard is down. The dream permits news."[6]

THE DREAMER

Jacob sees a ladder or a staircase extending between heaven and earth.[7] That is the first part of his nighttime vision. The second is that he sees angels of God ascending and descending on the ladder/staircase. And third, above the ladder stands the Lord, who says, "I am the LORD, the God of your father Abraham and the God of Isaac" (Gen 28:13). Then God makes an incredible promise, elaborating on the promise he made to Abraham. Jacob and his descendants will have the land; they will become a large family that will spread out in all directions; they will be the means of blessing all the nations. But best of all, God says, "I am with you and will watch over you wherever you go, and will bring you back to this land. I will not leave you until I have done what I have promised you" (v. 15). Waltke notes the three parts to this last personal promise: God promises to sustain Jacob's faith; God promises to protect him; God promises a homecoming.[8]

Jacob is the first person whose dream is explicitly described in the Bible. But it is not the last time he will have a revelatory dream. Later, in Genesis 31, he will explain to his wives that it was through a dream that God revealed to him the secret of animal husbandry through which Jacob was able to gain large flocks and herds by means of a daring breeding program.[9]

The meaning of dreams can often be traced to the day's events and concerns, what Freud called "the day's residue." His view was that dreams express unfulfilled wishes and instinctual urges originating in one's early childhood or in repressed sexual desires.[10] Dreams, then, are the royal road to the unconscious mind. Freud said in effect, "I dream, therefore I am."

In Jacob's case there is his uncertain assumption of the leadership of the family and the responsibilities of keeping the covenant. Who is he, after all, to have the blessing, though he undoubtedly craved his father's approval as an infant craves his mother's milk? But on the other hand, God is speaking here; God is revealing himself to Jacob through a dream. Significantly David in Psalm 16:7 says, "Even at night my heart instructs me."

In the history of God's revelation, it is obvious that people in the Old Testament (Pharaoh, Pharaoh's butler and baker, and Joseph) as well as people in the New Testament (for example, Mary's Joseph in Mt 2:13) were guided by God through dreams. Dr. Stephen Anderson, a psychiatrist, offers a fine summary of what dreams mean to us now that we have Scripture as a direct word from God:

Dreams can be extremely useful for understanding ourselves and for providing an impetus for change. God may also communicate with us through our dreams. However, dreams only make sense against a person's background and past, and most dreams require a detailed and intimate knowledge of the dreamer and his or her circumstances. . . . We are still far from knowing all there is to know about dreams. We do know that dogmatic interpretation of dreams is inappropriate and that, like works of art, dreams must often be allowed to speak for themselves.[11]

Anderson then quotes the seventeenth-century physician Sir Thomas Browne to indicate that our understanding of dreams has not changed much in the last three hundred years: "However dreames may bee fallacious concerning outward events, yet may they bee truly significant at home, and whereby wee may more sensibly understand ourselves. Men act in sleepe with some conformity unto their awaked senses, and consolations or discouragements may bee drawne from dreames which intimately tell us ourselves."[12] Jacob's dream was a revelation of God and himself at the same time. He encounters heaven on the run.

JACOB'S LADDER

Spirituals, songs and dozens of pieces of art have been created around the image of the ladder (or it may have been a staircase). But a significant one is based on the writing of John Klimax, author of *The Ladder of Perfection*. According to *The Ladder*, a monk should gain perfection by climbing thirty rungs of virtues, but the way is beset with temptations. Based on Klimax's book, a sixteenth-century icon from Mount Athos in Greece pictures a ladder between heaven and earth with the thirty rungs, each a spiritual quality to be attained before one can reach the next step. Monks are attempting to make it up the ladder one rung at a time. But demons on all sides are pulling them off the ladder. At the very top, for those who make it, Jesus is holding a scroll of Scripture with the text "Come to me all you who are weary and burdened, and I will give you rest" (Mt 11:28).[13]

Nothing could be further from the gospel of God—or from the vision given to Jacob in his dream. The good news is not that Jesus waits for us at the top of the ladder to welcome us when we have attained perfection. Rather, Jesus comes down the ladder to meet us where we are and brings us to himself and to God. "Come unto me" is spoken from the bottom of the ladder. Jesus, referring to this himself, tells Nathaniel, "You shall see heaven open, and the angels of God ascending and descending on the Son of Man" (Jn 1:51). That was the vision given to Jacob—a before-Christ gospel message. It is sheer grace.

Jacob has run away from his brother's murderous rage. Unbeknownst to him, he is heading to Haran, where Laban will exploit him. He is between a "death camp" and a "hard-labor camp."[4] In the narrative he comes to a "certain place" (Gen 28:11); the narrator holds back the original name of the location—Luz. He has come to a no-place place, a nameless place. But God has met him. His journey is now a pilgrimage. Whatever his experience at the old family homestead in Haran to which he is running, God will be working out his wonderful purpose. The no-place place becomes the axis of heaven and earth. So Jacob renames the place "Bethel," house of God. The grasper becomes a giver, as his vow to give to God a tithe indicates.

Jacob then makes a vow. It goes roughly like this: If God will (1) watch over me, (2) give me food and clothes, and (3) bring me safely home without my brother killing me, then (a) God will be my God, (b) this stone I have set up as a memorial pillar will be a sacred God-house, and (c) I will give God a tenth of everything. It doesn't take the intelligence of a rocket scientist to note that the vow is conditional—"if" (in contrast with the response of Abraham, who simply "believed the LORD"—Gen 15:6).

Many Christian commentators criticize Jacob for making a conditional vow. He should, they argue, have simply worshiped in gratitude and not made a solemn vow, certainly not one couched in "if" language. Significantly, though, God does not criticize Jacob's vow—nor do most Jewish commentators. The reason is profoundly theological. Jacob has just heard God make a promise to him. It is on the strength of that promise (articulated in terms of peoplehood, protection and God's presence) that Jacob is responding.

There at Luz the fugitive was found by God. The medium was a dream with a staircase between heaven and earth, with angels of God ascending (with requests and human wants) and descending (with help and protection from God). The message was sheer grace: "I am with you" (Gen 28:15), later twice repeated (31:3; 46:4) at critical moments in his life. The medium and the message were one and the same: uninterrupted communion with God. Jacob has a destination and a fellow traveler. Indeed God will not leave him until he has done what he promised. But where do the angels fit in?

THE ANGELS

Surprisingly in the postmodern West, angels are back in vogue. This renewed interest in angels is largely part of a recovery of "spirituality" after decades of soul-numbing materialism and scientism. I both welcome this recovery and worry about it. On the one hand, it is valuable to know that God has invisible servants and messengers to assist us in this complicated and confusing world. But on the other hand, Scripture warns us against worshiping angels and treating them as anything other than messengers of God, who alone deserves our undivided worship and attention. But what angels *are* baffles our understanding. In a fine article on angels, Thomas F. Torrance says this:

> As Gregory the Theologian once said, our minds go into a spin at trying to find the right way in which to speak of the elusive nature of angels. They are neither corporeal nor incorporeal in our sense even if they sometimes appear in human form, for, as Calvin pointed out, in depicting them the Scripture "matches the measure of our comprehension." They just are what they are as angelic beings existing before God and reflecting his light, hymning the majesty of the Godhead and contemplating his eternal glory. It is as such that angels are sent by God to fulfil a spiritual ministry as his heavenly messengers and joyful ministrants to us on earth. "Are not all angels ministering spirits sent to serve those who will inherit salvation?" (Heb 1:14).[15]

They constitute a great company and were created holy (though some, notably Satan, fell). Good angels are employed to stand in the presence of

God in worship (Mt 18:10), to rejoice in God's works (Lk 15:10), to execute God's will (Ps 103:20), to guide the affairs of nations (Dan 12:1), to watch over particular churches (1 Tim 5:21), to protect individual believers (Heb 1:14) and to punish God's enemies (Acts 12:23).[16]

In the Old Testament angels look after nations and their territories, a kind of God-sent earth patrol (Job 1:6; 2:1; Zech 1:8-17; compare Deut 32:8). The Jewish expositor Rashi posits that the descending angels in Jacob's dream are responsible for Jacob's homeland—to which he hopes to return safely—and the ascending ones patrol the foreign land to which Jacob is migrating. Thus the vision of angels was an assurance that God would be with him both where he was going and in the land to which he hoped to return—an interpretation supported by Genesis 28:15.[17]

Genesis 28 would not be Jacob's last encounter with angels. He saw a host of them twenty years later when he reentered the Promised Land at Mahanaim (Gen 32:1-2) and wrestled with an angel-man through the night at the ford of the Jabbok River (vv. 22-32).[18]

In an angel-soaked world, life itself is a spiritual discipline. Everyday life—waking-and-sleeping life as well as going-from-one-place-to-another life—is the spiritual discipline in which God continuously and graciously meets us. What Jacob experienced as a fleeting, extraordinary encounter under the older covenant becomes a window on the permanent, continuous and universal inheritance of those who follow Jesus. In the incarnate Christ, God is fully and finally "with us" as the angels of God continuously ascend and descend on the Son of Man, Jesus (Jn 1:51).

Angels help us to distinguish between the spiritual life and the "spiritualized" life. Spiritualized life is an add-on: God talk, religious activity, a pious veneer and theological prattle—talking *about* God, as Job's friends did. But spiritual life is God-inundated life in which people like Job—who spoke well of God (Job 42:7) by speaking *to* God—tell it all to God with holy boldness, communicating with God in the thick of life. This Jacob did. There is more to Jacob than mere deceit.

The gist of the experience is that the lines of communication with God are open. The extraordinary is found here in the ordinary. This common place is a window on heaven. This ordinary place becomes an "awesome place" (see Gen 28:17).

THE FEAR OF THE LORD

Jacob was afraid. Perhaps his fear was motivated by the recognition that he had defrauded his brother and manipulated his father. He was a sinner in the presence of a holy God (Is 6:5). But the fear of God is not merely fright. It is reverent awe combining nonrational numinous fear, love and trust, and the rational with ethics, justice and uprightness.[19] The Bible indicates that the fear of God (in this sense of awe that calls forth justice and righteousness) is the beginning of wisdom (Prov 1:7). Indeed such wisdom, according to Proverbs 3:19-24, leads to sound judgment and discernment and real peace.

> Then . . . when you lie down, you will not be afraid;
> when you lie down your sleep will be sweet. (vv. 23-24)

So this good fear transforms Jacob's camping place into "the house of God" and "the gate of heaven"—a place where God lives and a way to his heavenly destiny (Gen 28:17).

So Jacob takes the flat stone on which he rested his head and sets it up as a memorial pillar, a masseba.[20] He pours oil on it to consecrate it as the place where he received mercy and renames the place "house of God." This is not the only time Jacob will make a memorial with stones. Stones are, for Jacob, metaphors. They shape his life. As Robert Alter says, "Jacob is a man who sleeps on stones, speaks in stones, wrestles in stones, contending with the hard unyielding nature of things, whereas in pointed contrast, his favored son [Joseph] will make his way in the world as a dealer in the truths intimated through the filmy insubstantiality of dreams."[21]

How can ordinary places and ordinary time (like sleeping time) be inundated with God—not God talk or God religion but God? How can everyday life become the place where God lives, the open door to God's presence and the time for worship?

THE GOOD NEWS

First, this is a story of sheer mercy. Jacob deserves nothing. As someone has said, "I can understand God saying, 'Esau I have hated,' but I cannot understand how God could say, 'Jacob I have loved.' " Paul's conclusion on the matter is this: the promise "does not . . . depend on man's desire or effort, but on God's mercy" (Rom 9:16). Pilgrimage is not seeking God or finding the way to heaven; rather, it is the experience of being found and finding heaven interrupt us progressively until we reach our final destiny. In the last book of the Bible the apostle John discovered the same thing: "I looked, and there before me was a door standing open in heaven" (Rev 4:1). Heaven is open. Earth is crammed with it.

Second, we live in an angel-inundated world. These spiritual beings surround us as messengers of God, protecting, communicating, blessing. We live in a God-soaked world, a God-saturated creation. God sends his angels to care for us when we are tempted or in danger. We are aware of the help, sometimes aware of a miraculous intervention, even though we cannot see these heavenly messengers.[22]

Third, Jacob was a willing recipient of God's blessing. Esau, in contrast, did not care enough for the things of God to delay gratification of his hunger for a few minutes. Jacob cared enough to steal and cheat to get it. He was overly ambitious, an overachiever. But within this passion was a desire for the blessing of God that would in the end be violent in its intensity (Gen 32:26). Journeying saints take photos of the marker events of their lives. Pilgrims fall on their faces and cry, "This is an awesome place! How can I as a sinner be so near to so great a God?"

Finally, Jacob had a faith-full imagination. Like the younger brother in the parable of Jesus, Jacob could "see" home (Lk 15:17-20). Again Whyte has an insight. "Esau lost his birthright with all its blessings largely through his lack of imagination. The things that are unseen and eternal had neither substance nor evidence to Esau compared with the things that are seen and temporal."[23]

Pilgrimage is not a matter of place and time, of special moments and special places, but of seeing the invisible in the here and now. It is living in God's wide and expansive world rather than our own narrow and restricted world. It is embracing the God of Jacob (what inspiration in that phrase!) and shunning the paganism of Esau. It is wanting God and God's heaven so badly that we would storm the gates of heaven to get in, only to discover, as Pascal said ages ago, that we would not be seeking him if we had not already found him (or rather been found by him). Simone Weil said something similar that captures Jacob's encounter with the angels:

> We cannot take a single step towards [God]. We do not walk vertically. We can only turn our eyes towards him. We do not have to search for him, we only have to change the direction in which we are looking. It is for him to search for us.[24]

5

Courting—the Story of Rachel
Genesis 29:1-14

> *Only the rarest of human beings will be*
> *moved to marry by argument alone.*
>
> —AMY KASS AND LEON KASS

> *Today there is no socially prescribed form of conduct*
> *that helps guide young men and women in the direction*
> *of matrimony. This is true not just for the lower or under classes.*
> *Even—indeed especially—the elite, those who in previous*
> *generations would have defined the conventions in these matters,*
> *lack a cultural script whose denouement is marriage.*
>
> —AMY KASS AND LEON KASS

Silas, are you married?" Gail asked as she leaned forward on her chair in Pastor Silas's mud-brick house in rural Kenya. Stray slashes of light filtered through the thatched roof. It is the custom to have lunch with the pastor after speaking in a church. I had met Silas two years before, and remarking on his leadership qualities, encouraged a mature pastor to mentor this young schoolteacher. Now he was a tent-making, self-supporting pastor.

"No," he answered. Gail kept on inquiring, led (as we believe) by the Spirit.

"Would you *like* to be?"

"Yes," he said with a decisiveness that revealed a heart ready for romance.

Gail thought for a while and said, "I know a woman of the same tribe as yours who loves Jesus very much. She would be a wonderful wife for you."

"What is her name?" Silas asked, obviously more than a little interested.

"Elizabeth Oforo."

"I have noticed her." That comment from Silas might have been the end of it, an innocent exchange about marital readiness, but for what followed two hours later.

Seventeen people poured into our four-wheel drive to "help us" find the nearest road, as we were some distance from any recognizable track, near the Uganda border in a place with no telephone, no electricity, no automobile roads and only well-trodden footpaths. As we rumbled through bogs and plowed through dense copses, Silas leaned over to Gail in the back seat and asked, "Mama Stevens, would you mind writing a letter to Elizabeth Oforo to see if she would be interested in a relationship that could lead to marriage?"

"I will," Gail replied. Thus began one of the greatest romance stories of our lives.

There are only two ways to enter marriage. One is by arranging it yourself through courting (that old English word for friendly persuasion between a man and a woman); the other is by having an arranged marriage (which is the friendly persuasion by another person). Some think there is a third way—by prayer and magic through which God miraculously delivers a spouse without any human intervention. But that seems to be supported neither by Scripture nor experience.

Silas and Elizabeth were eventually to be married, as Jacob himself was, by a combination of both self- and other-person arrangement. Indeed each arrangement is unique, and there is no ordained method.

The Jacob-Rachel-Leah marriage was exceptional even among the patriarchs in two ways. Jacob married two sisters (which was not simple polygamy), and he got married to each of his wives differently—Rachel by a passionate, all-consuming romantic love, and Leah through her father's secret arrangement. The latter was the outworking of a devious plot on Laban's part that unwittingly played into the concern of God in the Genesis narrative: to build a family on earth that would bear the covenant and represent God's concern to bless the whole earth through that family.

Jacob had traveled from Beersheba with his father and mother's blessing to do this very thing—to find a bride and to find one in the right family, that is, a relative of Abraham and Jacob's mother, Rebekah. Samuel Dresner concludes, "The journey between heaven and earth is, then, intimately bound up with the journey to Haran to find a wife who can join him in the life of the covenant."[1] It is a journey that was taken a generation before.

HOW TO ARRANGE A GOOD MARRIAGE

Abraham, concerned with his advancing age and wanting to secure succession for the covenant within the family of promise, makes his servant swear by cupping his hand on his testicles (Gen 24:2-3)—a very ancient custom, deriving from the special sanctity of the reproductive organ, that two generations later would be done by Joseph (47:29).[2] The oath is to prevent Isaac from marrying a local pagan girl and so to compromise the covenant. The servant (traditionally named Eliezer) is a model marriage arranger (24:2-67). First, he prays that God will guide him, putting the preeminence on God's initiative. He seeks a bride for Isaac from the right family by traveling by caravan to Haran in Mesopotamia. Then he asks God for a sign not to strengthen his own faith but to be sure of God's guidance—let the woman, when requested for a drink, not only supply his needs but also that of his animals.[3] And so at a well that would later become a romantic meeting place for Jacob, Eliezer meets Rebekah, who is not only goodhearted and hospitable but also beautiful. He is taken to her mother's home, where through conversation and gift giving for the bride price, an agreement is made with her brother, Laban. Rebekah should return with this God-touched stranger to a faraway land, all on the basis of a promise from God. When asked if she agreed with this radical proposal, Rebekah said, "I will go" (v. 58).

Jewish authors maintain that this interchange is the scriptural source for the rabbinic ruling that a woman cannot be married without her consent.[4] It is noteworthy also that wherever the Christian faith has spread throughout the globe it has not always brought the arrange-your-own-marriage method. Often it has respected the arranged-marriage system already in place and working well (certainly with fewer divorces than in the West). But the church has brought consent, as symbolized in the pledge questions of the traditional marriage service: "Will you have this man/woman to be your lawfully wedded husband/wife?" No one can be compelled to make a covenant against his or her will. Rebekah gave her consent, and in a few short hours she was on her way to Palestine to meet and be joined to her husband, Isaac. It was not so simple for our friends Silas and Elizabeth.

NEGOTIATING AN ARRANGEMENT

Gail did write Elizabeth and received an astonishing reply. "I not only know the man but I love him." So we traveled to Elizabeth's town, where she was serving as a church worker.

"You need to meet with Silas, spend time with him and get to know him," we said.

"But that's not possible in our culture. The elders won't let young people be alone, because they assume they will have intercourse."

So we drummed up a Jacoblike scheme to get Silas to take the Friday overnight train to Nairobi, and we arranged to get Elizabeth there by car so the four of us could spend a day together in the anonymity of the city. The rendezvous took place at a public place—not a well but a train station. I reached down to pick up Silas's bag and carry it to the car, but Elizabeth pushed my hand aside and grabbed it first. Within her culture she had to give an important signal—I would be willing to carry your bags and your burdens. Then over tea in a hotel lobby Gail and I launched into the strangest premarital counseling session in our lives.

"In our country, we talk about expectations."

"First of all," Elizabeth interrupted, "we must talk about money. If there is a misunderstanding about money, about bride price, it will pollute the whole marriage." Then followed an hour's negotiation on family expectations in terms of goats and cows.

"Now can we talk about your expectations?"

"Next we must talk about monogamy," Elizabeth once more insisted. "I have never met a man from our tribe who was satisfied with one wife."

"I would be satisfied with you," Silas offered romantically. (Then Elizabeth recited the record of each of their fathers—two wives to the man.)

"What if I can only have girl children?"

"We will trust the Lord."

Then ratcheting up one final notch, Elizabeth asked, "What if I cannot have any children?"

Silas thought long and hard and replied, "We will accept that from the Lord."

Then we did get to expectations. Elizabeth told Silas that she expected him to wear a white shirt and tie every day. Silas told her that he expected her to keep them clean. On it went until, hours later, they announced that they had decided to have a relationship that could lead to marriage but that they had a serious problem. He wanted to marry in three months; she wanted to wait three years. Now we did shuttle diplomacy, first face to face and then with letters from Canada until after two years they were married—happily and fruitfully so. They are a delightful couple serving God as self-supporting church leaders and with a thriving family. But it was even more complicated for Jacob.

JACOB IN SEARCH OF A BRIDE

Jacob arrives, it appears, at the same well as his grandfather's servant, with a mandate to marry but with no bride price, only a staff in hand. Then Rachel comes to water the sheep. For Jacob it was simply love at first sight. There were other shepherds at the well waiting for all to gather before they rolled aside the massive stone covering the well to water their sheep. Jacob, overcome by a powerful emotion, single-handedly rolls away the stone that normally would take several men to move (yes, another occasion when Jacob speaks with stones), like uncorking a bottle.[5] Then he waters Rachel's sheep—a mirror image of Eliezer's "sign." And we don't know if he got rid of the other shepherds! But Jacob then ran up to Rachel and kissed her. No intermediary. No bride price. No bracelet or silver nose ring. Just masculine virility and passionate love expressed in a courting act.

Indeed, there is a parallel with Abraham's servant at the well, but also a significant difference. Eliezer came loaded with gifts (for the bride price). He also prayed, and when it was obvious that God had answered his prayer, he praised God. In contrast, Jacob comes empty-handed and seems not to pray. Instead, he relies on his own strength and is overcome by a powerful emotion. Instead of praising God, he embraces Rachel, seemingly unaware that God is involved in this meeting. But the narrative is rich: the contrast of extended journey and sudden meeting, the dry desert and the watery well, the lonely traveler and joyful communion.

THE KISS

Not surprisingly, Jacob's passionate embrace has been an embarrassment to many readers of the Bible. With the exception of the Song of Songs and the harlot's kiss in Proverbs 7:13, men and women in Scripture did not kiss before marriage. Brothers kiss. Parents and children kiss. But not unmarried couples. Rabbinic literature specifies that "all kissing is indecent save three: high office, parting and reunion."[6] Some rabbis rationalized it under the category of kinsmen (since Rachel was actually Jacob's cousin). And John Calvin maintained that the incident is actually an error in the text.[7] But drawing on the Jewish mystical classic *Zohar*, Dresner views the kiss as the meeting of material and spiritual, a divine-human encounter.

> To the mystic, the intimate aspect of that encounter is the goal of all religious striving, the heart of faith. It is through the experience of human affection, even the affection between man and woman, that the encounter with the divine and the life of the spiritual world is sometimes expressed. How else describe the divine than by means of the profoundly human?[8]

Then Dresner quotes *Zohar*: "No other love is like unto the ecstasy of the moment when spirit cleaves to spirit in a kiss, more especially a kiss on the mouth. . . . When mouth meets mouth, the spirits unite . . . they are one, and love is one. . . . Do not the kisses proceed from Him?"[9] The ladder and the kiss are one and the same.

Behind the physicality of biblical spirituality is an important truth—the biblical and Hebraic view of the person. A human being is not body, soul and spirit in three compartments like coaches linked together behind a locomotive. That unfortunate view, widely shared by Christians throughout the world, and usually with the depreciation of bodily life as "lower," actually came from the Greek world. The Greeks thought of the body as the shell for the soul, to be shucked on death (and by means of this putting off of the body, a person is saved through the immortality of the soul). In contrast, the biblical view is that the person is a unity.

People do not "have" bodies, souls and spirits; they *are* bodies, souls and spirits. The body is the person expressed. And to touch the body is to touch the person. It would revolutionize sexual behavior if we realized that we touched persons as a whole and not just bodies. As God is present in human affection, the human kiss is a sacrament of God's own embrace of humankind.

No wonder Jacob weeps aloud (Gen 29:11)! It is not hard to imagine why. Stirred by the sight of a lovely potential bride, on a divine mission, having had a transforming encounter with the living God, empty of money but full of longing, a journey completed with the woman of his dreams, Jacob had left home to find home. As the rabbis say, "The home *is* the woman."[10]

While Isaac "took" Rebekah, "married" her and *then* "loved" her (Gen 24:67), Jacob's love precedes marriage. This is not just a passing infatuation. Technically the word *infatuation* means temporary insanity, and the state generally passes after a year or two. A Greek father says to his daughter (who is in love) in the film *Captain Corelli's Mandolin*, "Love is what is left over when being in love has burned away."

Jacob's love endures seven years of hard work as the bride price (negotiated by Rachel's shrewd father). But these seven years of waiting "seemed like only a few days to him because of his love for her" (Gen 29:20). More significantly, Jacob's love endured the trials that were to follow. Love waits.

If it cannot wait till marriage, it is lust. Love suffers long, "is kind . . . is not self-seeking . . . always perseveres" (1 Cor 13:4-5, 7).

The contrast with our own day is most instructive, as Amy and Leon Kass note:

> To make naturally polygamous men accept the conventional institution of monogamous marriage has been the work of centuries of Western civiliza-tion, with social sanctions, backed by religious teachings and authority, as major instruments of the transformation, and with female modesty as the cru-cial civilizing device. As these mores and sanctions disappear, courtship gives way to seduction and possession, and men become again the sexually, famil-ially, and civically irresponsible creatures they are naturally always in danger of being.[11]

In other words, men are more likely to stray or have successive partners when there are not societal and religious structures that point to covenant marriage. Courting, once common in Victorian society and Pietist Amer-ica, was one way (though not the only way) to arrange your own marriage. Arguably it should be revived in some form.

THE LOST ART OF COURTING

Since *courting* is not a commonly used word today, it is important to define it. In their superb resource book on the subject, Amy and Leon Kass clarify that not all activities in which there is an erotic interest between two people of different sexes can be called courting. In its traditional meaning, courting is paying amorous attention to someone, wooing with a view to marriage. Thus courting can be distinguished from flirting or seducing, from having an affair or being in a "relationship," since none of these activities aims at marriage. "Accordingly, by courtship we mean that collection of activities aimed at (1) finding and (2) winning (3) the right one (4) for marriage." The Kasses further note that "finding means more than hunting out or locating; it also means *finding out* if the located one is really right."[12] This involves judgment and discernment and knowledge of oneself.

Courting also involves knowing what marriage is: a lifelong covenant by which two people belong to each other for companionship, procreation and shared service. Marriage, understood as a covenant, is characterized by faithfulness, exclusiveness and permanence—all critical matters for the relationship that leads up to it.

So courting is pursuing a relationship that could lead to marriage with clear intent, with affection appropriate for the level of commitment and with nonmanipulative persuasion by words, gifts, deeds and touch. Call this "dating" if you wish, but it is dating with intent (not "casual dating"), dating with self-control and dating with love rather than lust as the primary motive. It includes the determination to reserve sexual intercourse for its rightful context of full covenant marriage—in other words, to wait and to give and receive the tokens of love with integrity rather than duplicity, knowing all along that the relationship may not be consummated in marriage. So restraint and discipline are imposed. Again, the Kasses offer significant perspective on courting, giving us an apologetic for a process largely lost.

> Courtship took romantic or erotic love as its starting point, but sought to discipline it in the direction of marriage. . . . By holding back the satisfaction of sexual desire, courtship used its energy as romantic attraction to foster salutary illusions that inspired admiration and devotion. At the same time, it provided opportunities for mutual learning about one's character and, by locating wooer and wooed in their familial settings, taught the intergenerational meaning of erotic activity.[13]

Courting is really practice in being married. It provides the opportunity to learn and express attentiveness, care and faithfulness—all qualities that would be included in the promises made at a wedding: "to love and to cherish," "to be faithful to you alone," "for better or worse."

In contrast, the widespread practice of cohabitation, "living together," is not really a good preparation for marriage. It is not even a "trial marriage." It is an especially poor way of testing marriageability. Studies done by Walter R. Schrumm show that "the conditional nature of the living together arrangement begs for exploitation to occur, with the intimacy of substantial short-term gains making it too easy to rationalize one's behavior, to overlook or minimize things that are important to building a relationship in the long run or to disregard the long-term welfare of oneself or the other person."[14]

Even dating (as I have defined it above) is almost dead in much of the Western world. Allan Bloom calls dating a "petrified skeleton of court-ship."[15] So what we have left is "chance encounters, hookings up, and short-er and longer relationships."[16] This leaves most young people wondering who should take the initiative, or whether any initiative should be taken. And many Christians, spiritualizing the whole process, "leave it to God," often with a bitter result when it appears that God has let them down.

Dating and courtship are not strictly biblically mandated ways of getting married, though the Scripture might point to the value of a redeemed dating and courtship system. What the Bible shows is that all marriages are arranged, either by oneself or by others. It shows that there is nothing magical in mate selection and that God is at work in this process, as witnessed by the pregnant phrase in Genesis 2:22: "The LORD God . . . brought her to the man." Just as easily could the Lord God bring the man to the woman. The human initiative may come, at least as witnessed in Scripture, from either the man or the woman.

In the Old Testament the widow Ruth takes appropriate initiative, dress-es attractively, perfumes herself, gives Boaz a signal of her interest, speaks her heart (the Hebrew phrase for wooing is literally "speaking to the heart"—see Is 40:2) and empowers him to take the relationship further— all with a little help from her mother-in-law (Ruth 3).

There are, as we have considered, deep cultural reasons for the demise of courting. But there are also factors relating to the history of each person. Many today cannot bring themselves to court and be courted because of past hurts not yet healed and the fear of being rejected. Many are so repulsed by the lust world of the West—to bed on the first date—that they kiss dating goodbye and promise not to kiss until the wedding day. But just how, then, are they to find and to win the right one for marriage?

Another way of putting this is to say that marriages still ought to be arranged not just by one's biological family but also by one's spiritual family — the church community. They could sensitively introduce people to others, offer wise advice and counsel, and include matters of character and faith that are normally omitted by the professional and computerized dating and mating services.

But the other way, as I have said, is to take the initiative oneself. That certainly is what Gail and I did forty years ago. And I remember, after our first evening at the faculty music concert at McMaster University, returning to my residence bedroom and doing the equivalent of single-handedly removing the stone from the well. I did a backward somersault on my bed and landed with my feet squarely on the pillow. Jacob was not all wrong in his romantic initiative and, in due course, he would see that God was in it.

A GOD-SIZED PERSPECTIVE

Courting is not simply the invention of a romanticized society of a bygone day. It is native to the human heart and even corresponds to the heart of God, who courts, woos and wins (and wins back) his bride Israel (Hos 2:14-15). There is romance in the heart of God and a hunger for romance in the heart of God-imaging creatures. Of course it is experienced a little differently by men and by women, as the rather negative quote by the Kasses above suggests. Men are naturally more polygamous than women. And for women, sex is never merely accidental and incidental, because it is so closely linked with procreation. Indeed a woman in the sexual encounter — so profoundly expressed in its physical metaphor of penetration — must allow a man to come inside her person. She is incredibly vulnerable and must feel safe in the relationship. And the first sexual encounter should, for its proper meaning, take place within the safety and security of a lifelong covenant. For men it is a little different, though true love and civilizing influences would persuade a man to consider what it means for his beloved.

So the relation of the sexes in the delicious and delightful encounters of courting, while preparational (for marriage), are also inspirational. As we make space in our hearts for another, God dwells with us, welcoming and embracing.

Who better to recover godly courting than the sons and daughters by faith of the courting God? This courting God has wooed and won us for a romance that does not end with engagement but persists in an ever-deepening spiral of giving and receiving love, until we all experience full consummation at the wedding supper of the Lamb in the new heaven and new earth (Rev 19:7-8; 21:2). There and then all eternity will be the romance of God and the romancing of life.

The arranged marriage system, once the norm and still practiced in some parts of the world, can be just as sacred and sanctified as the story of Silas and Elizabeth suggests (and others we could recite). Ironically, Jacob's marital history was to exemplify both ways of getting married. And God was in both, though it didn't seem like it on the morning after the wedding night when he discovered in his bed not the beautiful Rachel for whom he had worked and waited seven years but her older weak-eyed or soft-eyed sister, Leah.[17] And having slept with her, he was now legally married—but to the wrong person. Or so he thought.[18] And so people think today—an issue we must now take up.

6

Marriage—the Story of Leah
Genesis 29:14-30

*Marriage is and remains the most important
voyage of discovery a human being undertakes;
compared with a married man's knowledge of life,
any other knowledge of it is superficial.*

—SØREN KIERKEGAARD

*[Today] when marriage occurs it does not seem to result
from a decision and a conscious will to take on its responsibilities.
The couple have lived together for a long time, and by an almost
imperceptible process, they find themselves married,
as much out of convenience as passion, as much negatively
as positively (not really expecting to do much better, since
they have looked around and seen how imperfect all fits seem to be).
Among the educated, marriage these days seems to be best acquired,
as Macaulay said about the British Empire, in a fit of absence of mind.*

—ALLAN BLOOM

At one time or another most married people wonder if they have married
the wrong person. This is especially so when two during courtship have suc-
cumbed to the powerful delusion called infatuation, a chemically heightened awareness that passes in a year or two. And when the drug does wear
off, reality sets in. Your spouse has bad breath, leaves socks on the floor, has
strange eating habits and is a morning person, and you wish he or she were

more or less talkative, less or more intuitive, more or less needing affection and less or more expecting intimacy. All this is normal and can be faced and accommodated much better in a long courtship (like Jacob's) than in a whirlwind romance.

WHAT YOU SEE IS NOT WHAT YOU GET

There are generally two problems with marriage: first, not getting what you expect, and second, not expecting what you get.

Even in a well-prepared marriage there will inevitably be conflict. It is impossible for two people to live in such geographical, vocational and emotional proximity without a conflict of interests and power, a parallel match for the conflict of expectations. The solution for this is not compliance—going along with the other. This is wrongly named submission. Submission is an act of free will in which one comes to embrace the interest of the other. Compliance is a psychological adaptation to pain. But there is always a sliver of resentment in the compliant person—a sliver that, left in place, leads either to the infection of depression (being "pressed down") or outright rebellion. Sadly many Christian women think they are submitting (Eph 5:22) when they are really complying; their husbands, imagining that "head" (v. 23) means making the decisions and being in charge, may even pride themselves on their biblical marital politics and imagine that it pleases God. Then the inevitable crisis happens, years or even decades later.

Catherine Booth, cofounder of the Salvation Army, gave a remarkable witness to a healthier and happier way. Certainly it is not a specimen of compliance under the name of "Christian submission." It is worth quoting at length:

> There were certain rules, which I formulated for my married life, before I was married or even engaged. I have carried them out ever since my wedding day, and the experience of all these years, has abundantly demonstrated their value. The first was, never to have any secrets from my husband in anything that affected our mutual relationship, or the interest of the family. . . . The second rule was, never to have two purses, thus avoiding even the temptation of hav-

ing any secrets of a domestic character. My third principle was that, in matters where there was a difference of opinion, I should show my husband my
views and the reasons on which they were based, and try to convince in favor
of my way of looking at the subject. This generally resulted either in his being
converted to my views, or in my being converted to his, either result securing
unity of thought and action.[1]

At such times, especially when resolution does not come easily (or at
all), it is tempting to think you have married the wrong person. This insid-
ious seed-thought may be advanced by reflective hindsight in which you
discover that you entered marriage for the wrong reason—to satisfy your
sexual appetites, to gain a provider, to find a substitute father or mother, or
to escape from your family of origin. Speaking to this and other wrongly entered callings, the Puritan William Perkins offers wise and God-sized advice. If you entered a calling for the wrong motive, the solution is to *repent*
of having the wrong motives and to *stay* in that calling for the right reasons.[2]

But for Jacob, the problem of his first marriage (to Leah) was that he did
in fact marry the wrong person. The essential ingredient—consent—was
lacking. He was tricked into marrying Leah when he had intended to marry
his beloved Rachel. This was an arranged marriage without the consent of
at least one partner. And the matchmaker (Laban) was as deceitful and
shrewd as the groom (Jacob). Commenting on the spirituality of this situation, Waltke says, "God's transformation of Jacob's character now begins in
the ambiguity of the beauty of romantic love being frustrated by an insen-
sitive father."[3] This gut-wrenching story does provide an answer to the question "Can we be truly blessed by God if we are seemingly trapped in an
unhappy marriage?"

MARRIED BY MISTAKE

Jacob works seven years effectively as an indentured slave to get Rachel.
Though Jacob is a blood relative of Laban, their work relationship reflects
rather the employer-employee bond, in this case Jacob's "working off" his
debt for the bride price. As a nephew, he might have expected his uncle to

treat him more generously, but instead Laban exploits him. But the years pass quickly because of his love.

On the wedding night, seven years later, Laban has a plan. Jacob the deceiver has met his match in the deceptive matchmaker. Laban slips the older sister, the one with the weak eyes, into the marriage tent, and Jacob consummates the marriage with one whom he thinks is his beloved Rachel but who in reality is her sister, Leah. He wakes in the morning and in effect cries, "How have you Jacobed me?"

Having looked at and longed for seven years to consummate his relationship with his beloved, it is hard to imagine how Jacob could have been duped in the marriage bed. Did he have too much wine at dinner? (The word used here to describe the feast comes from the root "to drink" and usually denotes a drinking feast.)[4] Was Leah heavily veiled, as even Judah later would not recognize his own daughter-in-law Tamar when she veiled herself as a prostitute (Gen 38:14-18)? Did Leah refrain from speaking even a word throughout the intimacy lest the ruse be discovered? And where was Rachel that night? Did she not protest to her father, or even cry out to her beloved about the injustice of it all? And why did Laban's wife not speak out, as certainly Rebekah, of the same stock, would and (in similar situations) did?

Dresner explores some of the history of the centuries of speculation on how Laban gets away with the dastardly deed. Some rabbis suggest that Laban makes sure he has an audience for the deception. All the family and friends are there (Gen 29:22). Undoubtedly the bride is heavily veiled. The marriage tent is dark. Jacob may have consumed too much wine. The two sisters may have similar physical characteristics except for the face, which is veiled (24:65). The bride's silence may be natural, given there was no intimate courtship as in modern times. The conversations through the night may be whispered, thus adding voice deception to the rest of the charade. But how could Rachel allow this to happen in the first place?

Some Jewish authors have speculated that Leah, the first-born, is actually pledged to Esau, the sensuous one. Her "weak eyes" or "soft eyes," they said, have lost their luster through weeping about the tragic prospect of marrying Esau. To save Leah the shame of marrying Esau, Rachel, torn between her love for Jacob and her compassion for her sister, tells Leah the secret signs by which Jacob and she had determined not to be deceived on the marriage night—touching Jacob's right toe or an earlobe.

The most radical suggestion of all—and the hardest to believe—is that Rachel actually hides under the nuptial bed, answering Jacob herself while Leah engages Jacob physically.[5]

However it is accomplished, Leah cannot be absolved of guilt even if her father demanded her obedience in the wretched scheme. Perhaps she secretly loves Jacob herself or saw this as her opportunity to get married or to "get the upper hand with her beautiful sister."[6]

It was a man's world, as Joyce Baldwin notes in her commentary. Laban arranges the feast and invites male guests. Laban supplies two maids for Leah out of the household. Laban brings his oldest daughter into the marriage tent. "Laban had dared to play this unscrupulous trick because he was certain that Jacob would never be content without the one on whom he had set his heart, and in this way Laban could bargain for further free service. Laban had his consoling suggestion ready."[7]

Jacob the deceiver is duped ("What is this you have done to me? Why have you deceived me?"). Indeed there is even a reminder in Laban's protestation that the older should marry first (Gen 29:26), that the first-born (yes, even Jacob's brother, Esau) had certain rights. Laban may have had the whole thing in mind from the beginning, as he does not specify which daughter he will give when he says, "It is better that I give *her* to you than to some other man" (v. 19).

LOOKING IN THE MIRROR

Jacob must have then, or shortly thereafter, seen in Leah's charade a mirror copy of his own dress-up as Esau in front of his own blind father. He had duped his brother before his blind father; now in the darkness one sister has been exchanged for the other. He receives what he had given, in spite of his protest, and perhaps his willingness to go the next mile, even the next seven years, was not only an act of desperation but also his sullen compliance with the poetic justice of the scene.

The Jewish midrash *Bereshit Rabbah* (70:17) emphasizes the oral deception involved in this, playing with words to veil the truth:

> All that day, they prepared for the wedding, with song and celebration. Jacob asked, "Why are you doing me so much kindness?" They replied, "You have done so much kindness through your presence among us," and they praised him and sang, "Ha, Lea! Ha Lea!" [hinting at the deception through the adulations of joy]. In the evening they came and put out the lights. He said, "What is this? Why have you put out the lights, while men and women are mingling with one another?" They answered, "What do you think—that we are dissolute as rams?" [Rashi: "We express our modesty by bringing the bride to the groom *in the dark*."] And all that night, he called her, "Rachel!" and she answered him. In the morning, "And behold, she was Leah" [lit.]. He said to her, "Deceiver, daughter of a deceiver! Did I not call you Rachel last night and you answered me?" *She replied, "Is there a master without students? Did your father not call you Esau and you answered him?"*[8]

God was throwing up mirror after mirror to Jacob so he could see himself and meet his God more deeply. Not only was Leah a God-polished mirror but so was Laban—a man who always had a plan for his own advantage, this time to get both daughters married and to get fourteen years of work out of Jacob

So for seven more years of service he can have Rachel. But first he must finish the wedding week with Leah, according to the custom of a week-long feast with the bridal couple enjoying their nuptials nightly in the wedding tent. But how hard this must have been for Leah, nightly sensing Jacob's pain, anger and even rejection! And how confusing for Jacob, required to be passionate with a woman for whom he felt nothing, while he anticipated the completion of this nightly duty would lead in short course to consummation with his true love. No man or woman can love with his eye on the clock or calendar.

For Leah, the second week must have been as hard as the first, as she saw her lovely sister take up the marriage bed, with Jacob now cherishing his true love. This sword through her heart would drive Leah to God, as evidenced in the names of her first five children, which roughly mean, with variations, "Now God, please may my husband love me, since I have given him a son" (Gen 29:31—30:6). And Jacob himself, in the complexity of his marriages, would be hounded by the heavenly Father through pain, through childlessness, through reaping the fruits of his own duplicity and through the pleading of God at his heart. But why did he not reject Leah after the first night? Would he have been righteous to do so?

ADULTERY OR BIGAMY?

Were Jacob and Leah guilty of adultery, or could they be considered as adulterous if Jacob had refused to continue the first week in the wedding tent? Luther answers negatively. Commenting on this, C. F. Keil and Franz Delitzsch suggest:

> Their union was not marriage at first, because there was no free consent between these two. It was not adultery, for Jacob consorted with one whom he certainly did not desire. Consequently, Jacob could on ethical grounds have rejected Leah and would still have been guiltless.[9]

The fact that Jacob didn't reject Leah, at least in bed, and went on to get Rachel the second week leads to a further question: Was this bigamy? Dresner says no.[10] It was two sisters marrying the same husband, something Scripture later prohibits in Leviticus 18 and 20.[11] But if bigamy is marrying more than one wife, then Jacob was a bigamist. As with many parts of the narrative, the grief caused as these two sisters were placed in such an untenable position is statement enough that this is not God's way. And the struggle of these two sisters is written eloquently in the names the wives gave to their children both through their own wombs and through surrogate mothers, their maids. "Now Jacob will love me." "The LORD heard that I am not loved." "God has vindicated me." "I have prevailed over my sister" (Gen 29:31—30:24).

The birth of Levi to Leah is particularly poignant. She named him "Now at last my husband will become attached to me, because I have borne him three sons" (Gen 29:34). Of the three parts of the marriage covenant instituted by God in the Garden of Eden (2:24)—*leaving* (father and mother—the public covenant), *cleaving* (in companionship—the personal covenant) and *one flesh* (sexual consummation—the private covenant)—Leah had "left" her father and was united physically with Jacob, but the covenant was empty of companionship (cleaving), and thus this union was surely something less than full covenant marriage. The phrase indicating she was hated, usually translated "not loved" (29:31) is legal terminology and literally means "to love less."[12] It is a term that usually means "rejection," though in this case Jacob remained faithful but without emotional love. For Leah it was an emptiness in her relationship with Jacob that drove her to God.

Many people today find themselves in a situation remarkably similar to Jacob and his two marriages (though today it is more common to have them one after another). In this Jacob can hardly be seen as a good role model in every respect. But he did this: he kept covenant with both Rachel and Leah. And making and keeping covenant is the key to recovering and nurturing a true marriage.

As I have tried to show in *Married for Good*, the most dangerous thing happening in North America and much of the industrialized world today is that people are entering marriage with the thought that they could leave it.[13] The quality of marriages may be higher today than in a previous generation, but the stability is lower. There are powerful cultural forces working against marriage itself, not only from the outside (making it financially, socially, occupationally and personally advantageous not to marry) but also from the inside (eroding people's confidence in making a vow that they will keep and a vow that will keep them). On the inside many hold unconsciously in their hearts an emotional loophole "in case it doesn't work out." To marry with the thought that you could leave the marriage is not to marry at all.

The Kasses give a partial list of the pressures we encounter today: the sexual revolution, made possible by effective female contraception; divorce, infidelity and abortion; the general erosion of shame and awe regarding sexual matters, promoted by the commercialization of sex and the sexualization of commerce; widespread morally neutral sex education in schools; and the explosive increase in the numbers of young people whose parents have been divorced.[14] But there is something stronger than these principalities and powers with which we must wrestle: a divinely designed and God-empowered covenant. Like Christianity itself, covenant marriage has not so much been tried and found wanting as it has been found difficult and often not tried (even by many who are legally married).

MARRIED FOR GOOD

There is much in this story to encourage the reinforcement and deepening of the marriage covenant.

First, there is need for *persistence*. Jacob persisted in his marriage to Leah, partly no doubt because he saw in it the justice within the injustice.

William Perkins, in his profound *Treatise on Callings* uses a pre-anesthesia illustration. He says that we should persist in our callings (such as marriage) as a surgeon persists in cutting his patient "even though his patient screameth much."[15] Years ago I went to Gail's old family doctor, a Second World War army physician. I had a painful, infected boil on my neck. The doctor examined it and announced he would "cut it out." As I lay on his operating table, he injected a local anesthetic and told me to tell him if it hurt when he cut. As he made the incision, I screamed. "The freezing didn't take," he said. So he tried again—another injection. More screaming. Another injection. This fiasco continued until, exasperated, Dr. Wilson said, "Darn. We'll just have to freeze and cut as we go." Perkins would have understood! And Jacob.

Over the years Gail and I have shared the lives of numerous married couples through marriage enrichment seminars, teaching, prayer, retreats for couples and personal counseling. We have come to see there is little difference between those couples who divorce and those who do not. All have their struggles and their joys. They all discover that they are incompatible. "Incompatibility" is a marriage myth. The one difference is that some persist in covenant fidelity not only "for better" but also "for worse," and they do so trusting that even the hardest times will yield the fruit of righteousness.

Second, there is need for *creativity*—creativity in companionship, in mutual care and in lovemaking. Leah, the less loved, nevertheless keeps the languages of love open and creative.

Genesis 30 contains a fascinating incident that turns around the mandrake fruit *(mandragora officinarum)*, which is believed to be an aphrodisiac. Leah's son Reuben found some in the field and brought them to his mother. But Rachel wanted it to increase her own desire and fecundity. In reality it did not help Rachel at all. When she did conceive, it was because the Lord remembered her (30:22). Evidently (as we learn from this story) Leah was already excluded from Jacob's bed, because she used the mandrakes to "hire" Jacob (from Rachel) for a night in bed. So when Jacob came in from the field, Leah took creative initiative and announced to him, "You must sleep with me. I have hired you with my son's mandrakes" (v. 16), already indicating the name of the son that will be born from that night's tumble *(sakar*, "to hire for wages"—Issachar).[16]

Marriage is like a dance. There is constant movement and change. One certainly is not married to the same person as he or she married ten years previously. So *being* married is a constant process of *getting* married and of finding appropriate ways of saying "I love you" at each stage.

Third, there is need for *contentment*. The rivalry between Leah and Rachel is illustrative. Each wanted what the other had. Rachel had Jacob's love but wanted children (like Leah). Leah had children by Jacob but wanted Jacob's passionate love (like Rachel). When Rachel said, "Give me children, or I'll die!" (30:1),[17] Jacob complained aptly to Rachel, "Am I in the place of God?" (v. 2). It is regrettable that this sad interchange is the only record we have of a conversation between Jacob and Rachel, given the romantic origin of their relationship.[18]

William Perkins also deals with the need for contentment in his "Treatise on Callings." The great sin in our callings (such as marriage) is the lust of the spirit—discontentment, coveting someone else's calling as better than one's own. The solution for this is to practice thanksgiving and to labor to see that God has given us what we need and that God (not a perfect situation) is our portion (Ps 73:26).[19]

Paul the Christian apostle speaks similarly about having learned in every and all situations "the secret of being content," which is this: "through [God] who gives me strength" and "in everything, by prayer and petition, *with thanksgiving*, [to] present your requests to God" (Phil 4:12-13, 6).[20]

As I write this, Gail and I are celebrating our fortieth anniversary on a remote island in the Great Barrier Reef, Australia. Just before we left Canada, her parents celebrated their sixty-fifth anniversary with most of the grandchildren and great-grandchildren present. Just fifteen years before, we were at the wedding church in Cana of Galilee, where the Italian priest, on hearing of their (then) fifty years, said, "Mama mia, fifty years of martyrdom." He was right, of course. Marriage is a living death, or rather life through death, as each loses himself or herself in another through self-giving, plowing oneself into each other not only physically but also personally.

Like the monastic life, marriage is a vowed life substituting community of property for poverty, sexual fidelity for chastity, mutual submission for obedience and an unconditional covenant for geographical stability. Many couples today, if they do marry, choose to write their own vows. Often they are soupy and sentimental: "I always want to feel this way toward you." Speaking to this, David Blankenhorn concludes, "The new vows are important philosophical authorizations for our divorce culture. They are both minor causes and revealing results of a society in which marriage as an institution is decomposing before our eyes."[21] The traditional vows had teeth in them: for better and for worse (there will be both), in sickness and in health, until death us do part. And where is God in all this?

GOD IN MESSY MARRIAGES

First, God is in our marriages *providentially*. Our married lives are not a bundle of accidents; we are not controlled by chance, luck or fate. God's providence means that God is overseeing, overcoming, working out his good purpose in the details of our lives.

The deception of Laban was turned by God into the means of building the family of promise: six sons and one daughter through Leah, two sons through Leah's maid, two through Rachel and two through Rachel's maid. From these four women came the twelve tribes. It takes the eye of faith (and often only hindsight) to see God's hand in complex human affairs, and especially in the most tawdry of everyday events. Speaking to this, Keil and Delitzsch point out there is more than romance (and the lack of it) in this chapter: "In the ordinary events of everyday life true faith finds its right sphere of activity, and the trivial things of one's daily task become great and important in them as man expresses his faith, as Jacob does."[22]

The narrative is full of dramatic irony. Jacob finds himself in the morning in bed with Leah, unbeknownst to him. Yet in another irony God uses the unloved wife to build up the family and, through her descendants, to give birth to the Savior of the world.[23]

Second, God is in our marriages *redemptively*. Part of this is the essential confrontation with ourselves that takes place in the intimacy of a life companionship. Marriage will find us out! God wants to bless Jacob as he wants to bless us, but he cannot do so until we are real. But the deception of Laban and the disguise of Leah serve as reality therapy. Ultimately, Leah is buried beside Jacob (a hint that, while loved less, she was honored). Rachel, the barren one, has two sons. Jacob goes through an encounter with God that leaves him limping but purified, fit to be the leader of the people of God.

Third, God is in our marriages *pastorally*, caring for each partner through one another. Marriage itself is a source of spiritual renewal because it offers three gifts to the spiritual life: sustenance, healing and growth.[24] God blesses and comforts the rejected wife, Leah. God opens Rachel's womb not once but twice. Maturity is not something that can be obtained through self-help books, high-powered seminars and consumer-oriented religion. It comes only in the long, thick experiences of life, seasoned by some of the hardest and most disappointing experiences, which, if directed Godward, become the crucible for faith formation and true holiness. This can happen in our marriages (or singleness); it can also happen in the workplace.

7

Work — the Story of Laban
Genesis 29:14-20; 31:10-13

> O Lord our heavenly Father, by whose providence the
> duties of men are variously ordered: grant to us all the spirit
> to labor heartily to do our work in our several stations,
> in serving one Master and looking for one reward.
> Teach us to put to good account whatever talents thou has lent to us,
> and enable us to redeem our time by patience and zeal;
> through Jesus Christ our Lord. Amen.
>
> — THE BOOK OF COMMON PRAYER

Whose work matters? To the world? To the church? To God? Among the readers of this book are businesspeople, investors, homemakers, politicians, retirees, teachers, tradespeople, doctors, pastors and lawyers. There are people whose work is studying — a strange work that you pay to do instead of receiving a salary for doing it. Does any of this matter to God? Or does some work matter more than others? We ask these questions especially because we are in a world where work is changing radically.

Jeremy Rifkin, in his disturbing study of work trends in the world, *The End of Work*, argues, "The wholesale substitution of machines for workers is going to force every nation to rethink the role of human beings in the social process." New technologies are replacing people faster than people are being relocated to other sectors, leading to massive unemployment — 800 million human beings now are either unemployed or underemployed. Rifkin asserts that the effect of this on the world's social and economic equilibrium is devastating. "Just outside the new high-tech global village lie a growing number of destitute and desperate human beings, many of whom are turning to a life of crime and creating a vast new criminal subculture."[1] Even the service industry, to which millions have been driven in the information society, will be largely displaced by technology, including the developing world. This raises the bar for us to see what work means when remunerated work is not available or when the work we do is less than fulfilling.

Over the years my own work has included making steel rivets by hand, preaching, filing, attending committees, listening, building houses, teaching, writing, grading papers and some domestic work. Is some of this holy work that lasts and the rest just fluff?

> Only one life, 'twill soon be past;
> only what's done for Christ will last.

That poem has driven generations into gospel work on the assumption that all other work will go up in smoke on the day of the great conflagration. But the Bible offers a different perspective.

WHOSE WORK MATTERS TO GOD?

The Bible opens with God hard at work—separating, designing, fashioning, communicating, beautifying, empowering. Adam and Eve were given, as their very first command, the dignity of being vice regents for God, taking care of the earth and developing the potential of creation (Gen 1:28; 2:15). Work is part of our dignity as creatures who are like God. It did not come about because of human sin. The Greek idea, that work is "unleisure" and a curse, has wormed its way deeply into the psyche of many God-fearing people, but it is flatly wrong, dangerously misleading. The Jewish people have always known this and have emphasized the dignity of work even for rabbis. As one saying puts it, "Whoever does not teach his son a trade teaches him to be a mugger."[2] Unfortunately people of faith too often do not have a spirituality of work. They see their daily work as incidental to holiness and a diversion from God.[3] But people in a Christian service career can think differently.

All around the world there is a hierarchy of occupations among God's people: missionaries and pastors at the top, followed by helping professionals, the trades (physically dirty but morally clean), business (physically clean but morally questionable—so it is thought) and marginal occupations like stock brokering. When was the last time stock brokers were prayed for in the church? This tragic but well-ingrained descending scale of "spiritual" importance has driven generations of young men and women into so-called full-time ministry to do work that will outlast the world. (In reality, there is no "part-time" service option available to the people of God.) And William Tyndale, the English reformer, had it right when he said, "There is no work better than another to please God; to pour water, to wash dishes, to be a souter [cobbler], or an apostle, all are one, as touching the deed, to please God."[4]

The average clock-punching church person spends eighty-eight thousand hours of his or her lifetime in the workplace from the first day of paid employment until retirement. Professionals, farmers, professors and homemakers spend even more time—the last being unremunerated. Yet even dedicated church members spend only four thousand hours of their lifetime in church-related meetings. And most of the church's life centers on those four thousand hours.

SLAVELIKE WORK

As mentioned before, Jacob is the first worker in the Bible—the first to have his work vividly described in its complexities and satisfactions. But more important, this story reveals God's interest in work. Jacob's work (and ours) is a way to God; it is blessed by God and becomes a ministry to God and our neighbor. This is all the more remarkable when one considers that Jacob's work was slave work—exactly how many will describe their work today: routine, monotonous, never-ending, inadequately remunerated, exhausting and just plain hard.

Jacob arrives in Paddan-Aram penniless, running from his brother and in search for a wife from the extended family home. But his father did not send him with the bride price. He has nothing to give for the gorgeous lady at the well but his sweat. So it appears he indentures himself effectively as a slave to Laban to get Rachel—working for seven years with no pay, no freedom and no dignity. He looks after his future father-in-law's animals.

When Jacob describes it, he uses slave terms. "Sleep fled from my eyes" (Gen 31:40). "The heat consumed me in the daytime and the cold at night" (v. 40). Later he says to Laban, "You changed my wages ten times" (v. 41).[5] He describes his work as "my hardship and the toil of my hands" (v. 42).[6]

Laban sees work only as a means of personal gain and ends up being possessed by his possessions. He is a polytheist (he worships "the God of Abraham and the God of Nahor," v. 53). He has neither God nor goods. H. C. Leupold says, "Laban . . . is a good illustration of the man who has fallen away from the true God, still knows of Him, feels impelled to heed His Word, but otherwise has put God on the same level with heathen deities, and lives a life as a renegade might live."[7]

LOVE WORK

The surprising reversal in the story is an irruption of hope and good news, a breaking in of a God-sized view of life. In Genesis 29:20 we have one of the purest statements of human love: "So Jacob served seven years to get Rachel, but they seemed like only a few days to him because of his love for her." Slave work can become love work. Love transforms all kinds of work into a ministry.

Working for the love of a woman or a man, for one's parents or children, for one's neighbor, for love of the earth, for love of nation and love of God— any of this can transform work into a ministry. And in the last day Jesus will say, in effect, "You changed my diapers, you visited me in prison, you made my dinner, you hosted me at a business reception, you put clothes on my back." As the parable says, "Whatever you did for one of the least of these brother of mine, you did to me" (Mt 25:40). Jesus (yes, God) receives our work, and not just religious work such as preaching, pastoral care, church planting and so on.

In 1 Thessalonians 1:2-3 Paul spoke to the Christians about their "labor prompted by love." Also, in developing what makes work Christian, Paul spoke about their "work produced by faith" and their "endurance inspired by hope." Faith, hope and love are what make work Christian and godly. Jacob worked for love, but did he work with faith?

FAITH WORK

After fourteen years, Jacob wants to do something for his own family. He has paid off the bride price; now he wants to work for wages. So he negotiates with Laban for a few more years of work. Their conversation is a masterpiece of diplomacy. Laban asks, "What shall I give you?" (Gen 30:31), but he really doesn't want to give Jacob anything. Jacob knows a cheat when he sees one, so he says, "Don't give me anything." But Jacob shrewdly offers a plan that would enable Laban not to give him anything but that at the same time (though Jacob does not reveal this) would enable Jacob to get what he needs for his family.

What happens is brilliant—entrepreneurial but surprisingly inspired by faith. Jacob has not forgotten his destiny as a promised person.[8] The results are not guaranteed, so Jacob must trust. But it is not a blind trust, a leap in the dark. God gives him an idea. Children of our creative God are inspired by the Holy Spirit. They should be the most creative people on earth—and not just in church work but also in world-making work.[9]

What happens next is shrewd, the kind of business deal that would make the toughest worldling admit that it ought to be commended (Lk 16:8). It is also mysterious, perhaps even magical. Jacob's work has been shepherding, and he has noticed that the sheep are mostly all white and the goats are mostly all black. Multicolored animals are rare. He makes an offer that Laban cannot refuse and he strategizes how to make it impossible for himself not to lose. Today we would call it win-win.

Jacob proposes that Laban will keep all the pure white sheep and pure black goats and also the presently alive mixed-color animals. Normally in the Near East goats are black (or dark brown) and sheep are white. What

Jacob will take for his own wages will be all *future* multicolored lambs or kids.[10] But for the present, Jacob will separate out all multicolored ones for Laban to keep.

Laban, like Jacob, knows a cheat when he sees one, so he does not trust Jacob with the separation of the flocks. So Laban separates out the multicolored flocks, takes them three days' journey away and puts them in the care of his sons (Gen 30:35-36). Effectively Laban has everything. He has all the animals—the blacks, the whites and the (present) multicolored ones. He has Jacob to care for some of his flocks, and Jacob's chances of generating a nest egg for his family are a remote possibility, or so Laban thinks. Such a deal! "Don't give me anything" (v. 31), Jacob explains. But Jacob has a plan.

Jacob could not have understood the principles of genetics, namely that recessive genes may emerge through mating. But his observations as a shepherd led him to believe that he could breed strong, *multicolored* animals in a big way through careful selective breeding. And he could do this with all-white and all-black animals (since Laban already had the first batch of multicolored ones and Jacob was still taking care of Laban's monochrome animals). Some research indicates that the vigorous animals are hybrids "whose recessive coloring genes emerge when they are bred together" and that "Jacob can distinguish the strong animals with the recessive genes by their copulating earlier than the weaker ones without that gene."[11]

Here is where it gets mysterious as well as cunning. The upshot is clear. Jacob succeeds in breeding multicolored sheep and goats from monochrome stock and ensures that the strongest sheep and goats are the multicolored ones—in other words, his! He does this by something that might be a primitive magic, by placing a multicolored post in front of the animals while they are mating on the assumption that what they see during intercourse determines their own color (Gen 30:37-40). Just as Rachel used "magic" with the mandrakes (to try to become fertile), so Jacob uses sympathetic magic by peeling the bark of poplar, almond and plane branches—all trees thought to have toxic substances and used medicinally in the ancient world. They were possibly able to hasten the onset of heat, making the animals ready to copulate.[12]

The dramatic irony in the narrative is heightened by the fact that Laban's name means "white."[13] "White" gets duped by white branches—white magic—just as, much earlier, "Red" (Esau) got fooled into giving up his birthright by red stew.[14] So Jacob selectively breeds the strongest animals, securing for himself the best and leaving the weakest for Laban (Gen 30:38-42). The narrator concludes: "In this way the man grew exceedingly prosperous and came to own large flocks, and maidservants and menservants, and camels and donkeys" (v. 43). Not surprisingly, Laban, the outfoxed fox, changes his attitude toward Jacob (31:1-2), and it is time for Jacob to leave.

Jacob's plan is brilliantly entrepreneurial. But where is God in this? Is there merely unbridled selfish ambition, a work of the flesh (Gal 5:20)?

Six years later Jacob, like Joseph, recalls a dream he received from God. As he sensitively and diplomatically draws his wives into the country to discuss in secret his desire to leave Haran and return to Canaan, he uses a multifaceted strategy. He notes that Laban's attitude has changed. He recalls how hard he has worked and how their father has cheated him, though he carefully makes no mention of the ultimate deceit—the exchange of Leah for Rachel. Then he appeals to divine providence: "God has taken away your father's livestock and has given them to me" (Gen 31:9).[15] Finally he tells what we have hitherto not known—that God gave him a dream that offered the secret of his success in animal husbandry.[16] God showed him that the strong animals mating were striped, spotted and speckled.

Jacob has been working out of faith and holy ambition. He has been doing the Lord's work on his father-in-law's ranch. Jacob has love and faith. But what about hope?

HOPE WORK

For Jacob, work related to the promise. Jacob is part of a holy plan, engaged in a divine project, enlisted in God-work. He has seen the promise of family amply fulfilled in his eleven sons and daughters (the first part of the promise). But the land remains unoccupied. As Wenham notes, "It is precisely the land, called by Jacob 'my land,' that gives the dynamic to the story."[17]

Several factors lead Jacob homeward. First, when his barren but beloved wife Rachel conceives and bears Joseph, Jacob now has a complete family and can return to the land fruitfully: "After Rachel gives birth to Joseph, Jacob said to Laban, 'Send me on my way so I can go back to my own homeland'" (Gen 30:25). God moves unexpectantly and graciously, making the barren fruitful. Jacob and Rachel know this child is from God. Indeed J. P. Fokkelman explains that "Rachel gives up the only thing that shows her precedence, the access to Jacob [through the mandrake incident with Leah], and after that God shows mercy."[18] Waltke adds that her "barrenness was partly a symbol of her self-will and envy and her oppression of Leah. As soon as she gives up the high-handedness of Jacob's policy and is prepared to bend, God grants her children."[19]

A second factor is that Jacob has a dream (at approximately the same time) in which God says, "Now leave this land at once and go back to your native land" (Gen 31:13). And God shows him just how he will accomplish this through a breeding program.

Each of the first two factors is a *pull* homeward. Then there is a *push*. "Jacob heard that Laban's sons were saying, 'Jacob has taken everything our father owned and has gained all this wealth from what belonged to our father'" (Gen 31:1).

God has promised to be with Jacob at Bethel (Gen 28:15). Now once again God promises to be with Jacob, but this time on condition that he return home (31:13). This is a pattern in biblical spirituality. The promise of God requires obedience and response. But through obedience there comes more grace and the need for new responsiveness—a delightful spiral of blessing.[20] He is doing God's work, going God's way, receiving God's blessing.

WORK YESTERDAY, TODAY AND FOREVER

Work is fundamental to our being God-imaging creatures. In this life we are supposed to work until we die. This does not preclude, of course, formal retirement from remunerated work. But it does mean that seniors (or middle-aged people who have reaped a bundle in a dot-com venture) are not supposed to waste the rest of their life in an orgy of leisure.

But what kind of work should we do? Should we leave the commercial realm and, now that we have our personal assets well in place, "go into the ministry"? (In fact many try to do this and find that they are still the same person they were in business!) Having given the first part of our lives to becoming successful, should we now give ourselves to something really significant? And what about the first part of our lives—is there no significance in "ordinary" work?

What makes work God-blessed is not that God's Word and name are spoken out loud but that the work is done with faith, hope and love. With these virtues (which are not human achievements but divine encouragements), even slave work can become holy work. So Jacob's work life is an Old Testament hint of Paul's advice: "Whatever you do, work at it with all your heart, as working for Lord, not for men, since you know that you will receive an inheritance from the Lord as a reward" (Col 3:23-24).

Throughout its history the church has had various lists of prohibited occupations: the military if it involved killing, gladiators, fashion designers (from the Puritan list), monks (from Luther's list) and prostitutes. Significantly there are no such lists in the Bible, with the exception of witchcraft in the Old Testament and, in the New, prostitution and extortion (1 Cor 6:9-10). When soldiers came to John the Baptist and asked "What shall we do?" he did not say to get out of the military but rather told them not to accuse people falsely and to be content with their pay (Lk 3:14). But not all work serves our neighbor either directly or indirectly or glorifies God. Some work is actually destructive, and we should not be doing it. The list is short. It takes all kinds of work to "keep stable the fabric of this world"—a phrase from the book of Ecclesiasticus (Gen 38:25-34).

What makes work last is not the religious character of the work (that the Word of God is proclaimed and souls are saved) but the fact that it is done for Christ (1 Cor 3:10-15). The biblical vision of the end of this world is not annihilation (the destruction of everything) and the creation of a brand-new world. The end, rather, is transfiguration. The resurrected body of Jesus is the prototype of this, the first fruits of the grave. In some way beyond what we can imagine, the work of our hands, heart and mind will pass through the purifying fire and, cleansed of sin, will find its place in the new heaven and new earth. The work may be sheep sorting or muffin making, selling or buying, processing information or food, creating a hospitable environment or building houses, teaching or doing accounts. All good work can be God's work and will last, even outlast this world, not by virtue of its religious character but because it is linked with God's kingdom, God's purposes and God himself.

> Only one life, 'twill soon be past;
> *only what's done for Christ will last.*

Ironically, that poem contains wonderful hope possibly unknown to the original poet.

And when we die and are resurrected, we will work in the new heaven and the new earth. Rudyard Kipling expresses this beautifully in his poem "When Earth's Last Picture Is Painted":

> When earth's last picture is painted and the tubes are twisted and dried,
> When the oldest colours have faded, and the youngest critic has died,
> We shall rest, and faith, we shall need it—lie down for an aeon or two,
> Till the Master of All Good Workmen shall put us to work anew.[21]

A good question to ask is: What kind of work do you think you will be doing in heaven?

Jacob is doing work that will last, preparing the way for the full coming of the kingdom of God on earth. In Christ all the promises of God find their "yes" (2 Cor 1:20). What "being in the land," "having a family" and "blessing the nations" meant to the patriarchs gets taken up in the summons and the blessing of being "in Christ." Working in the kingdom of Christ includes all three—stewardship of creation, peoplehood and worldwide blessing. Our work in this world is work under the King, for the King and to advance the kingdom—the sway of God's rule over all of life and creation. This refers not just to so-called Christian work but to all good work. Our work, whether remunerated or not, becomes the prayer

> Thy kingdom come,
> thy will be done on earth
> as it is in heaven.

8

Conversion—
the Story of the God-Man
Genesis 32:26-28

There is nothing so whole as a broken heart.

—HASIDIC SAYING

Our passion for romance comes to us in the form of two deep desires:
the longing for adventure that requires something of us,
and the desire for intimacy—to have someone truly know us for
ourselves, while at the same time inviting us to know them
in the naked and discovering ways lovers come to know each other
on the marriage bed. The emphasis is perhaps more on
adventure for men and slightly more on intimacy for women.
Yet, both desires are strong in us as men and women.
In the words of friends, these two desires come together
in us all as a longing to be in a relationship of heroic proportions.

—BRENT CURTIS AND JOHN ELDREDGE

Calvin begins his *Institutes* by asserting something sublimely simple: true religion is simply knowing God and knowing ourselves. One cannot know one without the other since a personal God can be known only in relationship. So this part of Jacob's story brings us to his conversion, or at least one of them, where Jacob comes to himself and God at the same time and in the process becomes truly God's person.

Coming to Brother

Jacob's reconciliation with Esau (Gen 32—33) forms the relational context for this deep interior work, just as the welcoming of the younger prodigal son in his return was, for the older prodigal, the relational context in which he could experience the welcome of the seeking Father who loves both Pharisees and publicans (Lk 15:11-32). As Kenneth Leech says, "'Where is your brother?' (Gen 4:9) has remained, across the centuries, a fundamental test of discipleship. 'Unless your . . . brother comes down with you, you will not see my face again' (44:23) might be seen as God's own words to his people. For it is in community that God makes his presence known."[1]

Jacob has been alienated from his brother for twenty years. But he must now face him as he reenters the Promised Land. So Jacob sends a messenger ahead to spy out the relationship. But he does so with very deferential words: "Your servant Jacob" (Gen 32:4).

The ambassador returns with an alarming report: Esau is coming with four hundred armed men. Does this mean he is bent on war or that he comes, in royal retinue, to meet his brother in peace? Jacob, true to his name, takes no chances. He prays and plans—a combination that Calvin and others find wholly consistent and eminently commendable. Having faith in God's power to answer prayer, Jacob does not sit back and do nothing. In the prayer Jacob relies on his greatest security—the promise—and reminds the Lord that he is the one who suggested returning! That is the prayer.

The plan is to divide the camp into two so that one may escape if the other is attacked. Then Jacob prepares a massive present for Esau, one composed of five groups of animals, each presented with the words "Your servant Jacob" (Gen 32:18; see vv. 13-21). In total there were 550 animals—a princely present. The words used for their presentation—"a present," "to find favor" and "to mollify" (or make atonement)—have a sacrificial bearing. As Wenham aptly notes, this sizeable present, the religious sacrificial language surrounding it, his personal submission ("your servant") and his actual words to Esau ("the present [blessing] that was brought to you," 33:11) all suggest that Jacob is attempting to return the blessing out of which he had cheated his brother twenty years before.[2] Now, with his family having forded the river, Jacob is "left alone" (32:24).

Until now Jacob has spelled out his identity in terms of wives and children, sheep and goats. He is the self-made person. Now he is stripped of that. Jacob is alone with himself. But he is not really alone in the universe. The big question for all of us is not "Is the universe friendly?" but rather "Is there a Friend in the universe?"

COMING TO GOD

What happened that dark night by the Jabbok Brook is emphasized by a play on three words that have a similar sound: "He struggled/wrestled" is closely related to the word *Jabbok* and probably even the name Jacob.[3] At Jabbok, Jacob jacobed.[4] It is a fight, a wrestling match with intimate embrace as each tried to gain the advantage. Does Jacob that night review his whole life, especially his relationship with Esau, and his own dissembling, role-playing, inauthentic performance? Does that physical struggle externalize a personal and spiritual battle within, one in which Jacob must come to terms with himself? But with whom does Jacob wrestle? The narrative is deliberately opaque and mysterious, as Jacob himself apparently does not know at first who has confronted him in the dark by the brook, who is grabbing the heel grabber.[5]

The reader knows, and Jacob himself gradually comes to know, that it is the Lord himself who is wrestling with Jacob. In Scripture "the angel of the Lord" (though it is a term not used in this text) always refers to God being actually present in some physical, personal and touchable way. The angel of the Lord anticipates the full coming of God in the flesh in Jesus Christ. It may well be the Son of God engaging Jacob. Consequently, Luther makes Jacob say, "Oh Thou Heavenly Father and Lord!"[6] God wants him. God comes to him.

Through the night Jacob has been fighting God without knowing it. But God wounds him, touching the socket of Jacob's hip. Now he knows it is

God he is encountering. He wants God with all his heart. Mysteriously the God-man attempts to leave. Jacob will not let this moment pass, nor let this personal presence disappear. So he says, "I will not let you go unless you bless me" (Gen 32:26). He is passionate for God.

I fear apathy more than anything—called by the ancients *acedia*, or spiritual boredom. Especially in church work and in a theological college we are in danger of *acedia*. We are tempted to be constantly handling the outside of holy things. Richard Neuhaus says, "Acedia is apathy, the refusal to engage the pathos of other lives and [the passion] of God's life with them."[7] Jacob is anything but apathetic. Jacob has a passion for the blessing of God and will lie and cheat and fight to get it. Esau is the epitome of spiritual ennui. He sold his blessing for a bowl of porridge. Perhaps there is nothing so damnable as apathy.

So in the Garden of Gethsemane Jesus takes the disciple's prayer on his own lips—"Thy will be done"—showing that submission is not the same thing as compliance to impersonal fate or karma, that praying for God's will is not passive but active. P. T. Forsyth once said that "we say too often, 'Thy will be done'; and too ready acceptance of a situation as his will often means feebleness or sloth. It may be his will that we surmount his will." Forsyth continues, "Does not Christ set more value upon importunity than on submission?" Forsyth refers not only to Jacob wrestling but also to the parable of the unjust judge, the incident of the Syrophoenician woman, Paul beseeching the Lord thrice, Abraham pleading—yes, haggling—with God for Sodom and Moses interceding for Israel. "We have Jacob facing God, withstanding him, almost bearding him and extracting revelation. . . . So the prayer that resists his dealing may be part of his will and its fulfilment. . . . It is a resistance that God loves."[8] Faith, as Jacob knows, is a fight.

COMING TO SELF

We are now at the climax of the struggle. The man asked Jacob, "What is your name?" This is the question Jacob has been avoiding for twenty years. It is also a question many people spend their life avoiding.

In *Death of a Salesman*, Mrs. Willy Loman provided this epitaph for her husband: "He didn't know who he was."[9] Jacob was also a man who did not know who he was, and he seemed determined not to find out. Many of us, like Jacob, live a false identity, one created around our jobs or adopted from media images, and we can spend decades in contriving such artful dodges. As R. D. Laing comments so insightfully, "It is as though we all preferred to die to preserve our shadows."[10] Tragically, the search for self in which the Western world now so passionately engages is a fruitless search since it is a search for what can only be given by another. Our identity is a gift of another's love.[11] And to set Jacob up for this gift, God had to plot a series of scenes to hold up mirrors to his life—the blessing by Isaac, Laban the deceiver and Leah impersonating Rachel.

It is all wrapped up in his name given at birth. The name derives from the root *akov*, which means crooked, indirect. It will be his characteristic always to have a plan, to lead from behind, to get in by the back door, to choose the way of the snake. Jacob defines himself as Esau's shadow, the one who comes behind, the one with a blurred identity. Zornberg calls him "a frivolous player with identities."[12]

In the narrative Jacob does not use his own name for twenty years—it seems deliberately, ominously, lucidly, provocatively—and this is a powerful hint that Jacob is not willing to admit who he is, that he has an incomplete, fragmented identity, that he is inauthentic. God wants to bless Jacob but cannot bless him until he will admit his own name. The evasion seems deliberate. In the story this requires twenty years of reality therapy.

When Jacob brings in the roasted goat, simulating his brother's hairy arms and neck, and when blind Isaac asks, "Who is it?" (Gen 27:18), Isaac and God are confronting Jacob with the question of his own identity. Jacob answers, in effect, that he is an impersonator, that he is taking on the role of the first-born, that he is someone else: "I am Esau" (v. 19).[13] When he meets the woman of his dreams at the well, he does not say his own name. "He had told Rachel that he was a relative of her father and a son of Rebekah" (29:12).

God's plot is to bring this man to himself in order to bring him to God and life itself. There can be no blessing ultimately for a trickster since there is no authenticity, no real person to bless. One who enters the world of seeming, of performance, of assumed identities cannot know God, because he does not know himself. With deep insight the Talmud links idolatry with this fundamental inauthenticity since idolatry is simply worshiping a semblance of God, an appearance. So finally in Genesis 32 when Jacob is asked by the God-man "What is your name?" Jacob admits for the first time in the whole story, "My name is Jacob." It is a disclosure of his personality. He takes off the mask. He is becoming real. He is not now Esau in disguise, not merely his mother's son. He is himself—the Heel-Grabber.

And then he is blessed by God.

Frank Boreham notes that John Wesley, in his monumental *Journal*, describes an incident before the light broke on his soul at Aldersgate Street. He went to America with some vague idea of Christianizing the Indians. Almost as soon as he set foot on the western continent, he made the acquaintance of Mr. Spangenberg, a German pastor. This devout and earnest man startled the newcomer by plying him with a succession of painfully penetrating and particularly uncomfortable questions. "Does the Spirit of God," he inquired, "bear witness with your spirit that you are a child of God?" Wesley was utterly bewildered and knew not how to reply. His confusion led the good German to ask his second question: "Do you know Jesus Christ?" Wesley hemmed and hawed and at length answered feebly that he hoped that Christ had died to save him, whereupon Mr. Spangenburg went one step further back. "Young man," he asked, "do you know *yourself?*" Wesley replied that he did, but he confessed that his answer lacked sincerity and conviction.[4]

Like the prodigal in Jesus' parable, Jacob can only come to the Father if he comes to himself. And like the New Testament prodigal, Jacob can only come to himself because he has a Father to whom he can come. It is a triple homecoming, to brother Esau, to God and to himself.

A NEW NAME

The God-man does more than bless him. He gives him a new name indicating his identity and his vocation: "Your name will no longer be called
Jacob, but Israel, because you have struggled with God and with men and
have overcome" (Gen 32:28).[15] Jacob wants the messenger's name. The angel of the Lord replies, "Why do you ask my name?" (v. 29), as though to
say, "Jacob, don't you realize who I am?"[16] And the angel does not say his
name, lest it be abused (compare Ex 20:7; Judg 13:17-18). This is Jacob's re-
baptism into Israel, the leader of the nation. The precise etymology of Israel
means "El [God] fights," but popular etymologies generally take the form
of a play on the name rather than an exact translation. So Jacob became the
one who has triumphed in his struggle against men (Esau and Laban being
conspicuous examples) and, most surprising of all, against God!

There is a great mystery in this. Jacob struggles with God, but it is God
who allows Jacob to overcome. This story sums up the national destiny and
experience of Israel—fighting with God but winning and being won.[17] Jacob "wins" and so does God![18] Israel fights God, and both Israel and God
win! This is illustrated by the confession of a Jew, Jessel Takover, who wrote
a prayer as he was preparing for the pogrom. These words were found on a
piece of paper at the end of the Second World War among the ruins of the
Jewish ghetto in Warsaw.

> I believe in you, God of Israel even if you have tried your best to dissuade me
> to believe in you. . . . I would like to say to you that at this moment, more
> even than in any previous period of our eternal struggle for survival, we, the
> tortured, the humiliated, buried alive, burnt alive, insulted, mocked . . . that
> we have a right to know: until when are you going to allow it to continue? . . .
> I die in peace but not appeased, embittered but not cynical, a believer but
> not pleading, a man who loves God but does not say Amen to everything. . . .
> All this will do you no good. You have done everything to destroy my faith,
> yet I am dying precisely as I have lived, saying, "Hear, O Israel, the Lord is
> our God, one Lord. Into your hands, O God, I commit my spirit."[19]

Jacob knows he has met God and calls the place Peniel because he has seen God "face to face, and yet my life was spared" (Gen 32:30). He is a changed man. Instead of prevailing over people by trickery, he prevails with God and people by words.[20] Humility replaces arrogance as he humbly bows before his brother seven times (33:3, 7). Courage replaces cowardice as he strides forth to meet Esau, not now behind all his cattle and family but in the very front. To his amazement Esau runs to meet him, throws his arms around him, kisses him and weeps (v. 4)—the very words Jesus used to describe the prodigal father in his parable running out to meet his homecoming prodigal son. He is reconciled to God, his brother and himself, all at once. Jacob, having wrestled with God the night before, now claims he sees "the face of God" in his brother's face, so graciously has he been received (v. 10). As James Stewart once said:

> It was Jephthah, not Jehovah, who said, "Why are you come to me now when you are in distress?" (Judg 11:7). God will not stop to inquire into the motives when a nation in peril of its existence or a whole recalcitrant generation returns to Him at last, any more than He inquires into the motives of one lost soul limping home from the far country. Even if the motive is mainly self-preservation—"How many have bread enough and to spare, and I perish here with hunger!" (Luke 15:17).[21]

The parable of the two prodigals in the New Testament is an evangelistic mission to good people. It is the story of a young man (the older son) who didn't want to go to heaven because his brother was there! To craft this parable, Jesus must have had in mind the Old Testament story of the two prodigals—Jacob and Esau. The Old Testament story, like the New, speaks to good believers whose hearts have not yet been broken with gratitude. The elder brother lives a good life but does not know the Father's heart. Esau is satisfied with the life he has created for himself. He does not care for the promise of God or the blessing of God. Jacob, on the other hand, returning from the far country, cares so much for the blessing of God that he would cheat to get it. And he gets it. And Jacob sees in the running, embracing and weeping brother the face of God, just as the younger son in

Jesus' parable experiences the embrace and tears of the father running out
to meet him. Perhaps Esau also saw the face of God in his brother returning from the far country.

Can we have Jacob's experience? No. We cannot experience someone
else's experience. But can we know God? Yes! But it is even more characteristic of our encounter with God that we know that he knows us (Gal 4:9).
True religion, as Calvin said, is knowing both God and ourselves. That was
what Jacob experienced and what we, in our own engagement with God,
will discover.

We are designed by our Creator to be mystics. And every true believer is
a mystic in the sense of communing with, interacting with and engaging
God *directly*, not indirectly through mediums or intermediaries. Paul spoke
of this in the New Testament as "Christ in me" (Gal 2:20; Col 1:27) and "I
in Christ" (2 Cor 5:17). Not everyone will have a Damascus road conversion, but each and every believer in Jesus enters into a real, interpenetrating
relationship with the living God. That is what mysticism means.

But this direct contact with God is not "union" mysticism in the sense
of being swallowed up in the Godhead (like a drop of water in the ocean).
That was what was offered by the mystery religions of the ancient world—
and by much that passes for spirituality today. But it is *communion* mysticism, the interpenetration of God and a human being, and the interpenetration of God and God's people. We are not lost and annihilated in the
relationship but are found, more ourselves than ever before. We get drawn
into God's communal love life. In the New Testament this is expressed in
the awesome words of John: "our fellowship is with the Father and with his
Son, Jesus Christ" (1 Jn 1:3). We are included in the communion of triune
God—Father, Son and Spirit. Speaking to this with great eloquence,
Thomas Torrance says this:

> The doctrine of the Holy Trinity [is] . . . the fundamental grammar of our
> knowledge of God. Why is that? Because the doctrine of the Trinity gives ex-
> pression to the fact that through his self-revelation in the incarnation God has
> opened himself to us in such a way that we may know him in the inner rela-

tions of his divine Being and have communion with him in his divine life as
Father, Son and Holy Spirit.[22]

This is the gospel, and Jacob eventually realizes it. God draws us into relationship with himself within the circle of God's own loving communion.
The God who is "us" is not solitary, is not abstractly "one" but a unified
communion of personal relationships. And this God gives us access to his
own personal life.[23] What could be better than this?

9

Sex—the Story of Dinah
Genesis 34

> *"Safe sex" is the self-delusion of shallow souls.*
>
> —AMY KASS AND LEON KASS

> *One can make a good case that biblical religion is, not least,*
> *an attempt to domesticate male sexuality and male erotic longings,*
> *and to put them in the service of transmitting a righteous*
> *and holy way of life through countless generations.*
>
> —AMY KASS AND LEON KASS

It is one thing to get the prodigal out of the far country, but it is quite another thing to get the far country out of the prodigal. It is one thing to possess a piece of real estate physically and legally, but it is quite another to overcome the culture of the land. Jacob is on his way home to the Promised Land. But to match the physical triumph for Jacob there must be a moral triumph. Healing the far country of the heart is a long process that only begins with a conversion experience such as Jacob so recently had at the Jabbok Brook. The story of Dinah, Jacob's only daughter, seeded ever so briefly in the narrative, is important precisely because Jacob is now on his way back to the land promised to him. She has a significantly feminine message to add to the family story.[1]

The critically important thing was to see that each generation did not compromise the covenant by marrying outside the covenanted people. It is for that reason, not mere favoritism, that Rebekah takes things into her own hands when her husband, Isaac, is about to bless Esau, who has made their life bitter by marrying Canaanite women (Gen 26:35). Rebekah, wiser than her husband and as shrewd as her son, saves Isaac from making a dreadful mistake, even if she does it through a deception. Further, it is for the purity of the covenant that Jacob is sent to a faraway country to find a wife among his kith and kin rather than the local women. Always in the narrative there is a connection between sex and religious practice, leading up to the sexual seduction of the Israelites by the Moabites (Num 25), a sad day that led to covenant pollution.[2]

And it is this concern that is uppermost in the troubling narrative about Dinah in Genesis 34. Jacob (now Israel) is on his way home. But what was Jacob doing setting up camp in Shechem when he was called to return to Bethel as he had vowed? As a result, his only daughter was raped.

THE HUMILIATION OF DINAH

The attraction of urban settlements to nomads is almost irresistible. Products of their flocks can be sold and traded in town. It is an easy step—all too easy—from commerce to connubiality, from shared enterprise to shared bed. Dinah steps out of the family circle and meets the women of the land, the settled Canaanite women, and "thus loosed the stone that became a landslide."[3] She is probably a nubile girl of about fifteen.[4]

Shechem, apparently one of the most eligible and honored bachelors in the town, sees her, seizes her and "violated her"—a word that indicates a social and moral debasing by which a woman loses the expectation of a fully valid marriage (Gen 34:2).[5] The order of the words' use by the narrator to describe this humiliation is significant: he saw her, took her, laid her,[6] and abused her (vv. 1-2).[7] Unlike the "normal" psychological reaction of hatred of the victim (as was the case in the rape of Tamar, 2 Sam 13:15), Shechem afterward "loved" the girl, even though it was obviously lust in possessing her in a way that depersonalizes her to fulfill his own sexual fantasy. The Bible, using a term meaning courting or wooing, says he "spoke tenderly to her" (Gen 34:3). So he interceded with his father to get the girl. When Jacob hears of it, he remains passive and keeps quiet,[8] perhaps because she is, after all, the daughter of Leah, the less-loved wife. For the story does begin by emphasizing that Dinah was the daughter of Leah (v. 1).

Jacob's sin is a double omission—not to speak up and not to act. And it will become apparent that he does little because he feels little. It is even unclear whether he bothers to summon the brothers from the field where they are working to alert them of the tragedy.[9] Apart from Jacob's passivity, there is a lot of busyness going on—the Hivites leaving their homes to see if they can make a deal with Jacob, the sons returning to their home from their work, while Jacob is inert, immobilized. And this inertness is a stark contrast to the endless mourning, the refusing to be consoled, that overcomes Jacob on a later occasion when Joseph, the son of his beloved Rachel, is deemed dead and Jacob can find no comfort except in the thought of reunion in the grave (Gen 37:34-35). Not so with Dinah's brothers! They are filled with grief and fury.

The brothers emphasize that the deed is disgraceful, that this is an outrage to Israel (the people of God), that Dinah is "Jacob's daughter" and that such a thing should not be done—it was intrinsically wrong (Gen 34:7). The brothers are not simply thinking of themselves. This is sin on multiple levels: the abuse of an innocent maiden, a familial dishonor, a disgrace to national dignity and against their faith. Still Jacob is silent.

Meanwhile Hamor, Shechem's father, and Shechem come to Jacob and his sons and, without giving any recognition that Shechem has committed a crime, ask for the hand of Dinah. They offer intermarriage, economic advantages and whatever gift (the bride price) Jacob might ask for Dinah, because Shechem wants this woman badly.

THE PLOT

The brothers take matters into their own hands and conceive a devilish plot to gain revenge. For Shechem the exchange of a bride price for mutual trade is a fair deal, with traded commodities being roughly equal. There are advantages for both sides. But the brothers disregard the economic advantages of intermarriage and deal with the issue (albeit deceitfully) strictly as a matter of national purity, at least in appearance. If they are to be one people, then Shechem and all the Shechemites must be circumcised along with the family of promise. Only then could they be "one people" (Gen 34:16), which is, after all, the real message of the story, though here presented in an ironic way. Integration requires submission to the covenant. And circumcision symbolizes the covenant (Gen 17:9-14).

Whether or not the brothers actually thought Shechem might agree to such a radical "bride price" is unclear. If the Shechemites did not, the Israelites might still have to take Dinah back by force. There is a threatening tone in the final words of the brothers: "But if you will not agree to be circumcised, we'll take our sister and go" (Gen 34:17).

The narrator says, "Jacob's sons replied deceitfully" (Gen 34:13). As we have seen over and over again, the story of Jacob is full of deceit: the deceit involved in getting Isaac's blessing, the deceit undertaken by Laban to get Leah married (and to get more work out of Jacob), the deceit expressed by Rachel when she lied about her menstrual period (when Laban was looking for his stolen gods). And here, once again, the deceiver (Jacob) is confronted with deceit in his own sons.

Shechem wants the family of Israel to "give" Dinah, but he had already "taken" her. And the narrator is holding back for the moment a significant piece of information that, when revealed, will make the brothers' deceitful and brutal action appear more justified: Dinah is, at the moment, with Shechem.[10] We will soon see that Shechem's offer is really blackmail.

In reality the brothers do not approve of intermarriage, and the offer of "gifts" in exchange for their raped sister must have driven them to the conclusion that they should get their sister out of Shechem's clutches, even if it involved bloodshed.[11] After all, Shechem's gifts were really a harlot's hire, as they pointed out to Jacob later (Gen 34:31). It was another case of deceit. But was this a *saving* deceit (as it was in the case of Rebekah's scheme to get the "right son" blessed by Isaac), like business bluffing, a justifiable sleight of hand to accomplish a greater good? Was this a justifiable deceit, like Jacob's plan to give Laban everything while scheming (in the context of a person too stingy to give him anything) to get what he needed for his family? Considering the fact that the brothers were greatly outnumbered and that Dinah was securely in the other camp, was this scheme a good shrewdness, an act of faith?[12]

For their part Shechem and his father present the option to the people in the best possible light, as super-salespeople. They do not delay to do what they could to get what they wanted. They completely ignore the circumstances of the rape. They emphasize the economic and familial advantages, appealing persuasively to the immediate benefits everyone will experience by becoming "one people" with the Israelites. Flagrantly violating the deal they have made with Jacob's brothers, they promise not only commerce but also control. "Won't their livestock, their property and all their animals become ours?" (Gen 34:23). Deceivers themselves, they add layer upon layer of deceit in an ironic way seen only by the reader. They argue that there need be no competition with this family, as the land is big enough for all. They have everything to gain and nothing to lose but their foreskins. So they submit to circumcision.

When, three days later, the fever is at its worst and the men are incapacitated, Simeon and Levi attack the city, killing every male, and retrieve Dinah, who was still in Shechem's house. Ironically, as Meir Sternberg points out, there is poetic justice in the discovery that "Shechem's punishment started exactly where his sexual crime did, and the self-inflicted soreness made the rest easy."[13] The names of Simeon and Levi, one name given with the meaning "because the LORD has heard that I [Leah] am not loved" and the other, "at last my husband will become attached to me" (Gen 29:33-34), underscore the fact that these sons of Leah are motivated by making things right with their side of the family, their neglected and marginalized side. Simeon and Levi are defending their sister's honor, indicating that Leah's children are as valuable as Rachel's.

But if there is righteous anger in the action of these two brothers, what follows by the "sons of Jacob" (presumably the rest of the sons of Leah) is sheer greed. They loot the town, acting like hyenas after Simeon and Levi have taken all the risk.[14] They are condemned in Genesis 49:5-7 for taking the matter into their own hands, and they lose leadership in the family of promise.

Now, Jacob notes, they are a stench to the people. He overlooks the morality, even the justice, of such retaliation and is concerned only with the negative consequences. And his complaint is all about "me" and "I." Jacob criticizes Simeon and Levi (though he ignores the greed of the others). They must tremble with emotion when they speak about "their sister" (rather than "your daughter"): "Should he have treated our sister like a prostitute?" (Gen 34:31). Sternberg summarizes where the guilt rests: "He who twiddles his thumbs about the rape and deems the gifts fair compensation is as guilty of making a whore of Dinah as the rapist and giver himself."[15]

Lust and sexual love—and how to move from one to the other! Why is sexual purity so important? And why is there no more difficult area in which to obtain righteousness than in the sexual area?

THE CALL TO SEXUAL PURITY

Crucial to the transmission of the covenant is the need for sexual purity. It is because human beings are identified so deeply, so personally with their sexuality—to the very core of their beings—that the issue of sexual holiness is intimately connected with spiritual integrity. For good reason ancients and many New Age experimenters today have regarded the sexual experience as essentially religious. It includes longing, hunger for union, self-abandonment and ecstasy (literally taking a person "out of one's existence"). It seems to obtain human transcendence, though the term "human transcendence" is really an oxymoron. From there the fertility cults of the ancient world would attempt to influence the gods to provide fertile soil, herds and families by means of offering union with a temple prostitute, male or female.

The ancient Greek world, into which the apostle Paul brought the gospel of Jesus, was saturated with religious sexuality and sexual religion. That is behind his admonition to avoid any partnership with unbelievers who, through their sexually perverted religious practices associated with the temples, would lead followers of Jesus away from single-minded devotion to God (2 Cor 6:14-18). It is certainly true today.

THAT PERENNIAL LONGING WITHIN

When God made humankind, he made them male and female "in his own image" (Gen 1:27). God himself is a loving community of Father, Son and Spirit. To express, insofar as human speech can, the mystery of this, Augustine described God as Lover, Beloved and Love itself. So, amazingly, God loves God. But because God is love, God made a creature that could never be like God or reflect God's nature apart from relationality. God built this primal desire into us for another so that we might know that we were never meant to live individually and in isolation but in community.[16] Males or females by themselves, whether married or single, are not the image of God but only males in relation to females and females in relation to males. We are like God in our need to be people-in-communion without losing our identities. The sexual desire expresses something godlike within us.

The union to which we are driven is not actually the urge to merge — becoming one with another so that our identity is lost, as a drop of water in the ocean. Rather, it is an appetite for communion, mutual immersion, a unity gained not in spite of diversity but because of it. Intercourse is a powerful symbol of this — the mutual penetration of persons. I emphasize *persons* because we do not have sex with bodies but with whole persons, which is why the violation of a woman in nonconsenting intercourse is such a brutal and painful invasion of the person, leaving a transcendental mark on the person so she can never be the same again. So deep and life-penetrating is the act of sexual intercourse that our infinitely wise God has created one and only one context for complete sexual expression: a lifelong covenant of companionship marriage.

Speaking to the vulnerability we experience in the sexual act, the Kasses note that sexual intercourse is by nature unsafe. "All interpersonal relations are necessarily risky and serious ones especially so. And to give oneself to another, body and soul, is hardly playing it safe. . . . Whether we know it or not, when we are sexually active we are voting with our genitalia for our own replacement and demise. 'Safe sex' is the self-delusion of shallow souls."[17]

Even the order of marital preparedness is significant in the fundamental text quoted by both Jesus and Paul: "For this reason a man will leave his father and mother and be united to his wife [cleaving], and they will become one flesh" (Gen 2:24).

LEAVING FATHER AND MOTHER

For Jacob, leaving father and mother in Beersheba and traveling to Haran involves more than a physical journey. He must detach himself from previous identities and securities in an act of abandonment if he is to cling to his bride. In almost every culture it is expected that a woman will leave her parents—as, for example, Rebekah left Nahor and Bethuel. But Scripture also calls men to self-abandonment.

The result of this mutual self-abandonment is a relationship characterized not by patriarchal hierarchy, as commonly proposed, but mutuality, shamelessness, harmony and equality. "A helper suitable for [Adam]" (Gen 2:18) literally means a person who is equal and adequate for the man; nothing of inferiority or subordination is implied. While sin politicized the relationship into one characterized by rule and revolt (3:16),[18] God's intention is otherwise. Sin makes men into masters, while God's grace creates equality and mutuality (Eph 5:21). The curse effectively gets reversed.

So when Adam names Eve (which he does so differently from naming the animals, through which he expresses sovereignty), she is given two names, signifying her two roles. She is Eve (from *hava*—life or life-giver), which signifies her procreative sexual role, and she is "woman" *(isha)*, which indicates her intellectual and spiritual role. Thus woman, created from Adam's rib, according to the figurative language of Genesis, is bone of bones and flesh of flesh with the man—next of kin. Adam sees himself in the woman and at the sight of her offers the first hymn of praise in the Bible—"at last" (Gen 2:23 RSV). She is his equal. This double role—companionable and procreative—means, as the ancient Jewish commentator Rashi (A.D. 1040–1105) proposed, that "a woman who cannot bear children still has her greatest purpose in living—her moral and spiritual role, equivalent to a man."[19] Consequently, Jacob is angry with Rachel when she invests her life energy in the procreative role that was denied her. But succession through fecundity was important not only to Rachel but to Jacob.

FECUNDITY

Jacob is called to be the father of a large family. The command given to Adam and Eve (Gen 1:28) to "be fruitful and increase in number" was repeated to Jacob at the covenant renewal at Bethel (35:11). But while Leah was fertile, Rachel was barren. In the Western Christian tradition barrenness was a religious ideal, practiced by priests, monks and nuns to live the life of heaven. The source of this was not Scripture but the Neoplatonic philosophy of the ancient world that disparaged the body, sexuality and marriage itself. In the contemporary Western world there is again barrenness, but this time by choice *within marriage* as women and men elect not to have children for reasons of a promising career or to pursue an unencumbered lifestyle. This is made possible by contraception, which is 99 percent reliable.

In contrast, the Jewish tradition (so deeply rooted in the Genesis narrative) and the Christian tradition (rooted in such texts as 1 Tim 2:15: "Women will be saved through childbearing," that is, in the context of their natural function) have rendered the idea of elected barrenness unthinkable. Speaking for the Jewish tradition, Dresner says, "To be able to have a child but to decide against doing so was considered by the later sages to be akin to shedding the blood of the unborn. Childless love was thought to be incomplete, and giving birth, the ability to transcend the self into another."[20] Thus Rachel's exasperated cry, "Give me children, or I'll die!" (Gen 30:1). It was the cry of a woman facing her own emptiness, at least for the first few years. It is not simply the outcry of a pampered wife who is denied a comfort. She is wrestling with something fundamental to her femininity. If nothing within, I am dead. Instead of angrily disclaiming that he is not God, Jacob might well have responded as Elkanah did much later: "Don't I mean more to you than ten sons?" (1 Sam 1:8). Along with the matriarchs who preceded her—Sarah and Rebekah—Rachel would know that the covenant could not succeed apart from an act of God, that each child is immediately precious.

Not surprisingly, Christian tradition has favored Rachel over Leah, arguing that Rachel is like Mary (contemplative and unencumbered) and Leah is like Martha (the active person in her childbearing). So it was thought, as Jacob preferred Rachel, Jesus preferred Mary. Spiritualizing it even more, the early church argued that Leah's dull eyes represent the blindness of the synagogues to the true Messiah, while beloved Rachel points to the victorious church just as Rachel become the mother of Israel.[21] But in reality it took both women to build up the family of God. That is something that it appears is in the mind of the brothers.

The brothers are not so much moved by the horror of intermarriage as with passion to make things right in the family, a matter that is threaded through the rest of Genesis. And the brothers have not, in retaliation, trusted the providence of God. So Jacob, afraid that having taken matters of justice into their own hands, "I and my household will be destroyed" (Gen 34:30), must move on.

This is the very thing God has been trying to get him to do—to come home, home from the far country and home from the far country of the heart.

10

Home—the Story of Bethel
Genesis 35

> *In my experience nothing tortures us so much as longing. . . .When we*
> *are forcibly separated from those we love, we simply cannot, like so*
> *many others, contrive for ourselves some cheap substitute elsewhere. . . .*
> *We find the very idea of substitutes repulsive. . . . All we can do is*
> *to wait patiently; we must suffer the unutterable agony of separation. . . .*
> *There have been a few occasions in my life when I have had to learn*
> *what homesickness means. There is no agony worse than this.*

— DIETRICH BONHOEFFER (WRITTEN IN PRISON)

> *Sometimes I feel like a motherless child,*
> *Sometimes I feel like a motherless child,*
> *Sometimes I feel like a motherless child,*
> *A long way from home.*
> *A long way from home.*

— AFRICAN AMERICAN SPIRITUAL

Jacob is going home. But will it be Shechem or Bethel?

"Homeward bound" is one of the most evocative phrases in human speech. The words draw from the deep wells of our hearts memories of home-cooked meals, warm family laughter, life-soaked space that has a comfortable familiarity because of someone's sacred art of homemaking. The smell of my mother's apple pies in the oven still haunts me. The best part of my workday is coming home. Gail is usually there to greet me with

aromas of familiar foods. Home to me means predictable space, certain belonging, comfort, kicking back and rest. With good reason servants of the
gospel speak about "coming home to God." Home means welcome—and
welcome based not on one's deserts or performance but on sheer belonging. Home is another name for grace.

HOMEWARD BOUND

In Robert Frost's poem "Death of a Hired Hand" the old servant comes
home to the farm to die. The farmer and his wife, sitting on their stoop, reflect on what this means. Says the farmer, "Home is the place where when
you have to go there, they have to take you in." But the farmer's wife had it
right: "I should have called it something you somehow haven't to deserve."[1]
Home is much more than "house." Indeed a house may not even contain
a home. Certainly a home cannot be bought or sold, in spite of the real estate ads to the contrary.

Sue Monk Kidd speaks quite deeply to the experience of homecoming:

> The image of coming home is a powerful, archetypal symbol for returning
> to one's deepest self, to the soul. To come home is to return to the place of
> inner origin, that original imprint of God within. Therefore coming home
> fills us with a sense of being in the right place, a sense of deep spiritual be-
> longing. We all have this profound longing to come home, whether we rec-
> ognize it or not.[2]

Home, however, is a complex thought; it is not always thoughts of un-
adulterated joy. Holiday gatherings—whether Thanksgiving or Christmas—and family reunions are for many events anticipated with a mixture
of pleasure and dread. Frequently the thought is laced with confused feelings. I remember as a twelve-year-old boy crying myself to sleep for several
nights as I overheard my parents fighting. Would they divorce? (They
didn't, and God blessed them in their senior years with a real and deep
companionship as they kept their covenant.)

Often we cannot locate our home in a single geographical place. After spending two or three years in a new place studying, students go "home" at Christmas only to discover that it doesn't feel like home, not as much as the circle of belonging they have more recently gained. Hotels sometimes advertise their wares as a "home away from home," but it is a virtual home. Missionary children and the children of people in foreign service sometimes feel they do not belong anywhere, neither in the country of service adopted by their parents (where they are aliens), nor in their "home" country. There, on occasional visits to relatives, they may also feel like "resident aliens"—that evocative term used in the United States for people who do not fully belong where they are, who are not quite citizens.

Homecoming is complex for Jacob, as it is for us. He had been settled in Haran. James Hastings describes the dilemma:

> Like Ulysses and his crew, he was in danger of forgetting the land of his birth, the tents of his father, and the promises of which he was the heir. He was fast losing the pilgrim spirit, and settling into a citizen of that far country. His mean and crafty arts to increase his wealth were honeycombing his spirit, and eating out his nobler nature, prostituting it to the meanest ends. His wives, infected with the idolatry of their father's house, were in danger of corrupting the minds of his children; and how then would fare the holy seed, destined to give the world the messages of God? It was evident that his nest must be broken up in Haran.[3]

A TRIPLE HOMECOMING

Jacob cannot find home at Shechem and with Shechem (the leader of the Canaanite clan that gave its name to the place). But where? There are layers of meaning in his homeward journey in Genesis 35. He is coming to his *homeland* (Canaan), to his *homestead* (his father's residence—Hebron) and to his *spiritual home* (Bethel). These three "homes" are, respectively, a place, a family and a spiritual posture. For the Christian there is also a triple homecoming, since "in the land" is now fulfilled in all that is "in Christ." This includes being at home with the family of God, having one's heart as a home for God to inhabit (as a temple of the living God) and living with heavenly mindedness as we view the new heaven and the new earth as our final and ultimate home. We are "resident aliens" on earth, with our final home on the other side of death. The psalmist rightly said, "Blessed are those . . . who have set their hearts on pilgrimage" (Ps 84:5).

Jacob needs to come home. He fled into exile knowing brokenness: he was alienated from his brother and his parents, and he was not even at peace with himself (as reflected in his consistent refusal to use his own name). Significantly, Jacob uses the word for peace and wholeness (shalom) at the first Bethel encounter when he makes a conditional vow: "If God will be with me and will watch over me on this journey I am taking and will give me food to eat and clothes to wear so that I return safely [in peace—shalom] to my father's house, then the LORD will be my God and this stone that I have set up as a pillar will be God's house, and of all that you give me I will give you a tenth" (Gen 28:20-22). God has now provided food, clothes, wives, children and abundant possessions. So he needs to return in peace to his father's house. With shrewd insight Laban has analyzed Jacob's underlying homesickness while he worked year in and year out in Haran. "Now you have gone off because you longed to return to your father's house" (31:30). When later Jacob comes to his father in Hebron, Isaac "breathes his last," as though he had been waiting for Jacob's return to die, perhaps even waiting for Jacob and Esau together to bury him (35:29), thus dying in peace (shalom) and bringing peace to Jacob. But there is a painful, even an eerie silence in the text—no words from Isaac after twenty years of absence.

The journey back to the land is now almost complete. Motivated inwardly by the promise given at Bethel (that the land would be his) and outwardly by the birth of Joseph (Gen 30:22-24), Jacob starts the long trek back. First he crosses the Jabbok and the Jordan. Then he is diverted tragically for a while at Shechem, the place where Jacob buys land for his tent and stays, possibly for ten years, and where Dinah is raped. The revenge of Leah's sons gets him on the move again. Like the tower of Babel story (chap. 11), this was both judgment and fulfillment. At Babel God confused the language of the homogeneous people group bent on staying together and forced them to get on with the job of filling the earth; the Dinah-Shechem fiasco, and the stench Jacob had become to the Shechemites, forced him to pack his bags and move on. It was judgment: God condemned the self-seeking compromise of the people involved (and let them reap the consequences). It was fulfillment: it motivated the people to get on with fulfilling the promise—by moving.

The journey *out* (from Beersheba to Haran) is matched with the journey *in* (from Haran to Beersheba and Hebron). This corresponds to the shape of the corporate journey of God's people (*out* of Egypt and *into* the Promised Land) and the shape of our personal journeys (liberation *from* sin and the clutching paralysis of the principalities and powers and *into* increasing maturity, conformity to the image of Christ, becoming fully human—the "promised land" of the believer).

THE HOMESTEAD

Coming to the homestead was complicated for Jacob by more than twenty years of absence and by his having to deal with his brother's brooding anger at being cheated out of the birthright. Jacob returned the stolen blessing, but Jacob turned down his brother's offer to live with him. They went their separate ways until they met again at their father's funeral (Gen 35:29). Subsequently they had to separate because the land couldn't support all their flocks and herds together (36:7). The final healing of Jacob's own family would not really happen until the very end of the Genesis story when, in Egypt, Joseph and his brothers would be reconciled and the children of Leah and Rachel would become one people.

Such a relational homecoming is not accidental to the spiritual journey but rather is central. We cannot come home to God without being at peace with our brother or sister. If Jacob one dark night wrestles with God in human form and then sees God "face to face," he will the next day see the face of God in his brother, Esau, as he embraces him and atones for his past sin (Gen 33:10-11). True spirituality is relationship with God and neighbor as encompassed in the two great commandments, to love God and to love our neighbor (Mt 22:37-39). Thus, Jesus said, if you are offering your gift at the altar and then remember that your brother has something against you, leave your gift, get right with your brother and then express your devotion to God (Mt 5:23-24)—the very thing Jacob was doing in going up to Bethel. This was returning to his spiritual home—but belatedly.

A VOW KEPT BELATEDLY

God speaks to Jacob a second time, just as he would to Jonah and Hosea. God had called Jacob not only to return to Bethel but also to *settle* there (Gen 35:1). Jacob had promised to do so. But the lush pastures of Succoth and the urbane way of life of Shechem had seduced him. Dinah's rape was a costly judgment, but it led also to a fulfillment of God's call, now repeated: "Go up to Bethel and settle there, and build an altar there to God" (v. 1). The rabbis say that a vow unkept is like a house whose beams are about to fall on the occupants.

Zornberg notes that the rabbis overlooked Jacob's stealing the birthright and his financial negotiations with Laban and reserved their harshest criticism for his delay in fulfilling his vow made originally at Bethel. On this Rashi says, "Because you delayed on your journey, you were punished by this, your daughter's fate."[4] Rashi's source, *Midrash Tanhuma*, explores the root problem of the delay: a vow made but not fulfilled. "There are three conditions where a person's ledger is examined: if one goes on a journey alone, if one sits in a house that is in danger of collapse, and if one vows and does not pay one's vow."[5] He then cites Deuteronomy 23:22 and Proverbs 20:25 on the danger of unfulfilled vows. Extrapolating on what Jacob's vow meant, the Midrash continues:

> When Jacob made his vow, he prayed to be preserved from the three cardinal sins: idolatry, immorality, and bloodshed. Because he delayed in fulfilling his vow, he became guilty of all three: idolatry—"Rid yourselves of the alien gods in your midst" ([Gen] 35:2); immorality—the story of Dinah; and bloodshed—"They [Simeon and Levi] killed every male [in the city of Shechem]" (34:25). This teaches you that delaying the fulfilment of a vow is a graver of-

fense than all three cardinal sins! "It is better not to vow at all than to vow and not fulfill it" (Ecclesiates 5:4).[6]

In the New Testament the same issue is raised by Jesus in a parable about a pair of sons. One son refused to work in a vineyard but then did so, while the other promised to work in the vineyard but did not (Mt 21:28-32).

When a vow is not kept, equilibrium is disturbed. The reason is that vows are nonrefundable. The whole person comes out of the mouth. One's word does not return void unless the person is of no consequence. Not to keep a vow is an offense against one's own integrity; it is to break oneself up. Indeed we do not break promises and vows; we break ourselves against them.

The Hebrew concept of word is not simply vibrations from the vocal cords or digitalized electronic bits that can be processed in a computer. It is both word and deed. Speaking the word implies that the action is as good as done. Behind the word is the person. The Hebrew (and biblical) view of persons is a total unity—a psychopneumosomatic unity (soul, spirit and body). So words are not just incidental things that come out of bodies. Words are an extension of the person, the self-giving of that person. To give one's word is to give the essence of one's person. If the person lacks integrity, his or her words will "fall to the ground" (be resultless, of little significance), as was surely *not* the case with Samuel (1 Sam 3:19).

To reverse a vow would be to destroy something in oneself. Faithful Jephthah in the Old Testament said, "I have made a vow to the LORD that I cannot break" (Judg 11:35). In the play "A Man for All Seasons" Thomas More, chancellor of England, is asked to approve the divorce of the reigning queen so that Henry VIII could have a yet another wife. Having given his loyalty by a vow to Christ and the church on the matter of divorce, he could not go back on it, even if it cost him his life, which it did. In a moment of penetrating reflection, More explains to his daughter, "When a man takes an oath, Meg, he's holding his whole self in his own hands. Like water. And if he opens his fingers *then*—he needn't hope to find himself again."[7]

That is why people make vows when they marry. Without a vow, a marriage is simply an unwritten, unspoken contract for mutual need-meeting, a contract that can easily be broken if one partner defaults. Covenant marriage is created and sustained by vows. We make vows not because we can keep promises but because in our weakness we are not able to keep them. We do not keep the vows; they keep us. They stir up our growing-cold hearts to love as an active verb and not just a romantic feeling.

Vows are the only way of securing the future. Vows are out of vogue today not only among the irreligious, who want to keep all their options open, but also among the religious, who fear that making a vow might be overly righteous. But Jacob's vow, Jephthah's vow (Judg 11:30-31) and Hannah's vow (1 Sam 1:11) are, as Calvin Seerveld says, "acts of faith, hope, love, in trouble, glorying, anticipating, praising God for the Lord's certain relief! A biblically conceived vow is not a ritual to win favors, but is the most rich, imaginatively believing way of offering one's fear, dismay, shame, weakness, humiliation, tiredness, yes that too, to God."[8]

Jacob's reasons for the delay are undoubtedly complex, and we are given only hints about them. After all that had happened to Jacob, we might have expected that he would proceed directly to Bethel, but the same Succoth pastures that captivated his grandfather charms him. As we shall soon see, there is idolatry in Jacob's camp—that implicit double mindedness and instability (lack of *shalom*) that comes from not having a "single eye" (Lk 11:33-36) toward God. Undoubtedly Jacob, like his later descendants about to take the Promised Land, is simply afraid and feels insecure after the massacre of the Shechemites (Gen 34:30), so the narrator notes that when he finally goes, a God-inspired terror falls on the towns and "no one pursued them" (35:5).

IMMOVABLE IDOLS AND THE MOVABLE GOD

The issue uppermost for Jacob as he approaches his spiritual home is idolatry. In this case it is images that are a focus of worship, such as the teraphim (Laban's household gods) Rachel had stolen. Did he know about them before the pilgrimage to Bethel?

Idolatry may not involve a physical object. It is simply making something one's ultimate concern other than the One who is ultimate. It can be money, sex, work, even family—whatever we are actually living *for*, that to which we look for meaning and purpose.

Psalms 115 and 35 deliver a stunning judgment of idols.

> They have mouths, but cannot speak,
> > eyes, but cannot see;
> they have ears, but cannot hear . . .
> > feet, but they cannot walk. (Ps 115:5-7)

Most damning of all,

> Those who make them will be like them,
> and so will all who trust in them. (v. 8)

It is an axiom of the spiritual life that we become like the god we worship. In a commodity society our idols come in packages, with glossy advertisements and technologically intriguing challenges. We buy and sell idols, fondle them and give them the devotion of our hearts. This results, as John Kavanaugh concludes, in the depersonalization of human beings and the personalization of things.

Persons relate to things as if they were persons; they relate to persons—including themselves—as if they were things. Having patterned ourselves after the image of our commodities, we become disenfranchised of our very humanness. Reduced to commodities, we lose the intimacy of personal touch. We cannot truly see or listen as vibrant men and women. We do not speak, limited as we are to the repetition of computed input. We do not walk in freedom, since we are paralyzed by what is. Such is the result of idolatry. Those who make idols and put their trust in them become like them.[9]

Worship something man-made, and you will become a diminished person. Worship doctrines, even Christian doctrines, and you will be inflexible, immovable and only half human. But, so says the psalmist:

> Our God is in heaven;
> > he does whatever pleases him. (Ps 115:3)

God is the most free, movable and moving Being in the universe. And those who worship the living God become truly free and truly alive, and are wonderfully flexible.

There is nothing healthier than having undivided love for God, a love above all other loves, and nothing more debilitating than being a polytheist in actual practice. Polytheism is the theological equivalent of polygamy. As polygamy is a distortion of marriage, so polytheism is a distortion of our relationship with God. Laban was essentially a polytheist, worshiping the god of Nahor as well as the God of Abraham (Gen 31:53). The problem of idolatry is the same as the problem of polygamy, as Jacob well knew. It leads to divided loyalties, disruption, brokenness and disunity.

RENEWAL

So how does spiritual renewal come about? It comes, as Jacob has learned and continues to learn, by renaming, by reclothing, by renouncing idols of heart, mind and body, and by receiving the promise again. At Shechem, Jacob assimilated; at Bethel, he separates. Jacob does this as he approaches Bethel, instructing his company to get rid of their gods, thus fulfilling in anticipation the second of the Ten Commandments. Further, just as Jacob's company dons clean clothes, so we need to clothe ourselves in the righteousness of Christ. This putting off and putting on is the warp and woof of personal and corporate renewal. But there is one thing more that Jacob does at Bethel.

He builds an altar and sets up yet one more pillar to commemorate the ladder he had seen there. The altar is the place of sacrifice of something precious in order to be right with God. It is humankind going to God, praying to God, giving to God. The ladder (symbolized by the stone pillar) is God coming to humankind, speaking to us, giving to us. So there is a mutual homecoming of God and humankind that brings Sabbath rest—*shalom*.

THREE FULL-TIME JOBS

At Bethel, God speaks to Jacob once again. He changes his name once

again from Jacob to Israel, perhaps indicating that now that he has reconciled with Esau, and reconciled with God at Bethel, he is *entitled* to use his
new name: "He who strives with God and man wins." Once again God re-
news the promise, telling him "to be fruitful" and (significantly) "to fill the
earth," both phrases reminiscent of the mandate given to Adam and Eve before the Fall (into sin). Back in Genesis 1 and 2 God gave three full-time
jobs to Adam and Eve, and through them to all human beings. It is the human vocation, the calling on all men and women.[10]

First, they (and we) are called to full-time *communion* with God. Adam
and Eve placed in a sanctuary garden were to enjoy God's presence continuously while eating, sleeping, working, fixing up the hedges and making
love. Even after they sinned, God walks in the garden in the cool of the day,
wanting to commune with his creatures.

The second full-time job is *community building*. God made them male
and female "in his image" (Gen 1:26). We are built for love, built for relationality, and we are Godlike (literally) when expressing friendship, loving,
building family and extending our love to the outsider, so creating community. This may be the arena where some people have gainful employment
(as child-care workers, town planners, pastors and counselors), but for all of
us it is full-time. I dare not think of myself as a part-time husband, father,
grandfather, brother or friend!

The third full-time job is *cocreativity*—developing the potential of creation by exercising dominion and stewardship over all creation (Gen 1:26-
28), taking care of God's earth and making God's world work. This involves
everything from agriculture to hairdressing, from making tools to developing computer programs, from crafting and firing clay pots to building sky-
scrapers and rapid transit systems—all the ways we enhance human life.
Some of us have remunerated employment in this area, but all of us are
stewards of creation all the time, every moment of the day or night. And this
too is under God, whose earth we care for as trustees and in whose presence
we work as co- or subcreators.

Peter J. Leithart has made the insightful observation that there are three concentric circles in Genesis 1—2: the Garden is in the center, with Eden surrounding it and then beyond that the other lands (see Gen 2:10-14). The Garden is the *sanctuary* and a place of worship; Eden is *home*; and the "other lands" are the *world*. The sanctuary was a place of refuge and safety, a place of nourishment and fruitfulness, and a place of beauty. In that sanctuary the tree of life was a special provision of food by which Adam and Eve would have continuous communion with God. God's purpose was that the man and woman would extend the sanctuary into the world, making the world, as Calvin once said, into the theater of God's glory. "Subduing the earth brings safety, prosperity and beauty. . . . Instead of guarding the pristine creation, humanity is called to guard the world once it has been subdued to human rule."[11]

This is what it means to be fully human and a Godlike creature. This world is not junk and we are not just passing through on our way to heaven. In fact heaven is not our final destiny, but rather we are headed for "a new heaven *and a new earth*" (Rev 21:1, emphasis mine)—a remarkably material future. This makes perfect sense of our daily work, as it will (if done in faith, hope and love and purged of sin) find its place in the *renewed* creation.

Remarkably, the promise/blessing given to Abraham and his descendants was a reinstatement and focusing of the original human vocation, as though Abraham and his descendants were called to model and implement a genuinely human existence on earth. Abraham received *communion* with God as his faith was credited to him as righteousness and God welcomed him, certifying that he really belonged to God by means of a covenant ceremony (Gen 15). Then Abraham was promised a family, a people who would ultimately bless all nations (22:18); thus he was called to *community building*—something he did rather badly in Egypt (chap. 20). But finally Abraham was given the land in *cocreativity*, not as a mere possession but rather as something to develop in such a way that there would be stewardship, economic and social justice—as developed in later legislation.

Communion. Community building. Cocreativity. All this adds up to a spiritual, social and very down-to-earth material calling.

Now at Bethel Jacob hears from God once again. God is with him—the pillar symbolizes this (communion). God calls him once again to be fruitful, reaffirming the community-building vocation, especially now that he has met with Esau and is returning home to his father. But finally God calls him to be fruitful and to fill the earth (Gen 35:11)—the cocreativity calling—which he should do both socially through raising his family and by creative work in the world. Joseph, his son, will do this in a spectacular way in Egypt, and this is the story to which we turn in the next chapter.

Jacob had a triple homecoming. He came to his *homeland* (Canaan), to his *homestead* (his father's residence—Hebron) and to his *spiritual home* (Bethel). Those who follow Jesus also "come home" in multiple ways. In the long run they look to their final homeland in the new heaven and new earth, which they will enter, along with their works (Rev 14:13), when Christ comes again. But the reality of that ultimate home, expressed in the irruption of the kingdom of God here and now (though coming later in fullness), means that they are already beginning to live a heavenly life. Further, believers come home to the family of God, where they are brothers and sisters. And finally, their life here and now, and forever, becomes a home for God as they become temples of the Holy Spirit. Jesus more than fulfils the promise to Jacob in these words: "If anyone loves me, he will obey my teaching. My Father will love him, and we will come to him and *make our home with him*" (Jn 14:23, emphasis mine).

Calling—the Story of Joseph
Genesis 37—50

My object in living is to unite
My avocation and my vocation
As my two eyes make one in sight.

—ROBERT FROST

I knelt down beside a Ph.D. student at the University of British Columbia. This young Indian man was brilliant, unusually talented and hungry for God. "Do you want to invite Jesus into your life?" I asked.

"I've been waiting two days for you to come and pray with me," he replied.

After praying, I turned to him and said, "You are now a disciple of Jesus. And as a disciple of Jesus, you have a vocation that is greater than becoming the prime minister of India."

"How did you know?" he asked.

"Know what?"

"That is my life goal." (He went back to India and became an influential person, both in leadership of the country and in the church, but not prime minister!)

Unfortunately the word *vocation* is badly used today, and had I the power to do so, I would eliminate it entirely and replace it with the other translation of the Latin word *vocatio*, namely *calling*. While *vocation* has come to be identified with occupation, the word *calling* invites the question "Who?" Who is doing the calling? The most fundamental fact about calling and living vocationally is that we are first called to Someone before we are called to do something. That lesson is one Jacob is slowly learning, culminating in wisdom in his old age as he goes down to Egypt to be reconciled with his son Joseph. Joseph himself is learning to live vocationally. It is something we desperately need and are in process of losing.

THE POSTVOCATIONAL WORLD

The signs are all around us. People identify themselves by their occupation: "I am a dentist." Then there is that wretched sentence "I am *just* a house-wife." Further, the few people who speak about being "called of God" turn out to be religious professionals, pastors and missionaries. Not many busi-nesspeople speak of being called to business, and if they did, they might be considered a little daft. God's call to do holy work certainly—so it is as-sumed—has nothing to do with making money. In many parts of the world careerism reigns, aided and abetted by the dominant popular philosophy of self-actualization—I have a duty to myself to be fulfilled and to choose a life path that leads to personal happiness and the expression of all my talents. In other parts of the world, life is approached from the perspective of luck or karma.

Luther's complaint against the priests and monks of his day was really along these lines: they are not called to be religious professionals; they have *elected* to go into the ministry or priesthood as a superior way, to gain merit or prove their seriousness as disciples of Jesus.[1] *Calling* implies the exact op-posite: we do not elect a calling; we are chosen and summoned. So in one sense it is an oxymoron to speak of "vocational choice."

Were we to see our lives as totally lived under the empowering invitation of God—including work, family, friendship, sleep, leisure, civic responsibil-ity and mission—our lives would be given dynamic direction and purpose. We would not make finding the perfect job our ultimate concern. Work or ministry in the church would not be everything. Instead of being driven peo-ple trying to prove our worth through intensive activity (often because we have grown up in a nonaffirming environment), we serve, work and relate for love and gratitude. We do so because we are persuaded that our lives are not a bundle of accidents but rather are responsive to a wonderful purpose unfolding under the gracious and life-giving summons of God.

In this sense God does not have a wonderful *plan* for our lives; he has something better—a wonderful *purpose*. If it is a plan, we will have to follow the plan meticulously, and if we make a mistake, we must go back to "Go" (which is usually impossible) and start again. Otherwise we will be doing "God's second best." Being part of God's purpose is like canoeing down a fast-flowing stream. We have mobility; we can back-ferry or front-ferry, moving from side to side. But we are being carried along, swept up and embraced by the flow. It was so with Jacob and with Jacob's son Joseph.

THE SPOILED BRAT

Joseph's life is always of interest because of its dramatic turns of events—a real rags-to-riches story. But besides its dramatic quality, Joseph's story engages us at the level of living vocationally. In its simplest level, the story is one of the eleventh son of Jacob who is the favored son, dressed (one more disguise) in a richly ornamented robe so that he does not have to work, as do his brothers. They hate him because of his favored position, because of his dreams in which they are pictured bowing down to him and also because he brought a bad report of them to his father (Gen 37:2). So one day when Joseph goes out to the field to find out how things were going, they try to do away with him, first by throwing him into a dry cistern to die of malnutrition and thirst, and then by selling him to passing Midianite traders carrying spices to Egypt. The brothers, by the same kind of deceit that has passed from generation to generation, bring Joseph's special coat, now stained with animal blood, to Jacob and, without actually lying, invite him to draw his own conclusions: "We found this. Examine it to see whether it is your son's robe" (v. 32). Jacob concludes that a wild animal has torn Joseph to shreds, when in fact it was his wild brothers who had torn him from the family. Jacob refuses to be comforted, because his life is bound up in the children of his favorite wife, Rachel, and with Joseph in particular.

Meanwhile Joseph descends to Egypt, where he is sold as a slave to work in Potiphar's house. There, as everywhere else, Joseph rises into leadership and is placed in complete charge of the household. But when seduced by Mrs. Potiphar, he runs away, leaving only his coat behind. Falsely accused (through another deceptive piece of clothing), he lands up in another pit—a prison. There he interprets the dreams of Pharaoh's butler and baker, inserting after his hopeful prophecy for the butler, "Mention me to Pharaoh and get me out of this prison. For I was forcibly carried off from the land of the Hebrews, and even here I have done nothing to deserve being put in a dungeon" (Gen 40:14-15). The butler forgets, at least for a long time, until Pharaoh himself has a disturbing dream and cannot get it interpreted by his wise men and magicians. Enter Joseph.

Joseph confesses, "I cannot do it, but God will give Pharaoh the answer he desires" (Gen 41:16). Many people imagine that God cannot be found in high-ranking political circles or in the boardrooms of multinationals. But Pharaoh himself says, "God has made all this known to you" (v. 39). Then, partly at Joseph's suggestion, Pharaoh hires Joseph to be second to himself to garner food during the seven years of plenty for distribution during the seven years of famine. According to the dreams of Pharaoh, these are predicted.

If ever there were a prison-to-palace story, this is it! Joseph receives an Egyptian name (Zaphenath-Paneah), an Egyptian wife with strong connections to the local religious cult, a chariot and almost unlimited power. In this role he saves the Egyptian nation and, as we shall see, saves even his own family. Joseph is a stunning example of a full-time servant of God in a so-called secular situation. Further, he is in "full-time ministry" without a specific, existential call of God, yet he is truly living out his calling.

The plot thickens as the famine proceeds. Joseph's brothers are sent by Jacob down to Egypt to buy bread. But Jacob, now with his favoritism transferred from Joseph to the one remaining son of Rachel (that is, Benjamin), sends all but Benjamin down to get food "because he was afraid that harm might come to him" (Gen 42:4). The sons present themselves before Joseph and bow low. Joseph recognizes them but keeps his Egyptian disguise (one more pretense), and using a translator as though he could not understand what they are saying, Joseph recognizes that his dreams are coming true. But he does not identify himself, disclose himself. Is he still struggling to forgive? Does he willfully hold back his identity because he needs to know whether his brothers have come to terms with what they have done to him? Does he wonder whether they have repented? He tries to find out by putting them through a simulation of his own dreadful experiences at their hands—accusing then of being spies (as he had "spied" for his father on them), throwing them in prison (as he had been cast into the pit in Dothan), then releasing them on condition that one (Simeon) stay behind as a hostage while the rest return to get the remaining brother, Benjamin.

Finally, after the passing of a long time, they persuade Jacob to let Benjamin, his one remaining son of Rachel, go to Egypt. There follows a recognition scene that is one of the most moving in all literature. It is Judah who finally breaks Joseph down and achieves a reconciliation of the brothers. Then Joseph says, "It was not you who *sent* me here, but God" (Gen 45:8) and "It was to save lives that God *sent* me ahead of you" (v. 5).[2] Joseph recognizes his life as a vocational expression more by hindsight than foresight, though there are early indications that God is leading him.

THREE ROLES

We have much to learn from Joseph about living vocationally. It is much more than occupation. First, Joseph has a *career*. For the first seventeen years of his life (from privilege to the pit), he follows in his father's steps as a shepherd "tending the flock with his brothers" (Gen 37:2). A career is an occupation that one normally expects to undertake for a long period, possibly one's lifetime, though today people have four or five careers (with several assignments in each career) and have to keep reinventing themselves. Then Joseph gets a *job* (this is the period from the pit to prison), working as a slave in Potiphar's household. A job is work undertaken simply to survive. For much of the world today, work is undertaken merely to survive, with no sense that people are fulfilling a higher calling or doing work that is fitting for their gifts and talents. But when Joseph is elevated from the prison to the palace, he discovers a *vocation*, a calling.

Vocation is much more than simply working. It is the summons of God to belong to him, to live God's way and to do God's work in the world. I have been a pastor, a student worker, a carpenter, a businessperson and a professor. But that is only part of my calling. I am also called to be a husband and father, a son and a grandfather, a friend, a citizen. I express calling by living my whole life to God's glory. So Joseph, possibly more clearly toward the end, realizes that he was sent by God as a missionary to Egypt. This holy mission was to undertake stewardship of the resources of the land not only for the Egyptians but also for the family of promise. Even slave work can get taken up into the calling of God and be given purpose.

Significantly Joseph is a model management consultant. He gains a global view, defines the problem, recommends strategy and undertakes to support the CEO (in this case Pharaoh) in the process of implementation. In this case Joseph really "hired himself on," which was not crass selfish ambition but taking inspired entrepreneurial initiative. But Joseph was tempted in the area of his calling.

THREE TEMPTATIONS

The first of Joseph's temptations was to be the *architect of his own fulfillment*. As a young man, he has a dream in which his brothers all bow down to him. Given an amazing dream of greatness, he uses it manipulatively on his brothers. One would think that after their reaction to the first dream (eleven sheaves bowing down to his sheaf) Joseph would hold the vision in his heart. But no, he blurts out the second one—the sun and moon (father and mother) and the eleven stars (his brothers) all bowing down to him. Added to this, Joseph tattletales (Gen 37:2), bringing a bad report of the brothers to Jacob. So they hate him all the more. It seems that he is trying to make the vision happen. When we have a great vision, a mission that grips us, a "call" on our lives, it is always tempting to scheme about the dream without waiting on God, without depending for our next move on the God who creates and sustains us. Joseph has to learn this the hard way.

His second temptation is in the *sexual* area. He is seduced by Mrs. Potiphar, invited to go to bed with her. No one would know if he had done it, and a liaison with an important person could possibly stand him in good stead in the long run. But he courageously addresses both his own conscience and hers: he has a duty to his master ("My master has withheld nothing from me except you"). Then he calls a spade a spade: "How then could I do such a wicked thing and sin against God?" (Gen 39:9). This happens day after day until she catches him by the cloak. He escapes without his cloak, which she then uses as evidence, just as Joseph's brothers had before used his torn cloak as evidence of his death. Temptation in the sexual area thrives in the workplace. But so do temptations to power and status. It needs to be named, as Joseph called it a sin against God and his neighbor. Sometimes we can fight it directly; often, like Joseph, we must flee.

Joseph's third temptation was to locate his *identity* in his occupation. In Egypt he was raised from prison to the palace by Pharaoh. Joseph has an Egyptian name, an Egyptian wife, Egyptian culture and an all-consuming job. He was Mr. Second-in-Command. Many people have surnames derived from an ancestor's occupation—carter, smith, bolter, carpenter, carver or weaver, for example. So it is understandable, though dangerous, to become identified with one's occupation. It happens at parties. "What do you do?" And so to be retired or unemployed implies having no identity at all. With great wisdom Augustine advised that if you want to find out who people are, don't ask them what they do but what they love.[3]

Regarding a career, it is easy to think we are the architects of our own fulfillment. In our jobs we can compromise morally. We can also allow ourselves to be solely identified by the work dimensions, whereas calling is much, much more. But Joseph also has resources for living vocationally, and so do we.

THREE RESOURCES

The first is an *empowering vision* of greatness. This is the "wonderful purpose" of which I spoke above. At seventeen Joseph received a dream from God. Some try to pass this off as youthful narcissism, the inflated ego of a spoiled brat. But his dreams are not merely a revelation of his egotistical and narcissistic young mind. These visions are God-given pictures of his purpose. They were a vision of greatness *under God*. Without such a dream, our lives are uninspired. Rules, like fences, can hem us in and keep us from the awful (though interesting) ways of sinning. Principles can guide us. But we need something more to inspire us. In the outback of Australia they say that a well is better than a fence. Put in a well where you want the animals to remain, and you won't ever need a fence. The call of God is like that. Let me illustrate.

Before our three children married and left home, we had the privilege of traveling to Greece, Egypt and Israel. In Greece we (along with some goats and heavily burdened farmers) took the local bus to Delphi, the site of the ancient oracle. In the ancient world people would come to Delphi to consult the will of the gods. A priestess, sitting on a tripod over a stone disk, would inhale the narcotic fumes from a leaf-laden fire below and give an answer. King Croesus came from Sardis in Turkey before he was to wage war and sought counsel from the priestess. She took a whiff and said, "A great king will fall in this war" (not saying whether it was Croesus or the other guy). A pregnant woman comes and asks whether she will bear a boy or girl: "Son . . . no—daughter" (leaving the matter totally up in the air again). The will of the gods for the Greeks was ambiguous, tricky.

Then we flew to Cairo. Sitting in a restaurant, we struck up a conversation with an American at the next table. "What are you doing here in Cairo?" we asked.

"I'm training the Egyptian fighter pilots."

"That's an interesting job. What is the biggest problem you face in your daily work?" (I love to ask this one).

He replied, "When the red warning lights come on in the cockpit, they do nothing."

"Why?"

"Because they say if it is the will of Allah for the plane to crash, it will do so. And my biggest challenge is to convince them there is something they can do." For within Islam the will of God is inexorable and the true worshiper is a submitter.[4]

We then crossed the desert in an Arab bus without air conditioning, past grim Bedouin settlements scarcely distinguishable from the blistering sand, until we came to the border of Israel. There we saw lush flowers, fruit trees and hay swaying in the wind. Literally the flowers were blooming in the desert. How come? The will of God for the people of God is not ambiguous and not inexorable. It is an empowering vision. And the true worshiper is inspired to take initiative to fulfill the wonderful calling laid on him or her. We are called to be part of God's transforming work on earth. It is a kingdom vision. What a resource!

The second resource is the *sovereignty of God*. Joseph confesses to his brothers, "You intended to harm me, but God intended it for good to accomplish what is now being done, the saving of many lives" (Gen 50:20). We are not a bundle of accidents. God has been involved in our lives from the moment of our conception onward. God gives our family background, education, life experiences, personality and talents sovereignly. Even the most untoward experiences can, by the power of God, be turned for the good of those who love God. The worst experiences of our lives, being in pits and prisons—physical, occupational, emotional or relational—turn out to be the best experiences, though it doesn't feel that way at the time. I play chess, but I do so badly. And when I play an expert, I feel perfectly free to make any moves I want—for about four moves. But then the expert has got me. God has got me.

There is a mystery in the story of Jacob and Joseph, the mystery of human freedom and God's providential action. It is epitomized in Joseph's summary of his life, quoted above: "You intended . . . but God" (Gen 50:20). In the same way, the text notes that Joseph had been taken down to Egypt (39:1), which is exactly where God wants Joseph to be. But God accomplishes his own inscrutable purposes through human actions taken "freely": a favorite wife, a favorite son, a murder plot by siblings, a providential passing by of a caravan, a job in Potiphar's house, a seduction by Mrs. Potiphar, a residency in the king's prison that brings Joseph in contact with royal servants, the providential reinstatement of the king's butler and an interpreted dream! Where does God's will stop and human will begin? Or is there any human freedom at all?

A Jewish midrash explores this in a provocative challenge to the concept of absolute human freedom:

> Do not read, "Joseph was brought down to Egypt," but "Joseph brought his father and brothers down to Egypt. . . ." This is like a cow whose owners want to place a yoke on her neck. She refuses the yoke, so what do they do? They take her calf away from her, and pull him to the field they want ploughed. The calf bellows for his mother, who hears and involuntarily follows her son. In the same way, God sought to fulfil the decree of the Covenant, so He engineered the plot of this whole narrative, and the family went down to Egypt and paid off this writ—"Terrible to man are Your plots" (*Tanhuma*, 4).[5]

Avivah Zornberg comments that the midrash presents human beings as participants in a drama of God's devising.

Thomas Mann once said, "It is possible to be in a plot and not understand it."[6] It is, says Zornberg, "the very nature of life inside a . . . plot, that one does not understand its whole structure."[7] That surely is our situation: human beings are for the most part unconscious actors in God's plot. We can resent this and insist that we must be absolutely autonomous, in complete control of our lives and future. Or like Paul at the conclusion of his reflection on the providential purpose of God in relation to Jews and Gentiles in Christ, we can live doxologically, which is really to live vocationally:

> Oh, the depth of the riches of the wisdom and knowledge of God!
> > How unsearchable his judgments,
> > and his paths beyond tracing out!
> Who has known the mind of the Lord?
> > Or who has been his counselor?

Who has ever given to God, that God should repay him?
    For from him and through him and to him are all things.
    To him be the glory forever! Amen. (Rom 11:33-36)

Further, Joseph's third resource was the *people of God*. With all his
Egyptian pomp and circumstance, his Egyptian identity and role, Joseph is
separated from his brothers. And while he undertakes the violent role-playing experience of putting his brothers through what they had inflicted on
him, he must be wrestling with whether and how he would be able to identify with them. So when he finally confesses, "I am Joseph," he throws his
lot in with the despised and poor people of God, the family of promise, and
once again he has an integrated identity. In the film *The Quarrel*, a rabbi,
in the final scene, notes that in Egypt Joseph was great and powerful. Only
the mighty Pharaoh was above him. Joseph had everything. But until his
brothers came, Joseph was alone.

There are no individual Christians. We are included through faith not just
in the church (as a human organization) but in the very family of God, adopted into the love life of the triune God. We cannot live vocationally alone. We
cannot even discern our vocations alone. One of the most neglected ministries
of the church is vocational discernment. In the family of God we can help one
another discern the leading of God, the passion and talents God has inspired
and the circumstances that affect our life path. We are called together.

JACOB COMES DOWN

All this transpired before Jacob himself was called to come down to Egypt.
He who had been called to occupy the land is now called to abandon it.
This is not a career move "up." It takes a divine revelation to assure him that
he is still on a pilgrimage and is not a settler. On the way he stops at Beersheba to offer sacrifices to the God of his father, Isaac. And once again God
speaks to him directly: "I am God, the God of your father. . . . Do not be
afraid to go down to Egypt, for I will make you into a great nation there. I
will go down to Egypt with you, and I will surely bring you back again. And
Joseph's own hand will close your eyes" (Gen 46:3-4).

The presence of God, the family of God, the land—these are essential parts of the promise. And God is reassuring Jacob that his move to Egypt is not a move away from God, not a move away from family (Joseph's hand would close his eyes) and not a permanent move away from the land (as Egypt would be the womb of the nation and the nation would come back). This must be encouraging for many of us who move, as is the average in North America, every four or five years. We can find God "in transit." But what about the final part of the promise-cum-call—the blessing of the nations?

When Jacob arrives in Pharaoh's cart, Joseph has his own chariot made ready and goes out to meet his father. What an emotional meeting it is— not unlike the meeting of Jacob and Esau years before, and like that described by Jesus in the parable of the two prodigals when the father threw his arms around his homecoming son. In this case it is the father who is homecoming and his son welcomes him. Joseph "threw his arms around his father and wept for a long time" (Gen 46:29). And Jacob himself feels that there is closure: "Now I am ready to die, since I have seen for myself that you are still alive" (v. 30).

But Jacob is not quite ready to die. First he must meet Pharaoh. The meeting of the old patriarch and the pharaoh surely must be one of the strangest in all time. The leader of a family from Canaan, with the rumor of angels and the call of God, meets one of the most powerful men on earth, the superpower of the day, and one who represents a pagan religion (though he had acknowledged the God of Abraham's spirit in Joseph). Jacob twice blesses Pharaoh, first when he enters Pharaoh's presence and then after Pharaoh inquires about his age and pilgrimage. "Then Jacob blessed Pharaoh and went out from his presence" (Gen 47:10), thus in effect blessing the Gentiles and the nations with the positive spiritual good he had to give from his long journey with God, as Joseph his son has blessed the nations through his stewardship of creation. Here the vocations of Joseph and Jacob are joined. Along with them, we are invited to live vocationally.

We can now summarize what we have learned about living with a calling. Who are called of God? All, especially now that Christ has come and invites all to walk worthy of the calling to which they have been called (Eph 4:1). Where does that calling take us? Into the world to serve God's purposes in all of our life circumstances. How do we fulfill our calling? By undertaking with Abraham, Isaac, Jacob and Joseph the human vocation to commune with God, to build community (family, neighborhood, church and nation) and to enter into God's continuing creation as stewards on earth through all the human occupations that enrich human life and unlock the potential of God's creation. Are some people called into "full-time" ministry?[8] There is no part-time ministry option available.

Dressing — the Story of Tamar
Genesis 38

Adornment is a mark of humanity.
Seashells and lilies of the valley do not need decoration,
and it is an affectation to clothe animals, who are never naked.
Clothing is a gift of God to humankind.

— CALVIN SEERVELD

In the book of Genesis people began to wear clothes
when they first became aware of their sin:
since the day Adam and Eve covered themselves with fig leaves,
clothing has been both a blessing and a curse —
a cursed blessing to be exact (Gen 3:7).

— KATHRYN LOCKHART

Clothes can be a mere covering of our shameful nakedness, a means of
protection, a symbol of worth (as is Joseph's striped coat) or an extension of
our bodily identity. Or they can be a disguise.[1] In the Garden of Eden,
Adam and Eve made their first makeshift aprons from fig leaves. But God's
first gift and first act of mercy to the sinful couple was to give them leather
clothes to protect them from the thorns and the abrasions of everyday life.
Their clothes also covered their shame and provided privacy. As Seerveld
says, "To this day clothing is a blessing that protects the privacy peculiar to
us human creatures made in God's image."[2] A recurring theme in the story
of Jacob (and all the persons in his life) is clothing. It is revealing not only

to the spiritual meaning of the story but also to our own experience of dressing every day.

THE DRESS-UP FAMILY

It seems that the members of the family of promise are always "dressing up" like others to secure an identity or a position they do not have in themselves. Jacob wore Esau's clothing to confuse his blind father, Isaac. Leah wore Rachel's clothing in the marriage tent. Judah, along with his brothers, had deceived his father, Jacob, with Joseph's cloak and the blood of a goat to convince him that Joseph was dead. Father and sons all use cloaks and goats for deception. Later, in the story we will now explore, Tamar, Judah's daughter-in-law, dressed up as a prostitute and seduced her father-in-law. Joseph's coat, grabbed by Potiphar's wife as he tried to escape from her seduction, became the means of his being incriminated. Joseph himself "dressed up" as an Egyptian vizier until he, too, had come to himself and confessed to his brothers, "I am Joseph." And in this story full of repeated symbols, Joseph, when he was reconciled with his brothers, gave each of them new clothing (to replace the travel-worn rags) as a sign of honor and affection. Waltke notes that this stands in striking contrast to the action of the brothers when they stripped off Joseph's clothes and threw him in a pit.[3] It was a sign of reconciliation. In the end Joseph also gave to Benjamin five sets of clothes (Gen 45:22)!

The story we now explore from Genesis 38 is a sordid one, with two primary characters: Judah, Jacob's son, and Tamar, Judah's daughter-in-law. The chapter begins with a suggestive note: "Judah left his brothers and went down to stay with a man of Adullam named Hirah" (38:1). Under the influence of his pagan friend, he fell in love with a pagan woman, the daughter of Shua, and married her at a place with the significant name Kezib ("Deception"), signaling that it was a moral as well as a geographical descent. For at Kezib, Judah was misled, partly through the seductive influence of his godless friend Hirah. This is in powerful contrast to the friendship of David and Jonathan, in which Jonathan "helped [David] find strength in

God" (1 Sam 23:16). A friend is perhaps the most influential minister in one's life, for good or ill, usually without intentionally being so.

TAMAR'S DESPERATE DISGUISE

At "Deception," Judah and Bat (daughter of) Shua have three sons: Er, Onan and Shelah. Judah finds a wife for Er—Tamar. But Er promptly dies.[4] According to custom, his brother Onan is to marry Tamar to ensure continuity in his brother's line. But Onan spills his seed on the ground in his "promiscuous" refusal to provide his brother with offspring. So he dies. Shelah is next in line, but while Judah promises him to Tamar, Judah holds back his son misleadingly so as not to lose (as he fears) yet one more son— one more deception. Then on top of it all, Judah's own wife dies.

Judah is sexually vulnerable after the death of his wife, Bat Shua. He is also spiritually and relationally vulnerable. When his mourning is over, and again under the influence of his pagan friend Hirah, Judah goes up to Timnah at sheep-shearing time. Apparently he does not realize that in failing to provide a husband for Tamar he is condemning her to perpetual widowhood with no possibility of remarriage. She is forced to undertake a desperate ploy. The Jewish commentator Norman Cohen suggests, "Hearing that Judah was coming up to Timnah, Tamar became infuriated. She was not able to get on with her life, but her father-in-law could pick himself up after Shua's death and start over again."[5]

Tamar puts aside her widow's clothes and dresses herself as a prostitute, disguising herself as Jacob had with Isaac and as Leah had in the marriage tent. With her head covered in a veil, Tamar positions herself at the entrance to Enaim (which literally means "eyes"). The "uncovering" of the sheep and the uncovering of Tamar are parallels in the story. Judah sleeps with her. And as pledge of payment to the daughter-in-law—cum—prostitute, Judah leaves his seal, cord and staff—symbols of his identity. He promises a goat in payment, though he cannot find the prostitute when he later sends his worldly wise friend to make his belated payment. Here is one more cloak and goat story.

Consequently, when Tamar's pregnancy becomes public, and when "righteous" Judah requires her death, she produces the symbols of his identity: "I am pregnant by the man who owns these" (Gen 38:25). His eyes are opened and he has to face himself in the guise of a harlot. Unwittingly he has played the role of Shelah in providing offspring for Tamar. And God has used Tamar to open Judah's eyes to the need to redeem the lost brother (Er) as Judah had not redeemed his lost brother (Joseph) earlier from the pit. There are moral symmetries in the story that are compelling. But significantly, this was the beginning of Judah's transformation.

In confessing for all to hear, referring to Tamar, "She is more righteous than I, since I wouldn't give her to my son Shelah" (Gen 38:26), Judah is making a step toward his brothers and at the same time toward God.[6] And in one more symmetry in the story, Tamar bears twins by means of Judah's seed, and yet once again the younger (or second)—in this case Perez (his name means "Breaking Out")—would stand in the line leading to the Messiah. Reflecting on how God consistently chose the second—Isaac instead of Ishmael, Jacob instead of Esau, Perez instead of Zerah, and later Ephraim instead of Manasseh—and on how God used this "mixed marriage" (Canaanite-Israelite) and later the Moabite Ruth and Israelite Boaz to fulfill his promise, Norman Cohen concludes, "Righteousness is not the product of family status or societal position, but rather of the actions of individual human beings regardless of their backgrounds. . . . Often it is the stranger in our midst who teaches us what God expects of us."[7] Tamar in her "dress-up" was such a stranger.

The Ministry of Dressing

It is often said that clothes "make" the man or the woman, meaning of course that the clothes project an image—often the image of a person whom someone would like to be but is not. It is well known, however, that many men dressed in "power suits" are inwardly insecure and that some women who dress seductively are afraid of sexual intimacy. In a sense, we cannot tell a lie when we put on our clothes. We are saying something truthful about ourselves. Like speech itself, which reveals the person, clothing can reveal what is happening inside. When Job is grieving, he strips himself naked. No clothes, in his case, expressed his utter vulnerability and desolation.

On the one hand, clothes can be a temptation. In the sordid incident mentioned above with Tamar there was, once again, deception through the use of a cloak. On the other hand, throughout Scripture, clothes, especially fine clothes, are an expression of joy, as when a bride and bridegroom celebrate through garments (Is 61:10). Washing our robes or donning white clothes is an expression of being cleansed inwardly of sin and shame (Rev 7:14).

Paul regarded dressing as a metaphor of salvation and a way of working out that salvation. He instructed his readers, "As God's chosen people, holy and dearly loved, clothe yourselves with compassion, kindness, humility, gentleness and patience. . . . And over all these virtues put on love" (Col 3:12, 14). We put off the old fleshly life (self-centered and God-denying) and we put on the Lord Jesus, just as we take off soiled clothes from a dirty job and don clean ones. We put on Christ, his righteousness, truth, word and integrity, just as the Roman soldier put on all the pieces of his armor (Eph 6:11-18). Indeed for Paul the ultimate clothing is the final resurrection body, which we are given when Christ comes again. This clothing provides us with the covering needed for being in the new heaven and the new earth (2 Cor 5:4)—there are no naked souls in heaven! We long and groan for this final clothing (v. 2). So clothing can express faith.

Clothing another person is a ministry. On the final day Jesus will say, "I needed clothes and you clothed me" (Mt 25:36). Not only the poor and needy (who often lack sufficient covering) can receive the ministry of being clothed but also family members.

Clothing is also a ministry to ourselves. Clothing enables us to express to our neighbor as well as ourselves the truth that we are in fact beautiful, God-imaging creatures. So every time we dress we can live a faith metaphor.

LOOKING GOOD

Kathryn Lockhart, formerly my assistant, crafted a fine article on clothing for our *Thoughtful Parenting* book. As well as offering some practical advice for parents on the question of clothing, especially with teenagers, Lockhart considers the typical image of Christians portrayed in movies and on television as prim and straight-laced, "with no style or adornment (except a large cross pendant), wearing . . . ill-fitting, drab-colored, mismatched garments."

> The contrast between the joyous good news they are supposed to be spreading and their dowdy, lackluster appearance is laughably unattractive. . . . Christians need to have a healthy concern for what is on the surface even though God can see straight through it. . . . When Christians present an attractive image, it is not to deceive but to demonstrate a healthy self-respect and to celebrate that each person is a unique creation of God.[8]

Many are helped to live the reality of putting on Christ through symbolically putting on the soldier's armor—the helmet, the breastplate, the belt, the sword and the sandals. We can prayerfully dress in the morning every day, clothing ourselves with righteousness, putting on virtue. In the evening we take off our clothes but remember that one day we will be clothed with a spiritual body (that wonderful oxymoron) for full bodily life in the new heaven and the new earth.

Dressing can be a temptation. It can also be a ministry. Clothes conceal and clothes reveal. Ask Jacob. Ask Judah. Ask Tamar.

13

Finishing—the Story of Judah
Genesis 42—50

> *The Christians who did the most for the present world*
> *were just those who thought most about the next.*
>
> —C. S. LEWIS

There is an end to which the whole story is striving, a goal that brings meaning to every detail of the mundane, the necessary and the trivial. Without a destiny, everyday life dissolves into a series of happenings that will have the half-life of a bubble. Nothing lasts, not even diamonds! In the Western world the reality of heaven is hardly considered. Our own generation lacks any sense of the end to which the travail of history might lead. Communism, with its materialistic utopian future, has failed. But much that passes for Christianity is boringly this-worldly, seduced by the siren call of the latest advertisement, seemingly up-to-date and "with it," yet in reality profoundly irrelevant because there is no end in view other than this present happiness. Earth is not "crammed with heaven."[1] It is just dirt. Some even worship it.

The outcome of all this, ironically, is hopelessness. Much of the doddering religion that passes for the faith resembles the situation revealed in Samuel Beckett's *Waiting for Godot* in which two tramps, Vladimir and Estragon, wait hopelessly by the side of a country road, wishing that the mysterious Godot would show up—which he never does. It has been suggested that Beckett wrote this play in response to Simone Weil's *Waiting for God*, in which she proposes that the heart of meaningful life is expectant waiting on God.[2] And God, for whom we wait, does "show up" and is leading history to a glorious consummation. Lesslie Newbigin puts it aptly: "The gospel [of Jesus] is vastly more than an offer to men who care to accept it of a meaning for their personal lives. It is the declaration of God's cosmic purpose by which the whole public history of mankind is sustained and overruled, and by which men without exception will be judged."[3]

In contrast with the trappings of faith in the secularized West, the hymns and songs composed by tribal Christians in Africa, by and large, concern the second coming of Jesus and heaven. Nothing could be more relevant. It is the heavenly minded who are of most earthly use. The theologian Jürgen Moltmann said that eschatology (the study of the End) is the most pastoral of all the theological disciplines. It shows us that we are not at the sunset of life but at the dawning of a new day.[4] How can this be?

PRACTICAL HEAVENLY MINDEDNESS

The vision of the End given to us in Scripture does several things for everyday life. First it shows us that the nitty-gritty affairs of life—making meals, dressing, working and dealing with our bodies—have meaning. The reason is that our future is not in a "spiritual" heaven but in a new heaven and a new earth. There is continuity between this life and the next. Not only is earth crammed with heaven but also heaven is crammed with earth (Rev 21—22). With this end in view, time itself is not a resource to be managed by squeezing out every useful second we can. It is a gift. We have all the time God has given, all the time we need. And there is more time for adventure and discovery than we will have in this life. Everyday activities, such as dressing, eating or making love, have significance because our personal futures are not to be disembodied souls but fully resurrected bodies. That was behind Paul's frequent exhortation to the Corinthians that what they did with their bodies mattered. The basis of this fundamental truth is the resurrection of Jesus. He was not a spook, not a phantom, but a real bodily person with scars in his flesh. He went fishing and ate with the disciples.

Hope, as proclaimed in Scripture, means that our work will last—and not just religious work and gospel work but any work done in faith, hope and love. It lasts because there is continuity between this world and the next. Even the kings of the earth bring their glories into the new heaven and new earth (Rev 21:24). The glory and honor of the nations is found in the Holy City (v. 26)—and it is a city! There will be a purging of our work, and of all creation, just as the flood was a time of purification that nevertheless did not eliminate the world. The fire of judgment (2 Pet 3:7) does not mean annihilation but transformation, for "in keeping with his promise we are looking forward to a new heaven and a new earth" (v. 13). Romans 8:19-22 proclaims that the earth groans and waits for liberation from bondage; this is associated with the revelation of the children of God. Isaiah prophesies that during the reign of the Messiah we will not cease to work:

> My chosen ones will long enjoy
> the works of their hands. (Is 65:21-22)

In the final judgment Jesus declares that he personally received even humble acts of service in our everyday life (Mt 25:31-40). Revelation 14:13 indicates that the deeds of Christians will follow them—"the indelible imprint" of their life's work, though Miroslav Volf wisely cautions that while God will somehow include our efforts in the new creation, we must not imagine that the "results of human work should or could create and replace 'heaven.' "[5]

THE FUTURE OF THE FAMILY OF PROMISE

In Genesis 49 Jacob looks to the future and blesses his sons. But it is often called an antiblessing because what Jacob actually does is to prophesy about the future of each of the twelve tribes. It is not a pretty picture. This is the occasion when he passes on the blessing and the promise of Abraham to another generation. But the two who stand out in the blessings are Joseph and Judah, a son from each of his wives. The future rests with these two, not with Reuben, the first-born.

Jacob effectively divides up the birthright and the blessing into two parts, giving the blessing (with its promise of abundance) to Joseph and the birthright and its leadership implications to Judah. To Joseph he promises "blessings of the heavens above, blessings of the deep that lies below, blessings of the breast and womb" (Gen 49:25). So Joseph gets the double portion of the first-born (1 Chron 5:1-2). Joseph is to be a "fruitful vine near a spring" (Gen 49:22), thriving even though he had experienced the bitter arrows of hostility from his brothers (v. 23). Joseph will have blessing of heaven and earth, blessing of breast and womb, blessings for men and blessings for women. Joseph is the "prince among his brothers" (v. 26).

The leadership of the family of promise is transferred to Judah. The "scepter" and "ruler's staff" are symbols of regal command.[6]

> The scepter will not depart from Judah,
> nor the ruler's staff from between his feet,
> until he comes to whom it belongs
> and the obedience of the nations is his. (Gen 49:10)

In this way the "normal" rights of Reuben were split between Joseph and Judah.

As though Jacob were wearing trifocal glasses, he has in view three ranges of fulfillment for Judah. On the *immediate* level (the closest range) Judah will be preeminent over his brothers (in that his brothers will bow to him as they once bowed down to Joseph). On the *intermediate* level (the midrange) the tribe of Judah will have preeminence in the Promised Land. Judah will become the leading tribe in the south and will give his name to the southern kingdom. All the sons of Jacob (including those from Rachel) will pay homage to him, as they did during the reign of King David (2 Sam 5:1-2; 1 Chron 5:2). And so with Joseph preeminent in the north and Judah in the south, we have a glimpse of the embryonic nation. On the *ultimate* level (the long-distance vision) Judah will bring forth the Davidic dynasty and a king superior to that dynasty—the Messiah himself, the face of Israel's race, and the one who will gain "the obedience of the nations" (Gen 49:10)—all the nations!

Jacob punctuates his blessing of all his children with his deepest prayer: "I look for your deliverance, O LORD" (Gen 49:18). Joseph will thrive richly (the double portion); Judah will lead. So there is a future for the people of God.

Joseph's preeminence we can easily understand.

JOSEPH THE BLESSED

Most Christian commentators identify Rachel's son Joseph as a Christ figure. And this is done with good reason. Joseph was a superior person, combining (it seems) all of the good qualities of his genetic pool—Abraham's dignity, Isaac's power of devotion, Jacob's shrewdness, Sarah's humor, Rebekah's entrepreneurship and Rachel's beauty. Joseph went through two life-through-death experiences—the pit of Dothan and the prison pit in Egypt—thus anticipating the life-from-death experience of Jesus on the cross.

Like Jesus, Joseph was the father's favorite son who was sent to his brothers, and although he was guiltless, he was sold for twenty pieces of silver. Like Jesus, Joseph descended into an exilic existence—Jesus into hell on the cross and Joseph into slavery in Egypt—so that the people might be saved. "It was to save lives that God sent me ahead of you" (Gen 45:5), Joseph said to his brothers.

Joseph we can understand. But why Judah?

JUDAH THE LEADER

Judah was the strongest personality and was the natural leader of the brothers. When the brothers conspired to eliminate Joseph the dreamer by putting him in a dry cistern to die of thirst and hunger (while they enjoyed a picnic on the top of the pit),[7] it was Judah who said, "What will we gain if we kill our brother and cover up his blood? Come, let's sell him to the Ishmaelites and not lay our hands on him; after all, he is our brother, our own flesh and blood" (Gen 37:26-27). In this case his voice prevailed, and he saved Joseph's life by selling him into slavery. He went along with this with his siblings, all guilty of conspiring to kill—something that would haunt him for years, like a stuck track on a CD. Leadership has its price. But as a leader, he was vulnerable—a vulnerability that he shared with Joseph. Women seduced both Judah and Joseph. Both had to come to themselves by means of a hard experience.

Both Joseph and Judah went down to a pagan land. Joseph went to Egypt, where he assumed in due course a complete Egyptian identity and where he deliberately tried to forget his family (as suggested in the meaning of his son Manasseh's name—Gen 41:51). In the same way, Judah "went down to stay with a man of Adullam named Hirah" (38:1). All this happened in "the far country," just as it did for the prodigal in Jesus' parable (Lk 15:13). Leaders are vulnerable, and finishing the race faithful is a challenge.

TO BE A FINISHER

My spiritual director died a few years ago. He was an extraordinary person, a pioneer and a deeply God-grasped man. I visited him week by week toward the end, and in the final visit, when I knew he would pass before I saw him again, I asked my own existential question: "How did you make it?"

"What do you mean?" he replied.

"You made it to the grave without falling. Every other Christian leader I have honored over the years has fallen to sex, money or power. How did you remain faithful to the end?"

With failing energy he began, "When I was exactly your age, I was beginning to be invited to speak to very large conferences." I remembered the first time I heard him speaking to three thousand people in Ottawa—it was electric. He continued, "Instead of trying to get publishers to print my work, they were coming to me asking me for manuscripts. And the Lord showed me that I couldn't take it. Fame and power would corrupt me. God directed me to go to places and people that no one else wanted to bother with, groups so small that no leader was interested." I recall how, after the three-thousand-member convention, he went to fishing villages in northern British Columbia and then to track down the Nestorians in northern Turkey. He started a pioneer work in Pakistan.

If even the apostle Paul could be shipwrecked in his faith, as he once intimated (1 Cor 9:27), certainly I need to know how to be a finisher. And there is much in Judah's story to inspire and persuade us not just to start the life of faith but also to finish it.

First, Judah's repentance in relation to Tamar was a significant step forward. Instead of defending himself self-righteously, he turned his sin into a "happy sin" *(felix culpa)* as a means of grace and renewal.[8] We can learn from our mistakes by repentance and not simply keep repeating them.

Second, Judah learns a lifestyle of self-denial rather than self-promotion. Twice he offers himself, as we shall see, in place of a brother—first, to his father (Jacob), promising to give himself as surety for Benjamin's safe return from Egypt (as required by Joseph, Gen 43:9), and then when he offers himself as Joseph's slave in order to release Benjamin (44:33). The irony of "successful" discipleship is that it is precisely by denying ourselves that we find life. By not promoting ourselves, we are in the end found in Christ.

Third, Judah, a natural leader, learns that the essence of leadership is service, not control. His greatest act of leadership was, as we shall see, to offer himself as servant to Joseph, and thus he served his brothers. How this contrasts with much that passes for consumerist Christianity in the Western world is obvious. It was said of one televangelist who fell through sex, power and money that he began his career by using money and prizing people but came to the place where he used people and worshiped money.

JUDAH AND JESUS—ONE FOR THE MANY

The relationship of the brothers occupies the most compelling and dramatic part of the story: chapters 42—45, where it seems that Joseph, himself "disguised" as an Egyptian lord, deceives his brothers with his adopted Egyptian identity, holding back his personal disclosure until the last possible moment. Indeed, with the passing of two years, and at the considerable pain and suffering of his brothers, Joseph's treatment of his brothers is one of the mysteries of the story. Some, like James Hastings, suggest that "the key to his whole method is that he was trying to find out whether they would behave in the same fashion as they had done before, and to prove to them, as well as to himself, that they would not."[9] Hastings sees this as a three-stage process: remembering of the past, reversal of the past and forgiveness of the past. In contrast, Zornberg sees Joseph himself as needing healing. Probably both are right, and as Waltke notes, "Joseph's motives in using harsh words against his brothers are ambiguous and probably complex."[10]

The story of Joseph in Egypt is a history of his continued, desperate attempts to re-member himself, that is, to reintegrate the broken pieces of his identity. He names his elder, Egyptian-born son Manasseh, explaining, "God has made me forget all my trouble and all my father's household" (Gen 41:51). He remembers only the pain of his father's home, his last vision, perhaps of his brothers' animal faces, tearing him apart—and he is grateful for oblivion. His son's name continually evokes the paradox of dismemberment: he is forgotten, but he knows.[11]

When the brothers (less Benjamin) go to Egypt for food, Joseph requires the brothers to bring back the youngest son, Benjamin, the last remaining son of Rachel. It is noteworthy that Jacob had disenfranchised the sons of Leah by saying "he [Benjamin] is the only one left" (Gen 42:38). Judah, who was unwilling to give Tamar her rightful place in the family but did give a pledge in order to lie with her, now gives *himself* as a pledge: "I myself will guarantee his safety; you can hold me personally responsible for him. If I do not bring him back to you and set him here before you, I will bear the blame before you all my life" (43:9). Jacob is convinced, and the boys return to Egypt for food.

Back in Egypt, the brothers face Joseph disguised as Zaphenath-Paneah, this time with Benjamin. Joseph, still scheming to see if his brothers will treat Benjamin better than they treated him, trying to find out whether they have changed, plants his divining cup in Benjamin's sack. When the cup is discovered, Judah expresses on behalf of the others a complete solidarity in sin: "What can we say to my lord? How can we prove our innocence? God has uncovered your servants' guilt. We are now my lord's slaves" (Gen 44:16). When Joseph protests that only the guilty one (Benjamin) should become his slave, Judah the innocent offers himself for the guilty one as a substitute, one for the many—a type of Christ's substitution of himself for all.[12] Joseph can control himself no longer.

Zornberg explores the meaning of Joseph's three occasions of tears in the presence of his brothers. He wants to be reconciled. He wants to be known by his brothers in a way that will heal the rifts of the past. So Joseph must find out what will be his brother's response to Benjamin under duress. "Will they abandon him, as they abandoned Joseph in the past? This question—of abandonment, of alienation, rather than of active cruelty—is the essence of Joseph's plot, in its final stage."[13] So when Judah offers to indenture himself as a slave in place of Benjamin, he weeps again.

> Each time he weeps, something opens up in him, an unplanned response, which is at first a mere parenthesis, as he turns away and then turns back to his tyrannical role. In the course of that "parenthesis," he knows himself lost and yet remembered by his brothers. As they speak of what was not in the past, a new relationship is suggested, woven of regret, empathy, and loss.[14]

The critical turning point is the speech of Judah, the longest speech in Genesis. Judah's appeal is not for himself but for mercy for his father (Jacob). He focuses on his father's reluctance to let Benjamin come, as demanded by Joseph. He believes that the loss of Benjamin (enslaved in Egypt) would kill his father (Gen 44:30-31). He reports that he offered himself as a pledge. And then Judah asks that Joseph allow him to fulfill his pledge by becoming Joseph's slave in place of the boy. But the emphasis is on the cost of the deed to his father. "How can I go back to my father if the boy is not with me? No! Do not let me see the misery that would come upon my father" (v. 34). Meir Sternberg explains what is happening on the inside of Judah and Joseph. "That Judah should adduce the father's favoritism as the ground for self-sacrifice is such an irresistible proof of filial devotion that it breaks down Joseph's last defenses."[15]

If Joseph could, he would have turned the screw once again, but his plot collapses. He breaks down, wails and reveals himself. "He surrenders his project, shrivelled, and reduced to human size. A sinister grandiosity had informed that project; now compassion, the benign infection of Judah's words, compels him to relinquish his secret idea."[16] Significantly, his first question is whether his father is still living.[17]

His frequent leaving the room to weep in private suggests that this lengthy plot was not all for the sanctification of the brothers. Joseph is working through his own feelings for having been so badly treated, as well as trying to find a way to get Jacob and Benjamin both to Egypt for reasons he now understands are implicit in the dreams he had twenty years before. From the reader's perspective, "the signs of penitence of Joseph's brothers hold the promise that full family reconciliation will one day be possible."[18] Also from the reader's perspective, "I am Joseph" is roughly parallel to Jacob's own confession years before, "[I am] Jacob." In each case knowledge of God and self came together.[19] With both Jacob and Joseph, there is a triple homecoming—to God, to self and to his brothers.

PEACE AND HOPE

As it turns out, the complete reconciliation of the family took many more years. Years later, after the death of Jacob, the brothers feared reprisals without the protecting presence of their father, just as Esau himself had planned revenge after Isaac died (Gen 27:41). So with the grand funeral completed, the brothers first send an intermediary, then come and fall down before Joseph and plead for mercy (50:16, 18). Joseph weeps and reassures them, and there is peace at last.[20]

Waltke offers "the anatomy of reconciliation" from this story and, at the same time, points to the ultimate hope that our little everyday events and deeds are part of a much larger purpose that, in the goodness of God, will result in the full coming of God's kingdom on earth and eventually a new heaven and a new earth.

It is about loyalty to a family member in need, even when he or she looks guilty; giving glory to God by owning up to sin and its consequences; overlooking favoritism; offering up oneself to save another; demonstrating true love by concrete acts of sacrifice that create a context of trust; discarding control and the power of knowledge in favor of intimacy; embracing deep compassion, tender feelings, sensitivity, and forgiveness; and talking to one another. *A dysfunctional family that allows these virtues to embrace it will become a light to the world.*[21]

14

Death — the Story of Ephraim
Genesis 48:1-22; 49:29-33

Every going to sleep is a little death, a rehearsal for the real thing.

— RICHARD JOHN NEUHAUS

*When man is no longer able to look beyond his own death
and relate himself to what extends beyond the time and space of his life,
he loses his desire to create and the excitement of being human.*

— HENRI NOUWEN

*Jacob . . . drew his feet up into the bed,
breathed his last and was gathered to his people.*

— GENESIS 49:33

Getting into this world and getting out of it are the hard parts. The in-between is pretty straightforward." Mal Smith leaned over the table in the cafeteria on the ferry and passed on this piece of homespun knowledge. But it came from a heavy heart. His sister-in-law was dying.

Coming out of the French Revolution is a saying that on the way to the guillotine one's mind becomes remarkably sharp. But in the Western world death has been sanitized, removed from the home to the hospital and by and large purposefully denied. Richard John Neuhaus is right. "It used to be said that the Victorians of the nineteenth century talked incessantly about death but were silent about sex, whereas today we talk incessantly about sex and are silent about death."[1] The fig leaf has slipped from the genitals to the final passage—a passage for which there is a need for a unique spirituality.

Death is the one everyday experience that is absolutely universal. We can count on it. Not all fall in love, marry and have children. But we will all die, and we will all experience the loss of others. Every wedding is an announcement of a funeral. The wedding vows are reality statements, often uttered by young people beginning a romantic journey, but laced with the words "until death us do part." But few notice it until their senior years when death is just around the corner. Peter de Vries would call us to "the recognition of how long, how very long is the mourners' bench upon which we sit, arms linked in undeluded friendship—all of us, brief links ourselves, in the eternal pity."[2]

The philosopher George Santayana said, "There is no cure for birth and death save to enjoy the interval."[3] This accurately expresses the practical theology of a generation that denies death, fails to believe in a new heaven and new earth and therefore is preoccupied with fitness, health and plea-sure. But the Christian approach, as J. I. Packer once said, is to "regard readiness to die as the first step in learning to live."[4] One of Jacob's great works, and one of ours, is to prepare to die.

The story of Jacob contains many deaths—those of his father, Isaac, his beloved Rachel, the nurse Deborah and finally Jacob himself. These are pre-sented to us in an unsanitized manner. There is a significant difference in these passings compared with the death-denying culture of the Western world: each person prepared to die and turned that death into a ministry. Specifically Isaac and Jacob, when they saw the end in sight, made sure their death would be a blessing to the next generation and a ministry to others.

Our questions about death are manifold. *What will happen to me when I die? Will I be alone? Will I have completed my lifework? What will be the legacy I leave behind?*

It is this last question—of legacy—that occupies people as they move into their senior years. It occupied Jacob as he approached death in far-off Egypt. In the teens we ask, *What will I become?* And in the twenties, *Whom will I be with?* And later, *What will I achieve?* There is the inevitable transition from questions of success and accomplishment to issues of significance and legacy. In the middle of our life paths, at the time of the much-heralded "midlife crisis," we ask hard questions about what we have really accomplished and whether what we have done has been worth the sacrifice. More poignantly, we ask what to do with the rest of our lives. Sue Monk Kidd draws on Jung's insights that "every mid life crisis is a spiritual crisis, that we are called to die to the old self (ego), the fruit of the first half of life and liberate the new man or woman within us."[5] And then what? All the books on the passages of life leave the over-sixties with a dotted line!

THE MYSTERY OF DEATH

Death is a mystery, not only because it is not experienced by people who are still alive (except as we grieve the loss of those close to us) but also because it challenges us with thoughts of transcendence at precisely the time when it appears that our life might be cut short. Death is not only the great leveler; it is also the great elevator. It lifts us to the beyond. For the Christian this is the hope of resurrection of our body and full participation in the new heaven and the new earth.

The author of Hebrews says that Jesus tasted death for everyone (Heb 2:9), clearly indicating that whatever death has become through sin — in all of its psychological and spiritual consequences (Mt 27:46) — Jesus experienced it on the cross. Death is more than the mere stopping of the heart, breathing and brain activity. We must deal with death as death *of a person*, not just of a person's shell.

More than our bodies die; so do our emotions, our personality, our capacity for relationships and for giving and receiving love. Do our spirits die or at least "taste" death? We simply do not know whether we enter into a "soul sleep" until the day of resurrection or persist in some kind of "intermediate state" (as it is called in theological texts) until Christ comes again and the dead are raised.[6] What we do know is that death is more than a merely physical phenomenon. The whole person dies.

In all of this we admit we are facing a formidable power. Death holds people in slavery to lifelong fear (Heb 2:15). The fear may have multiple sources: fear of pain, of the unknown, of experiencing something uncontrollable and unpredictable, of losing all that is familiar and dear to us. Many older people fear increasing withering, loss of dignity and loss of independence—all preludes to death. A profound fear we carry from our earliest infancy is the fear of being dropped; the fear of death is the anxiety that when we can no longer hang on, we will be dropped and will plunge into nothingness. Deeper still is the fear of unpredictable consequences after the grave if there is a God. We are ultimately accountable to God, and the happy continuation into the "next" life is contingent on our performance in this life. Death is fraught with eternal consequences.

Paul spoke of death as the last enemy (Rom 8:38; 1 Cor 15:26) because it seems death has a life of its own, making its pretentious claims on human hearts and holding them captive to their mortality. This last enemy was destroyed by the death of Christ, this death of death being certified by the resurrection of Christ. Death has been killed! For the person found in Christ, death is not fraught with temporal fear or eternal consequences, as it is for those who have not yet responded to the welcome of God. Yet we still must die.

Christian hope promises a renewal, not a replacement. Our bodies, souls and spirits are transfigured and "will be like his [Christ's] glorious body" (Phil 3:21). Christians see death in a sacramental way, as a physical experience through which a spiritual grace is mediated. In this case the spiritual grace is located in the promise of resurrection. Even personality defects in this life will be healed, but not by our becoming *different* persons.

THE ART OF DYING

My father died in my brother's arms after being unable to speak or eat for two years. Pneumonia—sometimes called "the old man's friend"—complicated his stroke symptoms. He was not afraid to die. But he seemed to be lingering, hanging on, for reasons we could not discover. Mom had died months before, and there was no unfinished business known to us or admitted by him. My brother embraced him and said, "Dad, it's all right to go." And within minutes he died peacefully, sleeping in Jesus. But he left us wondering about the mystery of death, its timing, its meaning and the strange way that we are created by God to hang on to life, sometimes even longer than we need. It is hard to tell yourself to die. Some long for death and are still with us. Do we have some part in it, something vaguely witnessed in Scripture as "giving up the spirit"?

There are several ways we can prepare to die. First, we must repudiate the death denial of contemporary Western culture. Deaths of relatives and friends provide good opportunities in a family context to discuss what death means and to declare the Christian hope. The thoughtful preparation of our last will and testament helps us prepare for death and contemplate what inheritance, material and nonmaterial, we are leaving behind.

Second, living Christianly involves the idea of dual citizenship: living simultaneously in this world and the next. We are equidistant from eternity every moment of our life from conception to resurrection. We treasure life as good and may really flourish on earth, but it is not the highest good. We resist death as evil, but not the greatest evil, because it is the way to a better world.

Third, we can number our days, as the psalmist said, not by calculating our expected life span by the latest actuarial tables and then squeezing all we can into the remaining years because there is nothing more (or because eternity is just more of the same). Rather, numbering our days means treating every day as a gift, being aware that it may be our last, yet investing ourselves and our talents in a world without end (compare Mt 25:1-13). We do not live on borrowed time but on entrusted time. So we live one day at a time, not bearing tomorrow's burdens and anxieties today (Mt 6:25-34) but trusting that God will be sufficient for each day that we live.

Fourth, everyday hardships give us an opportunity to learn to "die daily." Paul said that we are like sheep led daily to the slaughter. Through these pains, persecutions and weaknesses that we suffer, we are able to live in the resurrection power—dying to self and living in Christ (2 Cor 4:10-12, 16-18).

Fifth, we can practice progressive relinquishment. As we go through life, we relinquish childhood and youth, our friends and parents through death, our children as they leave home, and eventually our occupations and health. Most people will discover the hard words of the marriage vow, "until death do us part." We cannot die together, as is often our wish and dramatized in opera. Ultimately we must relinquish life in this world. We are left with the one treasure of inestimable value—the Lord. One of the Ignatian exercises invites us to contemplate our own death by using our inspired imaginations prayerfully in the Lord's presence, imagining the gathering of people around our deathbed, the funeral, the burial in the soil, the gradual decomposition of our body until all that we were as a person in this life has dissolved and we are ready for full transfiguration. Are we ready to die? Are there broken relationships to be mended, persons to be forgiven and debts to settle? Is there something we can do for someone that we have been putting off?[7]

One of our dearest friends was dying of cancer. All her family and friends had come and said their goodbyes. Then her husband said, "You have said goodbye to all the people who are important to you. You have no broken relationships. You can relinquish." She immediately went into a coma and passed away shortly.

The Discipline of Death

Jacob's final passage gives us a window on the ministry of dying. Jacob had lived in Egypt for seventeen years. But as his death approached, he desired to provide for himself by making Joseph swear with his hands cupped on his father's testicles that Jacob would not be buried in Egypt but would be carried to the land promised to his father, to his grandfather and to himself (Gen 47:28-31).[8] Then Jacob worshiped as he leaned on his staff, thanking God for his grace and care through his life, and drawing himself up in his bed using the staff that accompanied him when he first ran from his brother, Esau, and that he carried when he crossed the Jordan, having wrestled with the angel of the Lord. He worshiped knowing that God had substantially fulfilled his promise of the family, the land and the blessing of the

Gentiles, even in his own lifetime. His faith reached out to God in gratitude—the fundamental spiritual discipline. David, in his old age, similarly
worshiped in dying (1 Kings 1:47-48).

Death itself is a spiritual discipline that concentrates life into a focused
receptivity to God. On one hand, it spells the end of all the achievement
and performance one can accomplish in this life. On the other hand, it
points beyond to what will last and what is ultimately important. For David
it was the provision of a successor: "Praise be to the LORD, the God of Israel,
who has allowed my eyes to see a successor on my throne today" (1 Kings
1:48). For Jacob it was a memorial, a message and means of seeing the promise continued.

MONUMENT OR MEMORIAL?

The Egyptian pharaohs built monuments to themselves, their pyramids and
sphinxes all standing on the west side of the Nile to this day—silent senti-
nels to the greatness of the kings and queens. The whole of Egyptian life
was focused on death, on the sunset of life. Thus the tombs and pyramids
were placed toward the setting of the sun. But in contrast, biblical faith proposes that we are not at the sunset of life but at the dawn, the dayspring. Literally the best is yet to come. There will be resurrection; there will be a new
heaven and new earth created for us.

Permanence beyond the grave is not obtained by monuments, as Ab-
salom attempted to accomplish by building one for himself (2 Sam 18:18).
In contrast, memorials are sacraments in time and space that call forth
faith. The Hebrew idea of remembrance—incarnated in the words of the
Lord's Supper "remember me"—is not simply recalling a past event, trying
to refresh a memory; it is rather revisiting an event in such a way that the
past becomes present.[9] We relive the reality. The power and potency of the
event is carried into the present. And it strengthens our faith. Monuments
point to a person, to bring honor to that person's name; memorials direct us
to God to strengthen faith.

Jesus left no monument. He did leave a memorial—ordinary, everyday things that would reenchant everyday life as we feed on him moment by moment: ground wheat and crushed grapes.

Jacob had left memorials all along his journey. At Bethel he first encountered the Lord in the vision of the ladder showing that heaven and earth were connected, that God was not only *for* life but also *in* life. Jacob took the flat stone that had served for his pillow and set it upright like a ladder and left it there as a memorial. This was the *grace* memorial. Running from his father-in-law, Laban, and being apprehended on his way back to Canaan, Jacob sets up another stone as a pillar. Adding some more stones to make a heap, Jacob says this stone will be a witness and a marker of the agreement between Laban and Jacob that they will not harm each other or pass beyond that point to hurt the other. Mizpah literally means "watchtower" (Gen 31:45-52). This was the *safety* memorial. It pointed to the protection of God. When Jacob returns, after a tragic delay, to Bethel, he makes another memorial, this time a stone altar and yet one more pillar "at the place where God had talked with him" (35:14). This was his *coming home* memorial. Then, when his beloved Rachel dies in childbirth, he once more sets up a pillar on the road to Bethlehem to mark Rachel's tomb (v. 20). This was his *love* memorial.

Gail and I journeyed back to one such memorial a few months ago at Pioneer Girls Camp in Ontario, to the Bunny Hutch where she was a camper, to the campfire where she had confessed her faith—that site being a marker, a memorial of an important meeting with God. For many who follow Jesus, baptism is such a memorial, and the weekly or monthly Eucharist is a pillar, a sacrament in bread and wine that make the past present and recapitulates a meeting with God, so strengthening faith.

But for Jacob there was now only his staff in hand as he worshiped on his deathbed (Heb 11:21). He was the limping saint, wounded by God but strong in faith. He had left physical memorials in various places. But now he must turn to the question of succession. Who will carry on the family of promise? Who will do the work of the kingdom and represent God's interests on earth? What living memorial can he leave?

The story of Jacob is rich in symbols: the bowl of red porridge, symbolizing Jacob's use of food to gain the upper hand with his brother; the well in Haran, where in all probability his father's bride and his own were found; the Jabbok Brook, where he wrestled a blessing out of God. But no symbol memorializes his experience of the grace of God more than the crossed hands.

CROSSED HANDS

As Jacob's time draws near through illness, Joseph brings his two sons—half-Egyptian, half-Hebrew—to their grandfather for a blessing. Jacob has lost much of his vision, but when he hears that his son Joseph is present, he rallies his strength and sits up in bed. He reiterates the promise that God made when he appeared to Jacob: (1) God was with him in communion; (2) God promised to make him fruitful with a family, even a "community of peoples" (Gen 48:4); and (3) the land would be given as an everlasting possession to his descendants.

There are two scenes in the final act. First, apparently before Jacob realizes that his grandsons Ephraim and Manasseh are present, Jacob tells Joseph that he intends to adopt them into the family of promise—all the more extraordinary since they were born of an Egyptian mother. "Your two sons . . . will be reckoned as mine . . . just as Reuben and Simeon are mine" (Gen 48:5). In other words, they will not simply be grandchildren but, along with the other eleven sons, will be full bearers of the promise and equal in standing with Joseph himself. Joseph could never have anticipated this move on his father's part.

Then there is a second scene. Jacob catches sight of two people, possibly seventeen or eighteen years old, and asks, "Who are these?" Joseph responds that these are the two sons God has given him in Egypt. Jacob requests that they be brought near so that he could bless them. Jacob kisses them and embraces them, recalling that he never expected to see Joseph again, let alone Joseph's children. They are then placed on Jacob's knees, which is the position used for official adoption in the ancient world. This being done, Joseph removes them from Jacob's knees and bows his face to the ground. Then something deeply symbolic, laden with good news and saturated with grace, takes place.

Joseph brings the boys to their grandfather (now their father by adoption) in the manner one would normally expect: the older, Manasseh, is placed next to Jacob's right hand (this being the place of preeminence and the rightful position for the first-born), and the younger, Ephraim, is placed by Jacob's left hand. But then Jacob does something that was wrung out of his lifelong theological education. Luther said, "Living, or rather dying and being damned make a theologian, not understanding, reading or speculating."[10] It is an act that became a memorial.

Jacob crosses his hands, placing the right hand of priority on the younger boy and the left hand on the older. With his crossed hands, he blesses both sons, not just the older or the younger, praying that the angel who had delivered him from all harm might bless these boys, that they might be called by his name as well as those of Isaac and Abraham, and that they might flourish.

When Joseph notices that Jacob has placed his right hand on Ephraim's head, he becomes upset and tries to wrestle Jacob's dying hand away to put it on the head of the first-born, Manasseh. He rebukes his father and says that he had got it all wrong. "This one [Manasseh] is the firstborn." But Jacob says, "I know, my son, I know." Manasseh, too, will become a great people, but "his younger brother will be greater than he, and his descendants will become a group of nations" (Gen 48:18-19). Again he blesses them both, though he puts Ephraim ahead of Manasseh. And he blesses them together in a way that he hoped would be perpetuated as the blessing of the crossed hands:

In your name will Israel pronounce this blessing:
"May God make you like Ephraim and Manasseh." (v. 20)

Thereby he put Ephraim ahead of Manasseh while at the same time blessing both. What does Jacob now know?

"I know" is full of irony. Jacob had inveigled the blind Isaac to bless him without Isaac's knowing it. But now Jacob, himself almost blind, "knows and deliberately follows God's unconventional plan." As Waltke says, "If Isaac's unwitting blessing could not be reversed, how much more this conscious blessing?"[11] Jacob knows that grace does not follow natural preeminence, natural gifts, position in family and human prominence. God loves without partiality. His love is gratuitous—without human cause or predictability. Jacob knows from experience that being the younger, just as he had been the younger, is not a position of disadvantage. Jacob knows that God looks on character, not on privileged position. Jacob knows that God's ways are not our ways and that we cannot control God, cannot manipulate grace, cannot force God's hand, cannot make the blessing happen. God is totally surprising. Jacob knows that God is beautiful.[12] Jacob knows the gospel, and his crossed hands symbolize what, under the new covenant with Jesus, came to be expressed as "at just the right time, when we were still powerless, Christ died for the ungodly" (Rom 5:6).

This lesson was deeply plowed into my own heart in the years when Gail and I were involved in the inner city of Montreal. We had taken a prostitute into our home, cleaned her up and loved her. She began to follow Jesus. But one day Daisy gravitated back to her old haunt downtown.

I was angry. I was losing control. Then Daisy telephoned me from a sleazy bar on Saint Hubert Street. "Help," was all she could say. "Please come for me." I was still angry but figured that the effort of driving down to the red-light district, where there was no parking, was roughly equivalent to the effort I required of her to get out of the tavern and walk to a street corner where I would pick her up. Fifty-fifty.

I drove down but did not find her on the corner. I rounded the block another way and still another. No Daisy. Now I was really angry and drove self-righteously up the hill, thinking that one more multiproblem person had wasted my time. Then, like a head-on collision, God spoke to me: "When you were still helpless, when you could not do anything but cry 'Help,' when you could not meet me halfway, Christ died for you." I was smitten.

Ramming the car around in a U-turn, I drove down to the bar, ran in and threw my arms around her, much (I am sure) to the astonishment of the other customers.

I do not know how much help I was to her that day, but I can tell you that she helped me remember the gospel. It was crossed-hands stuff. All true Christian service is marked by crossed hands, full of unexpected surprises.

REMEMBERING RACHEL

With hands crossed, Jacob remembers Rachel. The memory, of course, was stimulated by the sight of Rachel's first child, Joseph, and Rachel's grandsons. She had never seen them, because she had died in childbirth in the prime of life. But there is more to this than one more preference for Rachel rather than Leah and the painful pleasure of remembering his most beloved wife.

Jacob says, "As I was returning from Paddan, to my sorrow Rachel died in the land of Canaan while we were still on the way, a little distance from Ephrath. So I buried her there beside the road to Ephrath" (Gen 48:7). This is no mere death notice. When Laban pursued Jacob with hostile intent, searching for his household gods and his runaway daughters, Jacob swore that whoever had the teraphim would die. We the readers know what Jacob does not know—that the teraphim are hidden under Rachel's saddlebag. When Laban enters her tent to search for them, she complains that she cannot rise, because she is having her period. This delightful humor reduces the "god" to the status of a menstrual rag. So Laban passes by and the two men make a pact that they will not cross over their "line in the sand" with hostile intent either way.

However, years later, when they are on the pilgrimage to Bethel, Jacob wants to clear the camp of idols. Gordon Tucker helps us capture the moment.

> Imagine the heart-stopping, life-changing effect it must have had on Jacob. There on the outskirts of Beth-El, in the very shadow of the first *matzevah*, the stone on which he had rested his head, Jacob discovers what we, the readers, have known all along: that he had unwittingly doomed his adored Rachel.[13]

The next thing we hear is that Rachel has died in childbirth (Gen 35:19). Was his oath her death sentence? Jacob's sorrow may have been doubly numbing. First, there is something deep in the male psyche, that a man's seed planted in his beloved should cause such pain in childbirth, and in this case even death. But then, added to this, but in an even deeper way, was the thought that Jacob had vowed her death unwittingly by his solemn word.

Did he carry this burden through the rest of his life? And does this help explain his neurotic and exclusive attachment to Joseph and Benjamin? It seems that the blatant favoritism cannot fully be explained by the premature death of the mother of the boys. There is more history to it than that. Rachel had, on the birth of her first child (Joseph), named him "Let me have another son." Rachel had exactly one more son, Benjamin, and then died. But what Jacob can do, by adopting Ephraim and Manasseh, is to provide her with more sons—a living memorial. And so, at the moment of his adopting Joseph's two sons "as his own" (not mere grandchildren) he provided Rachel with the sons she possibly could have had but for her premature death.

His statement "to my sorrow Rachel died in the land of Canaan while we were still on the way" (48:7) seems out of place in the adoption ceremony unless Jacob was doing something for his own soul in the lingering guilt he felt about her death.[14] We are witnessing death work going on. He was dealing finally and fully, if not enigmatically, with his own feelings of Rachel's untimely death—a death that he had unwittingly willed. And in doing so, in this discipline of death, Jacob brought rest to his soul.

But the death of Rachel, here remembered in his dying act, was a memorial saturated with gospel significance even more than Jacob himself realized.[15] Jeremiah, much later, chose this incident to capture the heart of God's passionate grieving love for his own people as they were to be scattered into exile much later. As Rachel was buried "along the way"—not in the tomb at Hebron beside her loving husband but as an exile—she could weep redemptively for the exiles as they passed this same road on their way to distant Babylon. Just as Jacob could cry at the bloodstained death cloth

presented by his other sons, symbolizing (so it was presumed) Joseph's untimely death at the paws of a wild animal, just so would Rachel weep without consolation for all the children of Israel.[16] It is the pain of a mother's
tears, refusing to be consoled, that would move the heart of God to redemp-
tive action.

Jacob penetrates the mystery of this mother's death and explains the irony
that Leah, the wife of his deception and not his chosen bride, was to be buried with him in the cave of Machpelah, while the only true wife of his intention and desire, Rachel, should be buried separately from him—
something interpreted by Jeremiah as "Rachel weeping for her children . . .
because her children are no more" (Jer 31:15). Thus the loss of children, not
just Rachel's but also the children of Israel, is a grief undertaken prayerfully
and hopefully. It is grief prayer. So the eleventh-century Jewish expositor
Rashi explains, speaking for Jacob:

> I buried her there. I did not even take her to Bethlehem, bring her into the
> Holy Land proper. I know you resent this. But know that it was at the com-
> mand of God that I buried her there, so that she might be a help to her chil-
> dren. When Nebuchadnezzar will send them into exile, and they pass by her
> grave, "there, on the road," Rachel will come out of her grave and cry and ask
> for mercy for them—as it is said, "A cry is heard in Ramah—wailing, bitter
> weeping—Rachel weeping for her children. She refuses to be comforted for
> her children who are gone. Thus said the Lord: Restrain your voice from
> weeping, your eyes from shedding tears; for there is a reward for your labor—
> declares the Lord: they shall return from the enemy's land. And there is hope
> for your future—declares the Lord: your children shall return to their coun-
> try" [Jeremiah 31:14-16].[17]

How is it possible that Jeremiah would choose Rachel to exemplify this profound thought?

As Dresner notes, Jeremiah did not originate this moving vision of Rachel
perpetually weeping from her grave (not only over her own lost children
but truly over all her own children of Israel) as the great mother of Israel. It

is a verbal memorial crafted out of the dying words of Jacob. Among ancient and modern people, symbolic moments and people of stature are remembered by monuments. But it was different with the Jews, who fear idols as people fear the plague. They must not make a representation, a monument. But as Dresner notes, "The ancient Hebrews were, nevertheless, sublime masters of art, but art of a different sort—the art of words."[18] While statues are restricted to a fixed place—the west side of the Nile—words can be taken wherever we journey—portable memorials for a pilgrim people. So Rachel "emerges in apocalyptic legend as the deliverer of her people,"[19] a memorial that points toward the End that is the Beginning—the coming of the child of Mary, the incarnation of the Prodigal Father, the Word made flesh, God-with-us right where we are.[20]

So in Matthew, when Herod slaughtered the innocent children in Bethlehem (in order, he hoped, to eliminate Jesus), Jeremiah's grief prayer is quoted as being a fulfilled prophecy:

> A voice is heard in Ramah,
>   weeping and great mourning,
> Rachel weeping for her children
>   and refusing to be comforted,
> because they are no more. (Mt 2:18)

A mother's tears will win a response from God. Her children will not disappear into the night. It is through pain, through loss, through frustrated love and frustrated mothering and fathering, through finishing our earthly pilgrimage with uncompleted tasks, in a no-place place, along the way, through encountering the incompleteness of everything in this fractured world, through a holiness that translates pain into strength, tears of sorrow into faith tears of hope—in this we are able to die hopefully. It is in this context that Jacob says, "I know."

He knows that the love of God is revealed in all the passages of life—through the tears of a mother, through the strained relationships of a family, through reconciliations, through provision, through work, through childless love and loveless fertility, through an untimely death, through pilgrimage on the way, through the surprise of seeing even your children's children. He knows that God's love is gratuitous.

Such love will not let us go. While we, along with Jacob, tell God we will not let him go until he blesses us, God assures us that he will keep his prodigal children forever. He will keep finding us in our everyday life and in all of life's passages.

This is beautifully expressed by Calvin Seerveld when he reflects on the alabaster sculpture of *Jacob and the Angel* carved by Jacob Epstein, a Jew, in 1941 in the middle of the Second World War and the Holocaust. The angel and Jacob are locked in an embrace, their bodies meaty and muscular. They are toe-to-toe, shoulder-to-shoulder, head-to-head, cheek-to-cheek. It is a real fight. But it is also a deep embrace. The angel's hands are strong, tightly clenched. But Jacob's arms are now limp, hanging downward in submission. So, says Seerveld, "The Holy Scriptures invite us treacherous, deceitful people to take hold of God and pull for blessing. When we finally give up our self-sufficient pride then the Angel of the Lord, whom we know as Jesus Christ, will hold us tight in an embrace of love from which nothing can separate us."[21]

Epilogue

True spirituality is not . . . a diversion from life.
It is essentially subversive, and the test of its genuineness is practical.

— KENNETH LEECH

We have followed the story of Jacob from the womb to the tomb. It is a God-inundated life—the prodigal God seeking his prodigal children. God pursues people in the very ordinary, even the boring stuff of life: rising, eating, dressing, working, dealing with our sexual appetites, relating, pursuing our calling and living with those nearest and dearest neighbors, our families. God meets us in the marriage bed and the deathbed. God also reveals himself in exceptional, transcendent moments—visions, dreams and night wrestlings. But what does it all mean?

First, it means that the purpose of God in all this is that we might become more fully human. God's interest is not to make us angels, saved souls or even saints but to make us thoroughly human. But are we not already human? Is "becoming human" oxymoronic?

We are already human in the fact that we are creatures, hungry creatures, vulnerable creatures—a bag of road kill, to be exact. As human beings, we are built for relationships and long for them. We have innate yearning for transcendence, a sense of wonder and a God-shaped vacuum in our souls. We bear the image of the living God, however twisted and distorted that reflection might be. But we are not fully human, not at least as we have seen humanity full-blown and wonderfully transparent in the life and ministry of Jesus Christ. Jesus loved meals, work, relationships, friendship and life itself. If we were to follow Jesus in everyday life, on the street corner and not just the sanctuary, the business meeting and not just the prayer meeting, we would become wonderfully human. This happens not by trying to imitate him, as though this were possible, but by being inundated with the Spirit of Christ—the communion-mysticism we have explored earlier.

Second, the story of Jacob shows us that ministry is not restricted to the sanctuary. We serve God and God's purposes (this is the real meaning of ministry) in the home, on the move, in the workplace, in a pagan world. With the exception of Jacob's return to Bethel, ridding the household of idols and making his offerings to God at that holy place, Jacob's ministry (and the ministries of those around him) took place in the warp and woof of everyday life. Tragically, people think that ministry is what "ministers" do—delivering the Word of God and the sacraments, edifying the saints and leading worship services. All of these, of course, are good things to do. But the story of Jacob shows us that ministry takes place in the thickness of time and in ordinary places. It is an every-person ministry in the whole of life for all of one's life—touching God on behalf of people and places, and touching people and places on behalf of God. Some people, not aware of the potential of ministering to God and from God in the whole of life, decide that they want to go into "full-time" ministry. But there is no part-time option available—not, at least, since Christ has come and inaugurated the universal priesthood of all believers.

Third, there is no ordinary life, nothing you can write off as godless and just plain boring. Contrast that with today's person-on-the-street definition of what it means to be a human being:

> I am an animal, an accidental and perhaps negative outcome of unguided evolution—in this predicament as a thinking animal, I may construct fictions and participate in rituals which console me and give me a sense of meaning and purpose. The best I can do is to live as if there were meaning beyond my own mortal, physical existence. I am the sole guarantor of the meanings I construct, including the moral laws by which I conduct my life.[1]

Such a view makes humankind into magicians, inventing the meaning of their lives.

If God has come in the flesh, and if God keeps coming to us in our fleshly existence, then all of life is shot through with meaning. Earth is crammed with heaven, and heaven (when we finally get there) will be crammed with earth. Nothing wasted. Nothing lost. Nothing secular. Nothing absurd. Not even the hardest family experiences (of which Jacob surely had his share). As Eugene Peterson says, "God doesn't take shortcuts to heaven by bypassing our troublesome humanity."[2] All are grist for the mill of a down-to-earth spirituality.

And spirituality, as we have been using the term in this book, is not the human spirit trying to reach beyond itself, as though we could progress an inch toward God on our own or transcend our own creatureliness. Christian spirituality is essentially responsive to the seeking love of the triune God who comes to us in all of life; it is lived experience of the infinite and personal God.

Finally, this story means that you and I do not have to be somewhere else, raised in a different family, in some other relationship, in some other workplace, in some other body, to be found by God and be inundated with life. Spirituality is not to be reserved for special places, special people, for the circumference of life. Spirituality is responding to the seeking God in the totality of our lives, in the center of the daily round, rather than the circumference. And such a down-earth-spirituality does not make us religious but fully human. This is a lifelong process (as we have seen with Jacob). So, as Jean Vanier has so aptly expressed it, becoming human must be "the life undertaking of us all."[3]

Appendix A

The Family Tree

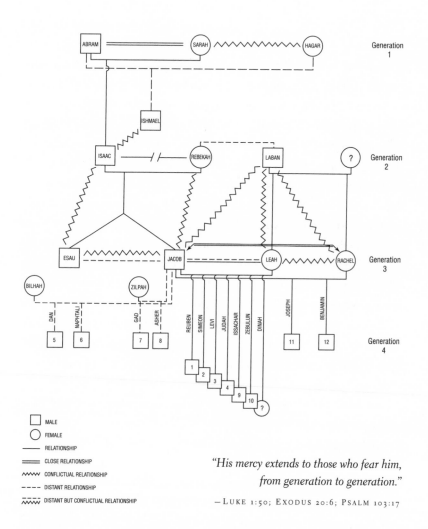

Generation 1
Generation 2
Generation 3
Generation 4

MALE
FEMALE
RELATIONSHIP
CLOSE RELATIONSHIP
CONFLICTUAL RELATIONSHIP
DISTANT RELATIONSHIP
DISTANT BUT CONFLICTUAL RELATIONSHIP

"His mercy extends to those who fear him,
from generation to generation."

—LUKE 1:50; EXODUS 20:6; PSALM 103:17

Appendix B

The Story in Brief
Genesis 25 — 50

Jacob strives with his twin brother in the womb, is born second (but is always trying to be first), steals his brother's birthright (which means the leadership of the tribe), steals his aging father's blessing, laps up his mother's favoritism (which causes envy and jealousy with his sibling), runs away from him purportedly to find a wife in the old family homestead in Haran (eastern Turkey). On the way, as a fugitive, he is met by the hound of heaven at a place called Bethel and sees a vision of heaven and earth connected. When he finally gets to Haran he falls in love, works for seven years to get his beloved Rachel but is duped on the wedding night when his father-in-law slips into the tent the weak-eyed older sister. He works for another seven years to get the one he wanted in the first place, schemes to get an inheritance for his growing family, and when his favored but infertile wife (who suffers rivalry with her very fertile sister) finally has a child, he thinks of home and makes a break for it. His beloved wife steals the household gods of her father (as title to the inheritance she feels cheated from) and Laban (his father-in-law) pursues them as they make their way back to Canaan, overtaking them, though restrained from violence by a heavenly vision. They make a pact.

Now Jacob has to meet his brother Esau, from whom he has been separated for twenty years. He is "scared spitless," and as a shrewd entrepreneur, plans to give an impressive gift and return the stolen blessing. He also prays. The night before his rendezvous he wrestles with God by the Jabbok Brook. While wounded by God in the encounter he wrestles a blessing out of God and gets a new name—God struggler, God prevailer (Israel). Now he is ready to return, as he promised twenty years ago, to Bethel, but the green pastures of Shechem, and the attraction of this pagan but prosperous community, seduced him to buy some land and set up his tent. In the process of delaying his return to Bethel his daughter Dinah gets raped, his sons retaliate and he has to get out of there quickly and make his way to Bethel to fulfill his much-delayed vow. At Bethel God speaks to him once again and having made things right with his brother he is now entitled to use the new name Israel. But tragedy strikes.

His favorite wife Rachel dies in childbirth. His father Isaac dies (the boys are reconciled finally at the funeral) and soon his favorite son Joseph gets kidnapped by the sons of his less-loved wife and is sent to Egypt, though Jacob is led to believe he has been killed by wild animals. In Egypt Joseph thrives, becomes second to Pharaoh, and through an amazing but fortuitous set of circumstances the family of Jacob seeks bread in Egypt and eventually discovers their long-lost brother. Jacob is brought to Egypt to be united with his son. The brothers, sons of Leah and sons of Rachel are reconciled. And the story ends with Jacob blessing his sons and grandsons to carry on the promise and purpose of the people called to represent God on earth and to do God's work.

Notes

Introduction: The Earthy Spirituality of Jacob

[1] Ronald S. Wallace, *The Story of Joseph and the Family of Jacob* (Grand Rapids, Mich.: Eerdmans, 2001), p. 102.

[2] Leland Ryken, *Words of Delight: A Literary Introduction to the Bible* (Grand Rapids, Mich.: Baker, 1987), p. 35.

[3] Ibid.

[4] J. P. Fokkelman, *Narrative Art in Genesis: Specimens of Stylistic and Structural Analysis* (Assen, Netherlands: Van Gorcum, 1975), pp. 118-19.

[5] Naomi H. Rosenblatt and Joshua Horwitz, *Wrestling with Angels: What Genesis Teaches Us About Our Spirituality, Identity, Sexuality and Personal Relationships* (New York: Bantam Doubleday Dell, 1995), p. 236.

[6] *Die last tragt mich,* quoted in Helmut Thielicke, *Und Wenn Gott Ware* (Stuttgart: Qwee Verlag Stuttgart, 1970), p. 238.

[7] Michael Fishbane notes that *blessing,* in its various verbal forms, occurs twenty-two times in Genesis 27:1—28:9. Michael Fishbane, *Text and Texture: Close Readings of Selected Biblical Texts* (New York: Schocken, 1979), p. 50.

[8] The Hebrew word *'aqab* (Jacob) means "to follow at the heel," or figuratively, "to assail insidiously," "to circumvent" or "to overreach."

[9] M. Craig Barnes, *Hustling God: Why We Work So Hard for What God Wants to Give* (Grand Rapids, Mich.: Zondervan, 1999).

[10] "The Jacob Cycle is a series of episodes in the life of Jacob framed by the genealogical lists of the excluded sons, Ishmael and Esau. It is thus part of a larger patriarchal cycle of *toledot* [genealogies] in the Book of Genesis, linking the earlier '*toledot*-account of the creation of heaven and earth' and the ante- and postdiluvian genealogies against a broader background" (Fishbane, *Text and Texture,* p. 40).

[11] At some points I have offered, in line with the Jewish tradition, a midrash or sermonic thought on the text.

[12] The story of Jacob is constructed with a structural symmetry that focuses on the climax of Jacob's wife Rachel becoming fertile (and so fulfilling God's promise of seed, blessing and land). Note the parallelism of AA', BB', CC', DD', EE'.

A Rebekah struggles in childbirth and seeks an oracle from God (25:19-34)
  B Interlude—Rebekah in a foreign palace; deception—covenant with neighbor (chap. 26)
    C Deception planned—The Blessing *[Berakhah]*; fear of Esau; flight (27:1–28:9)
      D Encounter with God at the border (Bethel)—blessing (28:10-22)
        E With Laban—deception, wages, Rachel barren; Leah fertile (29:1-24)
          F Rachel fertile; Jacob increases the herds (30:25-43)
        E' With Laban at border; deception (chap. 31)
      D' Encounter with God at the border (Jabbok)—blessing (chap. 32)
    C' Deception planned; fear of Esau—the blessing gift returned; return to land (chap. 33)
  B' Interlude—Dinah in a foreign palace; deception—covenant with foreigner (chap. 34)
A' Oracle fulfilled—Rachel struggles in childbirth; blessing; death (chap. 35)
Adapted from Fishbane, *Text and Texture*, p. 42.

[13] On authorship, see Bruce K. Waltke, *Genesis: A Commentary* (Grand Rapids, Mich.: Zondervan, 2001), pp. 22-29.

[14] Ibid., p. 39.

[15] Fishbane, *Text and Texture*, p. 62.

[16] Isaac Bashevis Singer, "Genesis," quoted in David Rosenberg, ed., *Congregation: Contemporary Writers Read the Bible* (San Diego: Harcourt Brace Jovanovich, 1987), pp. 7-8.

Chapter 1: Birth

[1] In Job 10:10 the creation of a person is metaphorically described as the curdling of milk into cheese. Scriptures that express the consummate wonder of conception include Psalm 139:13-16 and Ecclesiastes 11:5.

[2] See Carol Anderson, "Conception," in *The Complete Book of Everyday Christianity*, ed. Robert Banks and R. Paul Stevens (Downers Grove, Ill.: InterVarsity Press, 1998), pp. 205-9. See also the article "Pregnancy," pp. 792-95.

[3] The name Isaac strictly means "he laughs."

[4] The record of the three angel visitors telling Abraham and Sarah that they will have a child in their old age is in Genesis 18:1-15. Commenting on this, Gerhard Von Rad says:

> The narrative reaches its climax in the statement, "Is anything too hard for the Lord?" This word reposes in the story like a precious stone in a priceless setting. . . . The unbelieving and perhaps somewhat evil laugh, and now this word which indignantly punishes the way of thinking that mistrusts Yahweh's omnipotence. Of course Sarah did not basically renounce Yahweh with conscious unbelief; her laugh is rather a psychologically understandable incident, just as unbelief so often expresses itself. But this masterful, psychologically correct observation does not bring the narrator to excuse Sarah completely for her ignorance of the guests' identity. Rather, the unquestionable, decisive fact both for the narrator and reader is that a word of

Yahweh was laughed at. (Gerhard Von Rad, *Genesis: A Commentary*, trans. John H. Marks [Philadelphia: Westminster Press, 1961], p. 202)

[5] Michael Novak, "The Family Out of Favor," *Harpers*, April 1976, pp. 37-46.

[6] Bruce K. Waltke, *Genesis: A Commentary* (Grand Rapids, Mich.: Zondervan, 2001), p. 356. The name Esau is associated with "hair" by a wordplay. The connection with hairiness emerges more clearly in the name Seir (Gen 32:3). Strictly, Edom is cognate with "red," and thus "earthiness" may represent the common idea (David Clemens, unpublished notes).

[7] "This aspect of his name recognizes God's divine election. Jacob, however, will tarnish this honorable name with his deceit and self-reliant efforts to achieve God's good pleasure (see [Gen] 27:36; Hos 12:3-4), so the name also puns with *'aqab* 'to seize by the heel, go behind someone . . . to betray' " (Waltke, *Genesis*, p. 358).

[8] Amy A. Kass and Leon R. Kass, "What's Your Name?" *First Things*, November 1995, pp. 15, 18.

[9] The Hebrew word is very strong, indicating "crushing" or "smashing," as the woman in Judges 9:53 cracked a skull by dropping an upper millstone from a tower. Fokkelman says, "For Jacob and Esau any room is too small when they are together. The first battlefield is their mother's womb" (J. P. Fokkelman, *Narrative Art in Genesis: Specimens of Stylistic and Structural Analysis* [Assen, Netherlands: Van Gorcum, 1975], p. 88).

[10] Robert Alter, *The Art of Biblical Narrative* (New York: Basic Books, 1981), p. 53.

[11] Ibid., p. 53.

[12] Bruce Waltke notes, "There is significantly no account of Abraham, the most famous of the patriarchs, since there is no distinctive narrative for Isaac, though there is, surprisingly, a *toledoth* for Ishmael and even Terah." Noting the silence of the narrator about Isaac after the tragic episode of the blessing, Waltke says, "The silence is deafening. Isaac is given no memorial in Holy Scripture. He is saved only by the skin of his teeth (Job 19:20; 1 Cor 3:15)" (Bruce K. Waltke, "Reflections on the Life of Isaac and Retirement," *Crux* 32, no. 4 [1996]: 5-6).

[13] Alter notes that the verbs used to describe her actions at the well *(rutz* and *maher)* were used for the bringing of news of a stranger's arrival (Alter, *Art of Biblical Narrative*, p. 54).

[14] Ibid.

[15] Naomi H. Rosenblatt and Joshua Horwitz, *Wrestling with Angels: What Genesis Teaches Us About Our Spirituality, Identity, Sexuality and Personal Relationships* (New York: Bantam Doubleday Dell, 1995), pp. 240-1.

Chapter 2: Eating

[1] "I give you every seed-bearing plant on the face of the whole earth and every tree that has fruit with seed in it. They will be yours for food" (Gen 1:29).

[2] Leon R. Kass, *The Hungry Soul: Eating and the Perfecting of Our Nature* (Chicago: University of Chicago Press, 1999), p. 23.

[3] Data from Trends Research Institute, *Chicago Sun-Times*, July 27, 1999, *New York Times* June 22, 1997, and August 17, 1999, quoted in Bill Droll, ed., *Initiatives: In Support of Christians in the World*, no. 103 (September 1999): 1.

[4] See Carol Anderson, "Breast-Feeding" in *The Complete Book of Everyday Christianity*, ed.

Robert Banks and R. Paul Stevens (Downers Grove, Ill.: InterVarsity Press, 1998), pp. 83-90.

[5] Exodus 24:9-11 tells us Moses and the elders went up on Mount Sinai for the renewal of the covenant and saw the glory of God "like a pavement made of sapphire. . . . They saw God, and they ate and drank."

[6] The Hebrew expression for "venison in the mouth" is explained in C. F. Keil and F. Delitzsch, *Commentary on the Old Testament* (Grand Rapids, Mich.: Eerdmans, 1978), 1:268.

[7] Alexander Whyte, *Bible Characters: Adam to Achan* (Edinburgh: Oliphants, n.d.), p. 164.

[8] Ibid., pp. 171-72.

[9] In the third century Tertullian described Esau in believers of his own day:

> "Old" you are, if you will say the truth, you are so indulgent to appetite, and justly do you vaunt your "priority:" always do I recognize the savour of Esau, the hunter of wild beasts: so unlimitedly studious are you of catching field-fares, so do you come from "the field" of your lax discipline, so faint you are in spirit. If I offer you a paltry lentil dyed red with must well boiled down, forthwith you will sell all your "primacies:" with you "love" shows its fervour in saucepans, "faith" its warmth in kitchens, "hope" its anchorage in waiters; but of greater account is "love," because that is the means whereby your young men sleep with their sisters! Appendages, as we all know, of appetite are lasciviousness and voluptuousness. (Tertullian, "On Fasting," in *The Ante-Nicene Fathers*, ed. Alexander Roberts and James Donaldson [Grand Rapids, Mich.: Eerdmans, 1979], 4:113)

[10] Elaborating this incident on the basis of psychotherapy, Naomi Rosenblatt notes:

> [Esau's] preoccupation with the present moment also blinds him to his brother's jealous scheming. Jacob's behavior is equally telling. He understands that his brother is the slave, not the master, of his appetites—and he doesn't hesitate to exploit this weakness. As the physically weaker younger brother, Jacob has to press whatever strategic advantage he has, be it through guile or opportunism. Unlike his brother, Jacob is clearly a man who thinks about and plans for the future. Jacob knows that if he patiently bides his time, he will find a way to supplant his older sibling. What he hasn't yet grasp[ed] is the high emotional cost of such a gambit. (Rosenblatt and Horwitz, *Wrestling with Angels: What Genesis Teaches Us About Our Spirituality, Identity, Sexuality and Personal Relationships* [New York: Bantam Doubleday Dell, 1995], p. 240)

[11] The Hebrew word is very strong and suggests "fainting with hunger," as in Judges 8:4-5 and 2 Samuel 16:14 and 17:29. Jacob should have nurtured his brother rather than sell what he had. Psalm 41:9 (compare Jn 13:18) deals with "lifting the heel" [*'aqeb*] over a meal.

[12] Bruce Waltke comments:

> Accompanying the blessing of the birthright is also the responsibility to be the family protector, the leader of the family. This birthright is transferable; the youngest son can displace the eldest as in the cases of Joseph/Judah and Reuben, Ephraim/Manasseh, Moses/Aaron, David/his six older brothers, and Solomon/Adonijah. Since it concerns the future, its value is apprehended by faith. In Abraham's family, the one

who possesses the birthright inherits the Abrahamic covenant. The writer to the Hebrews treats these as a unity. Since Esau sells his inheritance rights he forfeits the
blessing (Heb 12:16-17). In sum, Jacob is inveigling the right to be heir of the family's
fortune and define its destiny. (Bruce K. Waltke, *Genesis: A Commentary* [Grand
Rapids, Mich.: Zondervan, 2001], pp. 363-64)

[13]Gerald G. May, *Addiction and Grace* (New York: HarperCollins, 1988), pp. 92-93.

[14]Waltke, *Genesis*, p. 364.

[15]Walter Brueggemann, *Genesis: A Bible Commentary for Teaching and Preaching* (Atlanta:
John Knox Press, 1982), p. 217.

[16]Rosenblatt and Horwitz, *Wrestling with Angels*, p. 245.

[17]Naomi Rosenblatt explores some of the possible human dynamics of this tension-filled
scene. It is possible, she hypothesizes, that the old man was not really convinced, that he had
seen the unworthiness of Esau to be the leader of the clan and that he might have gone
through with the charade knowing that Rebekah had provided the opportunity to disbelieve
his senses. He would not have had the heart to reject his favorite son (ibid., p. 249).

This seems to me unlikely, as Isaac trembles violently when he discovers the ruse. It is
significant that Isaac never raises the issue of the stolen blessing with Rebekah or even Jacob.

The fundamental psychological framework of Rosenblatt's interpretation is expressed in
the opening of her exposition: "Men who grow up with absent or emotionally distant fathers
often spend the rest of their lives compensating for the lack of a loving male role model in
their youths. If they are fortunate enough to have a strong and supportive mother, they can
become high achievers, though they often continue to strive for the approval of surrogate
father figures in the worlds of business, the arts, the professions, or politics. Other men face
a long uphill struggle against feelings of failure and inadequacy" (ibid., p. 235).

[18]The consideration of Isaac's preoccupation with touch and taste rather than words is considered in Avivah Gottlieb Zornberg, *The Beginning of Desire: Reflections on Genesis* (New
York: Doubleday, 1995), pp. 149-55.

[19]In calling Esau "my son," he seems to be disinheriting his other son, Jacob. Later, when Esau
does come in for the blessing (too late), Isaac puts all the blame on Jacob, whom he labels
"your brother" instead of "my son" (Gen 27:35).

[20]Rosenblatt and Horwitz, *Wrestling with Angels*, p. 247.

[21]"The Hebrew expresses the powerful turn of his destiny with a wordplay on the word "to
bless" *(barak)*. Esau the first-born *(haberakah)*, who longs for Isaac to bless *(barak)* him is
now reduced to weeping *(yebek)*" (Brian Morgan, "Falling Short of Blessing" [unpublished
sermon, Peninsula Bible Church, Cupertino, California, November 25, 2001], p. 4).

[22]Emphasis mine.

[23]Kass, *Hungry Soul*, pp. 208-9.

[24]The three temptation narratives in the Bible (Gen 3:1-19; Mt 4:1-11; 1 Jn 2:16) have a remarkable symmetry, as they expound the three testings of true godliness that take place in everyday life: (1) in provision ("food for food," "turn stones to bread," "the lust of the flesh"), (2)
in pleasure ("delight to the eyes," "throw yourself down," "the lust of the eyes") and (3) in
power ("desired to make one wise," "all the world will be yours," "the boasting of what one
has and does").

[25]Salvation is an open invitation to a table laden with food (Ps 23:5; 36:7-9; Is 25:6; Joel 3:18; Amos 9:13-14; Rev 19:1-10). Meals are important throughout Scripture. Sarah and Abraham cook for the strangers at Mamre (Gen 18:2-8); the widow Zarephath gives food to sustain Elijah (1 Kings 17); God feeds his people for forty years with manna in the wilderness (Ex 16:32-36).

[26]Robert Farrar Capon, *Supper of the Lamb: A Culinary Reflection* (New York: Smithmark, 1969), p. 27.

[27]Quoted in Reuven Kimelman, "Judaism and Lay Ministry," *NICM Journal* 5, no. 2 (1980): 47.

[28]Ibid., p. 51. See Matthew 18:20.

[29]See also Simon Holt, "Eating" (pp. 322-28); Patricia Kerr, "Hospitality" (pp. 505-10); and Mary Ruth Wilkinson, "Meal Preparation" (pp. 613-15), in Banks and Stevens, *Complete Book*. In addition to the references above, the following resources can be consulted: T. Barer-Strein, *You Eat What You Are* (Toronto: McClelland & Stewart, 1979); D. Bell and G. Valentine, *Consuming Geographies: We Are Where We Eat* (London: Routledge, 1997); Paul Brand, *The Forever Feast* (Ann Arbor: Servant, 1993); N. Charles and M. Kerr, *Women, Food and Families* (Manchester, U.K.: Manchester University Press, 1988); H. Davies, *The Bread of Life and the Cup of Joy: Newer Ecumenical Perspectives on the Eucharist* (Grand Rapids, Mich.: Eerdmans, 1993); J. Koenig, *New Testament Hospitality* (Philadelphia: Fortress, 1985); S. Mennell, A. Murcott and A. van Otterloo, *The Sociology of Food: Eating, Diet and Culture* (London: Sage, 1992); Henri Nouwen, *Can You Drink the Cup?* (Notre Dame, Ind.: Ave Maria, 1996).

[30]Kass, *Hungry Soul*, p. 228.

Chapter 3: Family

[1]Adapted from R. Paul Stevens, "Parenting," in *Thoughtful Parenting: A Manual of Wisdom for Home and Family*, ed. R. Paul Stevens and Robert Banks (Downers Grove, Ill.: InterVarsity Press, 2001), pp. 240-5.

[2]Quoted in J. Henley, "The Vocation of Parenting—with Surrogates," *St. Mark's Review* (winter 1990): 21.

[3]Emphasis mine.

[4]Bruce K. Waltke, "Reflections on the Life of Isaac and Retirement," *Crux* 32, no. 4 (1996): 7.

[5]Alexander Whyte concludes, "As we follow out the sad declension of Isaac's character to the end, it is forced upon us that it would have been well for Isaac, and for all connected with Isaac, that Abraham's uplifted hand had not been arrested by the angel of the Lord" (Alexander Whyte, *Bible Characters: Adam to Achan* [Edinburgh: Oliphants, n.d.], p. 151).

[6]Bruce Waltke notes, "The Hebrew word *[mesaheq]* is a variant form of the verb 'to laugh' *(sahaq).* The same variant is translated 'mocking' in [Genesis] 21:9. This play on Isaac's name may function to highlight the conflicts and triumphs of his life. Sarah 'laughed' *(sahaq-tishaq)* in unbelief at the announcement of Isaac's birth (18:12-15) and then in joy at his birth (21:5). Ishmael 'played in jest' when Isaac was weaned (21:9), and now Isaac 'plays in joy' with his wife" (Bruce Waltke, *Genesis: A Commentary* [Grand Rapids, Mich.: Zondervan, 2001], p. 369).

Commenting on the fact that Isaac had allowed himself to be publicly demonstrative with his wife, Brian Morgan notes the narrator's play on Isaac's name: " 'Laughter was tickling [causing to laugh] Rebekah.' The doubling of Isaac's name and the fact that the king is peering through his window (perhaps symbolic of a lens into the inner world) to discover the truth, may suggest that we have an insight into Isaac's real character. Sensual appetites can control this generally passive man" (Brian Morgan, "In the Footsteps of the Father" [unpublished sermon, Peninsula Bible Church, Cupertino, California, October 28, 2001], p. 3).

[7] Waltke, *Genesis*, pp. 370-1.

[8] Ibid., p. 372.

[9] Waltke comments on Esau's marriages and the question of bigamy.

> Although bigamy was not the Creator's ideal for marriage, Old Testament saints often had more than one wife (e.g., [Genesis] 25:1). Moreover, he cannot be censored for exogamy (i.e., marrying outside the kin group), since other saints, such as Salmon who married the Canaanite prostitute Rahab and Boaz who married Ruth, abandoned endogamy. However, as a son of Abraham, Esau is without excuse in marrying Hittites who are listed among the wicked Canaanites. He should have known that God condemned these people for their wickedness and would eventually give Abraham's offspring their land (15:16-20). He must have known how solicitously his grandfather acted to prevent his father from marrying these women (24:3). By marrying these women without regard to his ancestor's initiative and benediction, Esau again signals his lack of commitment to the Abrahamic vision of Israel's destiny and so his unworthiness to receive the blessing. (Ibid., pp. 375-76)

[10] Waltke, "Reflections," p. 5.

[11] Whyte, *Bible Characters*, p. 158.

[12] Waltke, *Genesis*, p. 351; see also chap. 1 n. 12.

[13] Walter Brueggemann, *Genesis: A Bible Commentary for Teaching and Preaching* (Atlanta: John Knox Press, 1982), p. 233.

[14] Simon Bar-Efrat explains the function of dramatic irony in Hebrew narrative: "Dramatic irony has a variety of functions, such as expressing criticism, stressing a shocking event or emphasizing a tragic situation. . . . Dramatic irony sometimes serves as a vehicle for the view that everyone received just deserts, in contrast to the view held by the character concerned" (Simon Bar-Efrat, "Narrative Art in the Bible," *Journal for the Study of the Old Testament*, Supplement Series 70, Bible and Literature Series 17 [Sheffield, U.K.: Almond Press, 1989], p. 125).

[15] Waltke, "Reflections," p. 13.

[16] The main point of the narrative is how the blessing got transferred, not the psychology of the participants.

[17] Naomi H. Rosenblatt and Joshua Horwitz, *Wrestling with Angels: What Genesis Teaches Us About Our Spirituality, Identity, Sexuality and Personal Relationships* (New York: Bantam Doubleday Dell, 1995), p. 251.

[18] Ibid., pp. 251, 255.

[19] The Hebrew [*tam*] can be translated "civilized" or "fine" (Waltke, *Genesis*, p. 362). J. P. Fokkelman notes how hard this word is to interpret. In some contexts it means "sound, un-

impaired, of character, incorruptible, sincere," but the moral qualifications seem not to be meant in Genesis 25:27. Rather, Jacob's singleness of purpose, his being "bent on one purpose," as evidenced both in his birth and in his later cattle-breeding program, seems to be what constitutes Jacob's "integrity" (Fokkelman, *Narrative Art*, p. 91). David Clemens argues that Fokkelman's interpretation is scarcely borne out by the immediate context and that the word might better be translated "domesticated" or "sedentary" (unpublished review, 2002). Brian Morgan suggests that the author might possibly have chosen the word (*tam*) as a pun on the word for "twins," which is *tomim* (unpublished notes, Cupertino, California).

[20]James R. Koch, "From 'The Sins of the Fathers (and Mothers)' to 'All My Children' " (unpublished manuscript, 1983), p. 1.

[21]On systems theory, see Edwin H. Friedman, *Generation to Generation: Family Process in Church and Synagogue* (New York: Guildford, 1985); Michael E. Kerr and Murray Bowen, *Family Evaluation* (New York: Norton, 1988); and R. Paul Stevens and Phil Collins, *The Equipping Pastor: A Systems Approach to Congregational Leadership* (Washington, D.C.: Alban Institute, 1993).

[22]Koch, "From 'The Sins of the Fathers,' " p. 19.

[23]Ibid., pp. 11-12.

[24]Ibid., p. 14.

[25]Even Ronald Wallace—who excuses and explains positively (as a ministry under the Word of God) Joseph's presumed tattletaling and his rough treatment of his brothers when they came to Egypt for food—admits that in subjecting the whole nation to Pharaoh, Joseph was wrong, being infected by the power that corrupts (Ronald S. Wallace, *The Story of Joseph and the Family of Jacob* [Grand Rapids, Mich.: Eerdmans, 2001], pp. 103-4).

[26]In his scholarly study Claus Westermann comments on the Hebrew use of "hate," saying, "We usually mean something that is a personal position or attitude. However, in Hebrew, the verb 'to hate' . . . is a deed or the inception of a deed. To practice this kind of hate is like pulling a bowstring taut—it has no purpose unless the arrow is unleashed. . . . Hate as a mere attitude would seem absurd to these people" (quoted in ibid., p. 16).

[27]Koch, "From 'The Sins of the Fathers,' " p. 20.

[28]Ibid., p. 21.

[29]In passing we might note that Koch attributes this breakthrough to the fact that what distinguished Joseph from the lives of the other patriarchs was that "he was the only character to have fully individuated from his family system." Koch offers further, "But the individuation was not the end in itself. God's plan of intervention and healing for the 'covenant family' required not only that Joseph be totally cut off from the decaying effects of his family tree, but that he eventually be drawn back into relationship with them as an instrument of confrontation, confession, absolution and recommitment" (ibid., p. 28).

[30]Michael Novak, "The Family Out of Favor," *Harpers*, April 1976, p. 40.

[31]Koch, "From 'The Sins of the Fathers,' " p. 32.

[32]Brueggemann, *Genesis*, pp. 212, 214.

Chapter 4: Sleep

[1]Thomas H. McAlpine, "Sleep," in *The Complete Book of Everyday Christianity*, ed. Robert Banks and R. Paul Stevens (Downers Grove, Ill.: InterVarsity Press, 1998), p. 906.

[2]Ibid., p. 908.

[3]Alexander Whyte, *Bible Characters: Adam to Achan* (Edinburgh: Oliphants, n.d.), p. 190.

[4]Brian Morgan, "Heaven on the Run" (unpublished sermon, Peninsula Bible Church, Cupertino, California, December 2, 2000), p. 3. Along the same lines Brueggemann notes, "The wakeful world of Jacob was a world of fear, terror, loneliness. Those were the parameters of his existence. The dream permits the entry of an alternative to his life. The dream is not a morbid review of his shameful past. It is rather the presentation of an alternative future with God" (Walter Brueggemann, *Genesis: A Bible Commentary for Teaching and Preaching* [Atlanta: John Knox Press, 1982], p. 243).

[5]Naomi H. Rosenblatt and Joshua Horwitz, *Wrestling with Angels: What Genesis Teaches Us About Our Spirituality, Identity, Sexuality and Personal Relationships* (New York: Bantam Doubleday Dell, 1995), p. 260.

[6]Brueggemann, *Genesis*, p. 243.

[7]Waltke notes that the precise meaning of the unique Hebrew word is uncertain. It could mean either a ladder or a staircase, such as the steps on the slopes of a ziggurat (Gen 11:1-9) (Bruce Waltke, *Genesis: A Commentary* [Grand Rapids, Mich.: Zondervan, 2001], p. 390).

[8]Ibid., pp. 391-92.

[9]It was a dream of greatness under God that kept Joseph going and enabled him to visualize how his life was purposeful under God's calling (Gen 37:5-11; 42:9; 45:5-8; 50:20).

[10]Naomi Rosenblatt argues, "The ladder expresses his desire for upward transcendence, for deliverance from earthly conflicts. . . . God promises him all that he has lost and has almost despaired of ever recovering: a family, a homeland, and most important, a feeling of being blessed" (Rosenblatt and Horwitz, *Wrestling with Angels*, p. 262). Jacob is not alone; he is special, wanted and chosen. But Rosenblatt, in true Freudian fashion, goes on to argue that the ladder is a phallic symbol "expressing Jacob's physical and sexual maturity. God's promise that 'your descendants shall be as the dust of the earth' is Jacob's wishful fulfillment of his desire for virility and power" (ibid., p. 263).

[11]Stephen Anderson, "Dreaming," in Banks and Stevens, *Complete Book*, p. 310.

[12]Ibid.

[13]*The Treasures of Mount Athos* (Thessalonika, Greece: Ministry of Culture; Museum of Byzantium Culture, 1997), p. 141.

[14]Waltke, *Genesis*, p. 388.

[15]Thomas F. Torrance, "The Spiritual Relevance of Angels," in *Alive to God*, ed. J. I. Packer and Loren Wilkinson (Downers Grove, Ill.: InterVarsity Press, 1992), pp. 123-24.

[16]A. H. Strong, *Systematic Theology: A Compendium* (Philadelphia: Judson, 1907), pp. 443-60.

[17]Gordon J. Wenham, *Genesis 16–50*, Word Bible Commentary (Dallas: Word, 1994), p. 222.

[18]Structurally, and as part of the narrator's art in telling the story, the encounter with angels leaving and entering the Promised Land forms a parallel, a chiastic pattern (Waltke, *Genesis*, p. 386).

[19]See Bruce K. Waltke, "The Fear of the Lord: The Foundation for a Relationship with God," in Packer and Wilkinson, *Alive to God*, pp. 17-33.

[20]Waltke notes that *masseba* (which denotes a single upright stone) is a wordplay on "resting" *(mussab)*. "In contrast to the Canaanite pillars that were thought to be repositories of deities' spirits and perhaps functioned to symbolize their fertility, this one commemorates the Lord's

theophany and promises" (Waltke, *Genesis*, pp. 392-93).

[21]Robert Alter, *The Art of Biblical Narrative* (New York: Basic Books, 1981), p. 55.

[22]A. H. Strong notes the practical results of living in an angel-saturated creation: (1) We gain a new sense of the greatness of God's resources and grace at work in creation; (2) our faith in God's providential care is strengthened to know that God sends his messengers to care for people being tempted, even when we sin; (3) we are taught humility since beings of greater intelligence perform such unnoticed services; (4) we are helped in our struggle against sin; (5) we are encouraged to consider the boundless possibilities of our future existence with such beings who praise and serve God unceasingly in heaven (Strong, *Systematic Theology*, p. 462).

[23]Whyte, *Bible Characters*, p. 162.

[24]Simone Weil, *Waiting on God*, trans. Emma Craufurd (London: Routledge & Kegan Paul, 1951), p. 145.

Chapter 5: Courting

[1]Samuel H. Dresner, *Rachel* (Minneapolis: Fortress, 1944), p. 24.

[2]Gerhard Von Rad, *Genesis: A Commentary*, trans. John H. Marks (Philadelphia: Westminster Press, 1961), p. 249.

[3]Von Rad quotes Hermann Gunkel: "Here childlike trust in God is combined with worldly wise calculation in a most charming manner" (ibid., p. 256).

[4]Dresner, *Rachel*, p. 29, TB Kidushin 11a.

[5]Waltke quotes Fokkelman: "God is indeed with him, leads him to the circle of relatives and inside it meets the woman who is to be his bride. Whenever Jacob acknowledges this and when he feels he is under God's special protection, he makes it clear with stones." However, notes Waltke, "unlike his stone pillar that commemorates God's encounter with him at Bethel ([Genesis] 28:16-19) and the stone heap that bears witness to his treaty with Laban in the sight of God (31:42-45), the stone in this scene is not connected to God by either Jacob or the narrator. The contrast suggests that Jacob is unaware of obvious Providence" (Waltke, *Genesis*, p. 401).

[6]*Genesis Rabbah* 70:12, quoted in Dresner, *Rachel*, p. 32.

[7]Quoted in ibid.

[8]Ibid., p. 33.

[9]*Zohar* 146a-147a, an abbreviated composite translation in ibid., pp. 33-34.

[10]Ibid., p. 35.

[11]Amy A. Kass and Leon R. Kass, introduction to *Wing to Wing, Oar to Oar: Readings on Courting and Marrying*, ed. Amy A. Kass and Leon R. Kass (Notre Dame, Ind.: University of Notre Dame Press, 2000), p. 14.

[12]Ibid., p. 5.

[13]Ibid., p. 10.

[14]Walter R. Schrumm, "Sex Should Occur Only Within Marriage," in *Current Issues in Human Sexuality*, ed. Harold Feldman and Andrea Parrot Eggleston (Beverly Hills, Calif.: Sage, 1984), p. 9.

[15]Allan Bloom, "Relationships," in Kass and Kass, *Wing to Wing*, p. 66. "Students do not date

anymore. . . . They live in herds or packs with no more sexual differentiation than any herds have when not in heat. Human beings can, of course, engage in sexual intercourse at any time. But today there are none of the conventions invented by civilization to take the place of heat, to guide mating, and perhaps to channel it. Nobody is sure who is make [sic] the advances, where there [sic] are to be a pursuer and a pursued, what the event is to mean" (ibid., pp. 66-67).

[16] Kass and Kass, introduction to *Wing to Wing*, p. 6.

[17] The "weak eyes" probably refer to softness, "lacking the fire and sparkle that Orientals prize as beauty" (Waltke, *Genesis*, p. 405).

[18] Amy and Leon Kass offer questions at the beginning of "Genesis 29–31: Jacob Finds a Wife":

> The story thus naturally provokes the question of which woman makes Jacob the better wife. Is falling in love with visible beauty a reliable guide for a good marriage? If eyes are windows to the soul, are they perhaps more revealing and relevant than beauteous form? Does Rachel's attachment to the (visible) household gods of her father (Chapter 31) have any bearing on the wisdom of Jacob's love? What does Jacob's response to Rachel's demand for children reveal about his own—and about Rachel's—understanding of marriage?" (Amy Kass and Leon Kass, "Genesis 29–31: Jacob Finds a Wife," in Kass and Kass, *Wing to Wing*, p. 317)

Chapter 6: Marriage

[1] *Life of Catherine Booth*, 1:96, quoted in James Hastings, *The Greater Men and Women of the Bible* (Edinburgh: Clark, 1913), 1:396.

[2] William Perkins, "A Treatise on Callings," in *The Workes of That Famous and Worthy Minister of Christ in the University of Cambridge, Mr. William Perkins* (London: John Legett, 1626), p. 762. A modern abridged version is found in William Perkins, *The Work of William Perkins* (Appleford, U.K.: Sutton Courtenay, 1969).

[3] Bruce Waltke, *Genesis: A Commentary* (Grand Rapids, Mich.: Zondervan, 2001), p. 403.

[4] The Hebrew word for "feast" *(misteh)* implies a drinking fest (ibid., p. 405).

[5] Samuel H. Dresner, *Rachel* (Minneapolis: Fortress, 1944), p. 46.

[6] Ibid., p. 43.

[7] Joyce G. Baldwin, *The Message of Genesis 12–50* (Leicester, U.K.: Inter-Varsity Press, 1986), p. 123.

[8] Avivah Gottlieb Zornberg, *The Beginning of Desire: Reflections on Genesis* (New York: Doubleday, 1995), pp. 185-86. Emphasis mine.

[9] C. F. Keil and F. Delitzsch, *Commentary on the Old Testament* (Grand Rapids, Mich.: Eerdmans, 1978), 1:798.

[10] Dresner, *Rachel*, p. 50.

[11] Abraham married his half sister, also prohibited later in Leviticus.

[12] Gerhard Von Rad, *Genesis: A Commentary*, trans. John H. Marks (Philadelphia: Westminster Press, 1961), p. 289.

[13] R. Paul Stevens, *Married for Good: The Lost Art of Staying Happily Married* (Downers Grove, Ill.: InterVarsity Press, 1986), p. 20.

[14] Amy A. Kass and Leon R. Kass, introduction to *Wing to Wing, Oar to Oar: Readings on Courting and Marrying*, ed. Amy A. Kass and Leon R. Kass (Notre Dame, Ind.: University

of Notre Dame Press, 2000), pp. 12-13.

[15] Perkins, "Treatise on Callings," p. 733.

[16] Von Rad, *Genesis*, p. 290.

[17] This cry is parallel to Rebekah's plea that her life would be "not worth living" if Jacob were to get a wife from among the neighboring pagan women (Genesis 27:46).

[18] Of all the patriarchs, only Isaac prays when facing infertility.

[19] Perkins, "Treatise on Callings," p. 760.

[20] Emphasis mine.

[21] David Blankenhorn, "I Do," in *Wing to Wing, Oar to Oar: Readings on Courting and Marrying*, ed. Amy A. Kass and Leon R. Kass (Notre Dame, Ind.: University of Notre Dame Press, 2000), p. 79.

[22] Keil and Delitzsch, *Commentary on the Old Testament*, p. 782.

[23] Waltke, *Genesis*, p. 406.

[24] I develop these in R. Paul Stevens, *Marriage Spirituality: Ten Disciplines for Couples Who Love God* (Downers Grove, Ill.: InterVarsity Press, 1989), pp. 18-21.

Chapter 7: Work

[1] Jeremy Rifkin, *The End of Work: The Decline of the Global Work-Force and the Dawn of the Post-Market Era* (London: Penguin, 2000), pp. xv, xvii-xviii.

[2] *Qiddushim* 1:11, in *Nashim* [The Order of Women], trans. Jacob Neuser, vol. 3 of *The Tosefta* (New York: Ktav, 1979), p. 244. Similarly, in *Genesis Rabbah: The Judaic Commentary to the Book of Genesis*, trans. Jacob Neuser (Atlanta: Scholars Press, 1985), 1:269: "All crafts did the first man [Adam] teach them."

[3] For an analysis of the contemporary situation, the biblical record on work and a biblical theology of work, see R. Paul Stevens, "Doing the Lord's Work," chapter five in *The Other Six Days: Vocation, Work and Ministry in Biblical Perspective* (Grand Rapids, Mich.: Eerdmans, 1999), pp. 106-30.

[4] William Tyndale, "A Parable of the Wicked Mammon," in *Treatises and Portions of Holy Scripture* (1527; reprint, Cambridge: Parker Society, 1848), pp. 98, 104.

[5] If Jacob got a lot of spotted animals for himself, Laban would say, "Let's make your wages the striped ones." But Jacob got striped ones in a big way. And on it went.

[6] Gerhard Von Rad argues that Jacob was neither a slave (given only maintenance and bodily protection) nor a domestic servant (normally remunerated). He is a relative under an economic obligation. It becomes apparent when Jacob requests to leave for Canaan that his status is slavelike. In Hebrew law the slave, when he was released, had to leave his wife and children behind. If he did not want to do this, he had to remain a servant (Ex 21:4-6). Jacob is not owned by Laban, but he is dependent. And he wants both to leave and to take with him his wives and children. Laban even says, "The women are my daughters, the children are my children" (Gen 31:43). Von Rad describes this as "a rather obscure legal situation" (Gerhard Von Rad, *Genesis: A Commentary*, trans. John H. Marks [Philadelphia: Westminster Press, 1961], pp. 285, 294-95).

[7] H. C. Leupold, *Exposition of Genesis* (Grand Rapids, Mich.: Baker, 1942), 2:846.

[8] The promise is found in Genesis 15:1-5; 17:1-8; 22:17-18; 26:24; 27:27-29; 28:13-15.

[9] For a theology and spirituality of entrepreneurship, see R. Paul Stevens, "Spiritual and Re-

ligious Sources of Entrepreneurship: From Max Weber to the New Business Spirituality,"
   Crux 36, no. 2 (2000): 22-33.
[10]Gordon Wenham notes that Jacob's offer is certainly less than the typical 20 percent of new-
   born lambs or kids that ancient shepherds received for their wages (Gordon Wenham, *Genesis 16—50*, Word Biblical Commentary [Dallas: Word, 1994], p. 256).
[11]Bruce Waltke, *Genesis: A Commentary* (Grand Rapids, Mich.: Zondervan, 2001), p. 420.
   Waltke bases his thoughts on N. Sarna's research (*Genesis*, JPS Torah Commentary 1 [Phil-
   adelphia: Jewish Publication Society, 1989], p. 212).
[12]N. Sarna, *Genesis*, p. 212, quoted in Waltke, *Genesis*, p. 420.
[13]J. P. Fokkelman, *Narrative Art in Genesis: Specimens of Stylistic and Structural Analysis* (Assen, Netherlands: Van Gorcum, 1975), p. 149.
[14]Waltke, *Genesis*, p. 420.
[15]Wenham notes that Jacob means this: "God has not simply transferred the herds from Laban
   to Jacob; he has done them a favor, giving them a much better life!" (Wenham, *Genesis 16—
   50*, p. 271).
[16]Wenham notes the parallel with the Bethel dream: (1) The language "saw in a dream and
   behold." (2) The vision, with even the word "mounting" / "going up" (Gen 28:12) being the
   same. (3) Explanation of the vision. Genesis 31:3 seems to place the vision just before Jacob
   speaks with his wives, though "at the time the flock bred" puts the vision back some years
   (Wenham, *Genesis 16—50*, p. 272).
[17]Ibid., p. 260.
[18]Fokkelman, *Narrative Art*, pp. 140-41.
[19]Waltke, *Genesis*, p. 416.
[20]Wenham, *Genesis 16—50*, p. 270. See also Gordon Wenham, "Grace and Law in the Old
   Testament," in *Law, Morality and the Bible*, ed. Bruce Kaye and Gordon Wenham (Downers Grove, Ill.: InterVarsity Press, 1978), p. 17.
[21]Rudyard Kipling, "When Earth's Last Picture Is Painted," quoted in *Working: Its Meaning
   and Its Limits*, ed. Gilbert C. Meilander (Notre Dame, Ind.: University of Notre Dame
   Press, 2000), p. 42.

Chapter 8: Conversion
[1]Kenneth Leech, *Experiencing God: Theology As Spirituality* (New York: Harper & Row,
   1985), p. 65.
[2]Gordon Wenham, *Genesis 16—50*, Word Biblical Commentary (Dallas: Word, 1994), p. 288.
   Wenham also notes how the structure matches the order of the quarrel in Genesis 27 (p. 289).
[3]Ibid., p. 295.
[4]The Jabbok Brook is the present Wadi es Zerka.
[5]Some Jewish commentators suggest it might be the angel of Esau, since Jacob's struggle with
   himself and his God was played out in relation to his brother.
[6]Quoted in Gerhard Von Rad, *Genesis: A Commentary*, trans. John H. Marks (Philadelphia:
   Westminster Press, 1961), p. 319.
[7]Richard Neuhaus, *Freedom for Ministry: A Critical Affirmation of the Church and Its Mission*
   (San Francisco: Harper & Row, 1956), p. 202.

[8] P. T. Forsyth, *The Soul of Prayer* (London: Independent, 1954), pp. 86-88.

[9] Arthur Miller, *Death of a Salesman* (New York: Viking, 1949), quoted in William Hulme, *Living with Myself* (Minneapolis: Augsburg, 1971), p. 69.

[10] R. D. Laing, *The Politics of Experience and the Bird of Paradise* (Harmondsworth, U.K.: Penguin, 1970), p. 81.

[11] Eugene Lowry, *The Homiletical Plot* (Atlanta: John Knox Press, 1980), p. 55.

[12] Avivah Gottlieb Zornberg, *The Beginning of Desire: Reflections on Genesis* (New York: Doubleday, 1995), p. 171.

[13] Some Jewish commentators, embarrassed by this direct falsehood, split off the first word, "I am" from the other two to protect Jacob's integrity, thus reading, "I am (the one who is bringing the food)—Esau is your firstborn." Zornberg offers another view, namely that by purchasing the birthright Jacob has become Esau in the birthright dimension (ibid., p. 172).

[14] Frank Boreham, *The Prodigal* (London: Epworth, n.d.), pp. 32-33.

[15] Wenham, *Genesis 16—50*, p. 304. Wenham notes that while Jacob's name was changed, both names continue to be used, though Jacob more frequently (thirty-one times) than Israel (twenty times). "Whereas in prose Jacob always refers to the historical individual, Israel sometimes refers to the people ([Gen] 46:8; 47:27; 48:20). . . . When Israel is used of the individual, it seems to allude to the position as clan head (43:6,8,11; 46:1; 48:2), whereas Jacob seems to be used where his human weakness is most obvious (e.g. 37:34; 42:4,36; 47:9)" (p. 351).

[16] Bruce Waltke, *Genesis: A Commentary* (Grand Rapids, Mich.: Zondervan, 2001), p. 447.

[17] Wenham, *Genesis 16—50*, p. 303.

[18] Calvin applies this to Christian experience:

> What was once exhibited under a visible form to our father Jacob is daily fulfilled in the individual members of the church, namely in their temptations it is necessary for them to wrestle with God. He is said, indeed, to tempt us in a different manner from Satan; but because he alone is the author of our crosses and afflictions . . . he is said to tempt us when we make trial of our faith. . . . He having challenged us to this contest at the same time furnishes us with the means of resistance, so that he both fights *against* us and *for* us. In short, such is his apportioning of this conflict that while he assails us with one hand, he defends us with the other; yea, in as much as he supplies us with more strength to resist than he employs in opposing us, we may truly and properly say, that he fights *against* us with his *left* hand, and *for* us with his *right* hand. For while he lightly opposes us, he supplies invincible strength whereby we overcome. (John Calvin, *A Commentary on Genesis*, trans. J. King [1847; reprint, London: Banner of Truth, 1965], 2:196, quoted in ibid.)

[19] David Jacobus Bosch, *A Spirituality of the Road* (Scottdale, Penn.: Herald, 1979), p. 34.

[20] Waltke, *Genesis*, p. 446.

[21] James S. Stewart, *A Faith to Proclaim* (London: Hodder & Stoughton, 1953), p. 40.

[22] Thomas F. Torrance, *Trinitarian Perspective: Toward Doctrinal Agreement* (Edinburgh: Clark, 1994), p. 1.

[23] Waltke speaks of what Jacob's encounter teaches us about knowing God: (1) It may be marked by ambiguity. (2) It does not mean ease of conflict. (3) It defies human understanding. (4) God in humility makes himself available to humanity. (5) "When they stop wrestling

with God and start clinging to him, they discover that he has been there for their good, to bless them" (Waltke, *Genesis*, p. 448).

Chapter 9: Sex

[1] In the Bible there are not only strong men but also enterprising women: a queen (Esther) who delivers a whole people, a harlot (Rahab) who saves Israel's leaders and a general (Deborah) who leads an army.

[2] Read the midrashic embellishment of the disaster of Baal-Peor in Samuel H. Dresner, *Rachel* (Minneapolis: Fortress, 1944), p. 125. See also Exodus 34:15-16 and Deuteronomy 7:3.

[3] Gerhard Von Rad, *Genesis: A Commentary*, trans. John H. Marks (Philadelphia: Westminster Press, 1961), p. 326.

[4] Waltke estimates from the text that the rape of Dinah took place about a decade after the family left Haran. Jacob's long delay and fascination with the pagan city cost him horrendously (Waltke, *Genesis*, p. 459).

[5] Von Rad, *Genesis*, p. 326.

[6] The verb is in fact a transitive word, which should more properly be translated "laid her" *(va'yishkab otah)* rather than "lay with her" *(va'yishkab ittah)*. Further, as Meir Sternberg shows, there is a symmetry in the way the narrative is composed so that the verbs of abuse (took, laid, abused) are parallel to the words of endearment with which the perpetrator of the assault is described as caring about the woman: his soul clung to Dinah; he loved the maiden; he spoke tenderly to her (Gen 34:3-4) (Meir Sternberg, *The Poetics of Biblical Narrative: Ideological Literature and the Drama of Reading* [Bloomington: Indiana University Press, 1985], pp. 44-47).

[7] David Clemens notes that the word translated "seize" is a relatively neutral word (Deut 22:13), while "abuse" is more forceful and is used of rape in Judges 20:5 (cf. 19:24), 2 Samuel 13:12, 14, 22 and 32 and Lamentations 5:11 as well as of compelled marriage in Deuteronomy 21:14. On the other hand, there appears to be an element of mutual complicity in its usage in Deuteronomy 22:24 and perhaps 22:29. Both passages, in their phraseology, are reminiscent of Genesis 34:1-2, as is Ezekiel 22:10-11. According to Clemens, then, it is unclear whether Dinah was a totally unwilling participant. She may have been passive, as Jacob was in his response. This has a bearing on whether Shechem was practicing blackmail. It is clear that Shechem was engaging in sexual intercourse inappropriately (David Clemens, unpublished notes on Genesis 25—50).

[8] The verb *hekherish* means "keep still" and has in other contexts connotations of inertness or neglect (2 Sam 19:11; Esther 4:14; Hab 1:13) (Sternberg, *Poetics of Biblical Narrative*, p. 448).

[9] Ibid., p. 453.

[10] "Later, at a critical moment, the narrator will suddenly lay bare the iron fist hidden all along in [Hamor and Shechem's] verbal glove, thus persuading the reader that Jacob's sons had good reason to counter by guile and violence" (Sternberg, *Poetics of Biblical Narrative*, p. 457).

[11] Sternberg reflects on the importance of determining the weight of the narrator's judgment that deceit was involved.

> Does the deceit cover the whole speech or a part only? And which part? What do the brothers really aim for in driving such a hard bargain: to enter into an alliance on

their own terms or inoffensively ("with deceit") to scotch an offensive alliance with their powerful neighbor by setting the most exorbitant conditions they can think of? Does the deceit confine itself to the specific proposal or extend to its rationale? . . . It is to good effect, therefore, that the narrative keeps this gap open and the whole inner life opaque almost to the end, where the brothers finally emerge as prevaricators rather than hypocrites. (Ibid., pp. 458-59)

[12] Reflecting on this, Sternberg comments:

With Dinah in Shechem's hands, the option of polite declining is closed to her guardians. And once the brothers refused to submit to the Hivite version of a shotgun wedding, they were left no avenue to the retrieval of their sister except force. Hence also the need for "deceit." Considering the numerical superiority of the troops behind "the prince of the land" — "two of Jacob's sons" faced a whole city — no wonder the brothers resorted to trickery to make odds more even. (Ibid., p. 468)

[13] Ibid., pp. 466-67.
[14] Sternberg suggests that "the greed betrayed by the plunderers reduces them to the moral level of the Hivites, a demotion reinforced by analogical linkage to the 'deceit' verse" (ibid., p. 471).
[15] Ibid., p. 475.
[16] In contrast to this, Dresner notes how the ideal of virginity had its origin in a reading of the biblical account of Adam and Eve as destined to live a virginal, angelic life as seraphim, "presocial creatures not meant to engage in sexual congress," and that only "because of the fall did they abandon their angelic status and copulate in the manner of lower creatures" (Dresner, Rachel, pp. 76-77).
[17] Amy A. Kass and Leon R. Kass, introduction to Wing to Wing, Oar to Oar: Readings on Courting and Marrying, ed. Amy A. Kass and Leon R. Kass (Notre Dame, Ind.: University of Notre Dame Press, 2000), pp. 15-16.
[18] See "The Problem of Headship," in R. Paul Stevens, Married for Good: The Lost Art of Staying Happily Married (Downers Grove, Ill.: InterVarsity Press, 1986), pp. 111-31.
[19] Quoted in Avivah Gottlieb Zornberg, The Beginning of Desire: Reflections on Genesis (New York: Doubleday, 1995), p. 303.
[20] Dresner, Rachel, p. 81.
[21] Ibid., pp. 66, 224.

Chapter 10: Home

[1] Robert Frost, "Death of a Hired Hand," The Poems of Robert Frost (New York: Random House, 1946), pp. 41-42.
[2] Sue Monk Kidd, When the Heart Waits (San Francisco: Harper & Row, 1990), p. 89.
[3] James Hastings, The Greater Men and Women of the Bible (Edinburgh: Clark, 1913), 1:419-20.
[4] Quoted in Avivah Gottlieb Zornberg, The Beginning of Desire: Reflections on Genesis (New York: Doubleday, 1995), p. 220.
[5] Ibid., p. 221.
[6] Ibid., p. 222.

[7]Quoted in R. Paul Stevens, *Married for Good: The Lost Art of Staying Happily Married* (Downers Grove, Ill.: InterVarsity Press, 1986), pp. 51-52.

[8]Calvin Seerveld, *Take Hold of God and Pull* (Carlisle, U.K.: Paternoster, 1999), p. 70.

[9]John Francis Kavanaugh, *Following Christ in a Consumer Society: The Spirituality of Cultural Resistance* (Maryknoll, N.Y.: Orbis, 1984), p. 45.

[10]See R. Paul Stevens, *The Other Six Days: Vocation, Work and Ministry in Biblical Perspective* (Grand Rapids, Mich.: Eerdmans, 1999), pp. 89-105.

[11]Peter J. Leithart, "Snakes in the Garden: Sanctuaries, Sanctuary Pollution and the Global Environment," *Stewardship Journal* (fall 1993): 24-32, reprinted in Scott Rae and Kenman Wong, *Beyond Integrity: A Judeo-Christian Approach to Business Ethics* (Grand Rapids, Mich.: Eerdmans, 1996), pp. 490-8.

Chapter 11: Calling

[1]See Klaus Bochmuehl, "Recovering Vocation Today," *Crux* 24, no. 3 (1988): 25-35.

[2]Emphasis mine. Significantly, the Latin word for "send" is *missio*, the word from which we get the English word *mission*. Joseph has a mission from God.

[3]Cited in Walter Hilton, *Toward a Perfect Love* (Portland, Ore.: Multnomah, 1985), p. xxv.

[4]Richard John Neuhaus states:

> In the Quran (or Koran), the canonical book of Islam, Muhammad (570-632) shows how a general feeling of Fatalism may be transmuted into a theologically profound reverence for the Will of God—and death transmuted into the opportunity for participating in God's judgment. . . . The entire process of death and judgment is foreshortened for the shahid (the witness) who is killed in the service of God. Longing for the status of witness (talab ash Shahada) is therefore intense, and it can be attained either by violent death on behalf of Islam or by various forms of self-surrendering devotion. (Richard John Neuhaus, "Fate as the Will of God," in *The Eternal Pity: Reflections on Dying*, ed. Richard John Neuhaus [Notre Dame, Ind.: University of Notre Dame Press, 2000], pp. 74, 77)

[5]Quoted in Avivah Gottlieb Zornberg, *The Beginning of Desire: Reflections on Genesis* (New York: Doubleday, 1995), pp. 254-55.

[6]Thomas Mann, *Joseph and His Brothers*, quoted in ibid., p. 255.

[7]Ibid.

[8]See the section on "The Ecclesiastical Call," in R. Paul Stevens, *The Other Six Days: Vocation, Work and Ministry in Biblical Perspective* (Grand Rapids, Mich.: Eerdmans, 1999), pp. 152-58.

Chapter 12: Dressing

[1]On the importance of clothing, see Mike Starkey, *Fashion and Style* (Crowborough, U.K.: Monarch, 1995).

[2]Calvin Seerveld, "Adornment," in *The Complete Book of Everyday Christianity*, ed. Robert Banks and R. Paul Stevens (Downers Grove, Ill.: InterVarsity Press, 1998), p. 22.

[3]Ibid., p. 572. See also 2 Kings 5:5, 22.

[4]Waltke explains the chronology. Joseph is seventeen when he enters Egypt. Judah's story be-

gins when he sells Joseph into Egypt. Assuming he had children right away, Er is about eighteen when he dies. If Tamar waits a year for Shelah, the twins are born about twenty-one years after Judah's original marriage. This means, says Waltke, "that Judah's confession of wrong against Tamar occurs near the same time as the confession of all the brothers in their wrong against Joseph (cf. [Gen] 38:26 with 42:21). Perhaps Judah's confession regarding Tamar prepares him for the other. The scene provides an essential piece in the characterization of Judah, whose greater Son will rule the universe" (ibid., p. 508).

5 Norman Cohen, *Self, Struggle and Change: Family Conflict Stories in Genesis and Their Healing Insights for Our Lives* (Woodstock, Vt.: Jewish Heights, 1995), pp. 164-65.

6 The rabbis argue that Judah's moral progress through this event was a major reason why the messianic line emerged from Judah (Mekhilta d'Rabbi Ishmael Beshallah, parashah 6). Cohen's conclusion on the righteousness of the second child is found in *Self, Struggle and Change*, p. 168.

7 Ibid.

8 Kathryn Lockhart, "Clothing," in *Thoughtful Parenting: A Manual of Wisdom for Home and Family*, ed. R. Paul Stevens and Robert Banks (Downers Grove, Ill.: InterVarsity Press, 2001), p. 50.

Chapter 13: Finishing

1 A phrase from the poem by Elizabeth Barrett Browning, quoted in Elizabeth A. Dreyer, *Earth Crammed with Heaven: A Spirituality of Everyday Life* (New York: Paulist, 1994), p. 1.

2 Sue Monk Kidd, *When the Heart Waits* (San Francisco: Harper & Row, 1990), p. 139.

3 Lesslie Newbigin, *Honest Religion for Secular Man* (London: SCM Press, 1969), p. 49.

4 Jürgen Moltmann, *Theology of Hope: On the Grounds and Implications of a Christian Eschatology*, trans. J. W. Leith (New York: Harper & Row, 1967), p. 31.

5 Miroslav Volf, *Work in the Spirit: Toward a Theology of Work* (New York: Oxford University Press, 1991), p. 92.

6 Numbers 21:18; 24:17; Psalm 45:7[6]; 60:9[7]; Zechariah 10:11.

7 Amos uses this image for the complacent people enjoying bowlfuls of wine and using the finest of lotions but not grieving "over the ruin of Joseph" (Amos 6:6).

8 In the liturgy of the Easter vigil, Christians call the fall of our first parents a "happy fault," or in the Latin, *felix culpa*. "O happy fault that gave us such a great redeemer!" the liturgy exults.

9 James Hastings, *The Greater Men and Women of the Bible* (Edinburgh: Clark, 1913), 1:510.

10 Bruce Waltke, *Genesis: A Commentary* (Grand Rapids, Mich.: Zondervan, 2001), p. 543.

11 Avivah Gottlieb Zornberg, *The Beginning of Desire: Reflections on Genesis* (New York: Doubleday, 1995), p. 273.

12 Norman Cohen notes some of the extraordinary parallels in the story: (1) The same Hebrew word for "pledge" (*'arab*) is used both in Judah-Tamar and Judah-Benjamin. (2) The brothers carry to Egypt as a gift to Joseph the same spices that had been part of the Ishmaelite caravan that took Joseph to Egypt. (3) As Judah "adopted" the half-Canaanite Perez into the royal line, so Jacob adopted the half-Egyptian Ephraim and Manasseh by placing them on the knees—a formal procedure (Norman Cohen, *Self, Struggle and Change: Family Conflict Stories in Genesis and Their Healing Insights for Our Lives* [Woodstock, Vt.: Jewish Heights, 1995], p. 207).

[13] Zornberg, *Beginning of Desire*, p. 309.

[14] Ibid., p. 307.

[15] Meir Sternberg, *The Poetics of Biblical Narrative: Ideological Literature and the Drama of Reading* (Bloomington: Indiana University Press, 1985), p. 308.

[16] Zornberg, *Beginning of Desire*, p. 337.

[17] Exploring the wealth of Jewish commentary on the vexed question of why Joseph held out on the brothers and why he did not communicate with his father, at least when he came to power, Zornberg offers a simple but (to her) totally convincing answer:

> Joseph is paralysed by the prospect of his brothers' shame, if he reveals himself to his father. This is a genetic sensitivity: his mother, Rachel, according to a classic midrash, had been so horrified at the idea that her sister, Leah, masquerading as Rachel, should be shamed on her wedding night, that she gave her the secret signs that Jacob had given her, to prevent just such a deception (Rashi, 29:25). To prevent his brothers' shame, Joseph has, like his mother, kept silent, while his heart yearned to express itself. When his brothers actually appear before him for the first time, passivity and silence are neither possible nor necessary. From this point on, Joseph engages in an active project of discovery, the aim of which is to produce evidence that will allow his brothers to endure his "resurrection" without shame. (Ibid., p. 333)

[18] Gordon Wenham, *Genesis 16–50*, Word Biblical Commentary (Dallas: Word, 1994), p. 413.

[19] Zornberg reflects on the difficulty Joseph had in convincing his brothers of his identity (Gen 45:12). He calls them to come close to him (v. 4) and says, "You can see for yourselves . . . that it is really I" (v. 12). The midrash (*Mereshit Rabbah* 93:8) suggests that despite his eloquence Joseph has to show them his circumcision before they will credit his words. Rashi (Rabbi Shelomo Yitzhaki, foremost commentator on the Torah, 1040–1105) comments: "'Your eyes see' my glory; and that I am your brother, for I am circumcised like you; moreover, that '*my mouth is speaking to you*' in the Holy Tongue." Thus, according to the midrash, Joseph used two proofs: his circumcision (visual) and his speaking Hebrew (aural) (Zornberg, *Beginning of Desire*, p. 344).

[20] "He weeps because they think they need a mediator, because they are afraid of him, because they ascribe to him the attitude of v 15, because he hears his father's voice, because he recalls his youth persecuted by their hate, and because it is they who remind him of this through their submissiveness. These his last tears are really their tears" (Wenham, *Genesis 16–50*, p. 490).

[21] Waltke, *Genesis*, pp. 565-66, emphasis mine.

Chapter 14: Death

[1] Richard John Neuhaus, introduction to *The Eternal Pity: Reflections on Dying*, ed. Richard John Neuhaus (Notre Dame, Ind.: University of Notre Dame Press, 2000), p. 2.

[2] Peter De Vries, *The Blood of the Lamb* (New York: Little, Brown, 1996), pp. 168-238, quoted in ibid., p. 4.

[3] Quoted in T. K. Jones, "Death: Real Meaning in Life Is to Be Found Beyond Life," *Christianity Today*, June 24, 1991, p. 30.

[4] Quoted in Jones, "Death," p. 30.

[5] Janice Brewi and Anne Brennan, *Mid-Life: Psychological and Spiritual Perspectives* (New

York: Crossroad, 1982), p. 19, as quoted in Sue Monk Kidd, *When the Heart Waits* (San Francisco: Harper & Row, 1990), p. 9.

[6] On the intermediate state, see John W. Cooper, *Body, Soul and Life Everlasting: Biblical Anthropology and the Monism-Dualism Debate* (Grand Rapids, Mich.: Eerdmans, 1989).

[7] Much of the above is found in Gail C. Stevens and R. Paul Stevens, "Death," in *The Complete Book of Everyday Christianity*, ed. Robert Banks and R. Paul Stevens (Downers Grove, Ill.: InterVarsity Press, 1998), pp. 273-78.

[8] Waltke notes that "thigh" in "put your hand under my thigh" is a euphemism for genitalia (Gen 46:26; Ex 1:5; Judg 8:30). In these verses, notes Waltke, a literal translation for "descendants" is "those coming out of his body [*yereko*]. The word for 'my thigh' in Genesis 24:2 is *yereke*. When facing death, the patriarchs secure their last will by an oath at the source of life (see Gen 47:29). The reason for this gesture is uncertain, but perhaps it is chosen because the oath involves the certainty of the posterity God promises" (Bruce Waltke, *Genesis: A Commentary* [Grand Rapids, Mich.: Zondervan, 2001], p. 327).

[9] To remember "in biblical thought, means to transport an action which is buried in the past in such a way that its original potency and vitality are not lost, but are carried over into the present" (Ralph P. Martin, *Worship in the Early Church* [Grand Rapids, Mich.: Eerdmans, 1978], p. 126).

[10] Martin Luther, *D. M. Luthers Werke*, Kritische Gesamtausgabe (Weimar, 1883-) 5.163:28-29, quoted in Alister E. McGrath, *Luther's Theology of the Cross: Martin Luther's Theological Breakthrough* (Oxford: Basil Blackwell, 1985), p. 152.

[11] Waltke, *Genesis*, p. 600.

[12] This wonderful phrase comes from the theologian Karl Barth.

[13] Gordon Tucker, "Jacob's Terrible Burden: In the Shadow of the Text," *Bible Review*, June 1994, pp. 25-26.

[14] Tucker argues that the Hebrew of "to my sorrow" can be translated as "to die on account of." Thus Genesis 48:7 could be rendered: "When I was returning from Paddan, Rachel died on my account while I was still journeying in the land of Canaan, when still some distance short of Ephrath."

Tucker further argues that Jacob cannot die until he has unburdened himself of the guilt he feels over her death. "Great as his need is to confess, [Jacob] cannot simply say to Joseph on his death bed that he killed his mother. So he phrases his confession in a way that Joseph can well be expected to hear *metah 'alat* simply as 'died suddenly' or 'died to my sorrow,' while Jacob actually intends the same phrase to convey his confession, that Rachel 'died on my account.' " Tucker suggests that the "exquisite ambiguity allows Jacob both to shed his burden before Joseph, and probably to conceal it at the same time. Only in this way can we understand the enigmatic language of Genesis 48:7" (ibid., p. 28).

[15] Not only is Rachel memorialized but also her descendants through Ephraim became the leading tribe in the northern kingdom (with the other son of Rachel becoming the leading tribe in the south). From Ephraim descended Joshua, Jeroboam, Saul and Esther.

[16] Samuel H. Dresner, *Rachel* (Minneapolis: Fortress, 1944), p. 152.

[17] Quoted in Avivah Gottlieb Zornberg, *The Beginning of Desire: Reflections on Genesis* (New York: Doubleday, 1995), p. 213.

[18] Dresner, *Rachel*, p. 157.

[19] Ibid., p. 162.

[20] Writing of this, Bernard Anderson says:

> Whereas Rachel, the Mother of Israel, was formerly deprived of her sons, she will
> have a posterity . . . and therefore the future in the land promised to Israel's ancestors.
> . . . The Woman will enfold a man (a son) as a sign of [the Lord's] gracious gift of new
> life in the land. . . . In a miracle of divine grace, Rachel will receive her son back. . . .
> The old age, symbolized by Rachel weeping for her lost sons, will be superceded by
> a new age . . . in which the woman will be the agent of new . . . hope. [The symbol
> of that] Woman is Rachel. (Bernard Anderson, "The Lord Has Created Something
> New," in *Essays in Jeremiah Studies* [Indiana, 1984], pp. 376-80, quoted in ibid., pp.
> 169-70)

[21] Calvin Seerveld, *Take Hold of God and Pull* (Carlisle, U.K.: Paternoster, 1999), p. 218.

Epilogue

[1] Maxine Hancock, "To Be Fully Human," *Crux* 36, no. 4 (2000): 35.

[2] Eugene Peterson, *Leap over a Wall: Earthy Spirituality for Everyday Christians* (San Francisco: HarperSanFrancisco, 1997), p. 8.

[3] Jean Vanier, *Becoming Human* (Toronto: Anansi, 1998), p. 1.